HENRY BRADSHAW SOCIETY

Founded in the Year of Our Lord 1890
for the editing of Rare Liturgical Texts

VOLUME CIII

ISSUED TO MEMBERS FOR THE YEARS 1983–4

AND

PUBLISHED FOR THE SOCIETY

BY

THE BOYDELL PRESS

A PRE-CONQUEST ENGLISH PRAYER-BOOK

(BL MSS Cotton Galba A.xiv and Nero A.ii (ff.3–13))

Edited by

BERNARD JAMES MUIR

1988

First published for The Henry Bradshaw Society 1988
by The Boydell Press
an imprint of Boydell & Brewer Ltd
PO Box 9, Woodbridge, Suffolk IP12 3DF
and of Boydell & Brewer Inc.
Wolfeboro, New Hampshire 03894-2069, USA

ISBN 0 9501009 5 1

British Library Cataloguing in Publication Data
A Pre-Conquest English prayer-book: (BL
MSS Cotton Galba A. xiv and Nero A. ii
(ff.3–13)). —— (Henry Bradshaw Society,
ISSN 0144-0241; v. 103).
1. Devotional literature
I. Muir, Bernard, James   II. British
Library. Manuscript. Cotton Galba A.XIV
III. British Library. Manuscript. Cotton
Nero A. II IV. Series
242   BV4832.2
ISBN 0-9501009-5-1

Library of Congress Cataloging-in-Publication Data applied for

ISSN 0144-0241

Printed in Great Britain by
St Edmundsbury Press, Bury St Edmunds, Suffolk

TABLE OF CONTENTS

PREFACE

When I first turned to this undertaking I was aware that it would be demanding: I felt that I should be a palaeographer, a liturgist, an historian, a latinist, a literary scholar, and more, to bring it to a happy conclusion. Luckily, I was young enough to think I could do it at the time. Eventually I realized the exact proportions of the project, and though humbled, persisted because I thought it unlikely that there were many scholars today who would have mastered all these disciplines and would also be interested in the manuscript. Moreover, this manuscript has received little attention in the past because of its poor condition, and apparently was held to be unimportant; it neither contained a major text, nor was it an example of a certain type of liturgical book. However, those who have examined the preliminary draft of this edition, liturgists among them, have remarked that the manuscript is significant in a number of ways, but principally because it is *not* a formal liturgical book, and yet is intimately related to the liturgy.

This edition is not primarily a study of the manuscript. It is a critical edition of the texts, restoring and identifying them and making them available to others. It explores sources and influences, and makes suggestions concerning the nature of the compilation and its position in the English devotional and liturgical tradition. It opens the door to further study by specialists from various disciplines, a door that has been only slightly ajar since Edmund Bishop first published his account of the manuscript in 1907.

Finally, there are a few acknowledgements to make: I should like to thank the staffs of the following libraries for their help—The British Library, Corpus Christi College Library, Cambridge University Library, the Bibliothèque Nationale, and the bibliothèques municipales of Rouen and Orléans. The British Library has kindly granted permission for the manuscript to be printed. The University of Melbourne offered generous support for a research trip to England and France in 1983 and a generous subvention towards the costs of publication. A number of scholars have responded to inquiries over the years, and these I thank as a group for their assistance. In particular, I acknowledge the patience and encouragement of both Reverend David Tripp and Michael Lapidge of the Henry Bradshaw Society, and the guidance and support of Roger Reynolds. Paul Moore offered helpful advice on some difficult passages in the Latin, and George Russell made some valuable suggestions concerning the Introduction. Lastly, I take this opportunity to thank Edmund E. Colledge, O.S.A., a friend and colleague, who first suggested this project, and supervised it in its preliminary form as a doctoral dissertation at the University of Toronto (1981), and to whom it is dedicated.

University of Melbourne
All Saints Day
1984

INTRODUCTION

The text presented here is a critical edition of British Library MSS. Cotton Galba A. xiv (complete) (hereafter referred to as G) and Cotton Nero A. ii (ff. 3–13) hereafter referred to as N.[1] The leaves from N have been placed at the beginning of the edition since they contain a calendar and computational tables that would normally appear at the beginning of a liturgical manuscript. After these two items there are a poem, a prayer, and two hymns (see 'Contents'). As it is presently bound, G consists of two computational texts (nos. **9** and **10**) followed by approximately 100 identifiable texts of various types: prayers, hymns, medical recipes, litanies, and biblical florilegia—in both Latin and Old English.[2]

N survived the Ashburnham House fire of October 23, 1731 unscathed. G was not so fortunate; it was badly burned and suffered extensive damage from the water used to extinguish the fire. Its binding has been completely lost with the result that in the post-fire period it has received three different foliations.[3] A major part of this edition has been the reconstruction of the text, first by identifying the texts—which often lack an incipit, a desinit, or both—and then the collation of these with identical or similar texts found in other

[1] The Nero (henceforth N) folios were first associated with the Galba (G) manuscript by Neil Ker (Catalogue of Manuscripts Containing Anglo-Saxon, Oxford, 1957, p. 200). In a recent article Michael Lapidge has argued that the Nero folios were never part of G ('Some Latin Poems as Evidence for the Reign of Athelstan', ASE 9 (1981), 61–98); see the 'Description of the Manuscripts' for further discussion of this matter. As the following note in N indicates, it is a modern compilation: 'Volumen hoc fragmentorum a Roberto Cotton collectum continet diversos Tractatus quae proxima in Pagina sequuntur' (f. 2); it is not clear how the eleven leaves from N included in this edition became separated from G before the fire (see below), or why Cotton decided to include them in this (Nero A.ii) collection of miscellaneous religious writings.
[2] In its present state, about 85 per cent of the texts in G are in Latin.
[3] For a discussion of the foliation see Appendix B. A most informative and vivid description of the fire and the subsequent treatment of the damaged manuscripts, written by one Mr. Winnington, is found in volume 1 of the Reports of the House of Commons 1715–35 (published in 1803), pp. 445–507; this report is reprinted in C. G. C. Tite's edition of Thomas Smith's Catalogus of the Cottonian manuscripts (see Bibliography).
[4] See the statement of editorial policy, p. xxv.

manuscripts from the period,[4] where possible, those which are contemporary, or nearly so, with *G* and *N*, and preferably from England or the Frankish realm.[5] Since, in the process of rebinding, many of the folios of *G* have been wrongly arranged, an attempt has been made here to re-establish the original sequence, so far as possible, from information in the pre-fire catalogues and from internal evidence (see pp. xi–xiii and *Appendix B*). The most remarkable discoveries among the texts are nos. **14** and **15**: no. **14** is a new witness for the 'Altus Prosator', a Latin abecedary poem often attributed (doubtfully) to St. Columba; no. **15** is another abecedary poem, the 'Adiutor laborantium', which is here also attributed to Columba.[6] For the rest, the texts are primarily interesting for the versions of traditional material which they present, for what they reveal about the devotional tradition and education in England in the post-Benedictine Revival period, and for what their arrangement within the manuscript discloses about the nature of devotional collections from this period (see 'Genre' and 'Analogues').

Several texts that are well-preserved and recognizable units within the manuscript have already appeared in print (e.g. the Calendar),[7] and all the decipherable items written in Old English have been edited previously at least once.[8]

Description of the Manuscripts

There are two good descriptions of *G*—very distinct in style: the first is the charming and sometimes lyrical one by Edmund Bishop, which

---

[5] A description of the analogues used in the reconstruction of *G* is given below (pp. xxvii–xxxi).

[6] See the introductory remarks to no. **14** for further discussion of this attribution.

[7] The following texts have been printed separately:

no. **1** F. Wormald, *English Kalendars before A.D. 1100*, London, 1934, pp. 28–41; also in F. A. Gasquet and E. Bishop, *The Bosworth Psalter*, London, 1908, pp. 165–71.

no. **5** W. de Gray Birch, *Cartularium Saxonicum*, London, 1887, II. 331.

nos. **11** *and* **12** *Ibid*. II. 332–33.

no. **34** H. Logeman, 'Anglo-Saxonica Minora', *Anglia* 11 (1889), p. 97.

no. **61** W. H. Frere, *The Leofric Collectar* II, London, 1921, pp. 618–26.

nos. **64**, **65** *and* **68** R. A. Banks, 'Some Anglo-Saxon Prayers from British Museum MS. Cotton Galba A.xiv', *N&Q* 210 (1965) 207–13.

no. **68** L. Gjerløw, *Adoratio Crucis*, Oslo, 1961.

[8] For bibliographical information see the introductory remarks to each text, which can be located by consulting the 'Index'.

first drew attention to the manuscript;[9] the second is the succinct and technical one by Neil Ker.[10] The following description is indebted to both of these to some degree.

There are 154 folios in *G*; these are edited here, along with the first 11 folios from *N*. No definitive statement may be made safely concerning the collation of *G* because of the extent of the damage to the manuscript, because no catchwords or signatures were used, and because the folios are now mounted individually in modern binding.[11] The folios measure approximately 138×103 mm.; the writing-area of the well-preserved folios is 122×85 mm. They range in length from 11 to 18 long lines (except for nos. **40, 61** and **63** which are in double columns—see plates 5 and 6). There are only two significant instances of marginalia, the longest of which has been reproduced below (p. 211). Ker has analysed the many hands in *G* and *N*, and concluded that certain texts have been entered in both manuscripts by the same hand, a statement with which I agree. In punctuating, the point and diagonal slash were used, separately and in combination. In a number of texts there are accents marks, but these appear to be used unsystematically (see plates 1, 2 and 4).

As indicated above (note 1), it has recently been argued that the folios from *N* were never part of *G*. To review the evidence, the same hand has made entries in both manuscripts (*N* ff. 10ᵛ–12ᵛ and *G* f. 125ʳ), but this does not necessarily mean that *N* was part of *G*; *N* may have been written in the same centre (Winchester) for another monastery which did not have an adequate scriptorium. The Calendar in *N* 'appears to be in the same backward-sloping hand as a Computatio Grecorum in Galba f. 2' (Ker, p. 201). Both manuscripts have the same odd abbreviations for October and November ($\overline{OCB}$ and $\overline{NOB}$). One text appears in both *N* and *G* (nos. **6** and **11**), but such repetition of material is not unusual in miscellanies or anthologies; in

[9] E. Bishop, 'About an Old Prayer Book' in *Liturgica Historica*, Oxford, 1918, pp. 384–91 (reprinted from *The Downside Review* for March 1907).
[10] N. Ker, *op. cit.* pp. 198–201.
[11] As with many of the severely damaged Cotton manuscripts, each folio was traced on stiff paper; the shape of the particular folio was then cut out and the folio itself was fixed in place with sticky tape (which has badly discoloured over the years so that now it obscures many letters and short words which might be read otherwise—see plates 7 and 8). Sir Frederic Madden's notes in BL MSS. Add. 62572 and 62576 indicate that the folios in *G* were set in place in 1855, and that it was bound in 1863; at this time the foliation series 1–137 was cancelled, and it was renumbered 1–155. *N* was rebound and repaired in January of 1865.

fact, another text is repeated within G itself (as nos. **27** and **69**). It has been suggested that the appearance of saints German (4 times), Gildas (twice), Petroc and Winnoc—all saints venerated in Celtic or British areas—in the Calendar be interpreted as evidence that N was intended for St. Germans in Cornwall, just as the absence of the names of saints Swithun and Æthelwold would seem to argue against a Winchester origin (Lapidge, p. 85). It should be noted, however, that saints Winnoc and Petroc appear in Litany II of G (f. 93^v), and that St. German appears in *both* of the litanies (ff. 77^v and 93^r). In addition, a large number of names in the litanies are no longer legible, and some of these illegible entries might also have been Celtic or British. The Celtic character of a number of items in the manuscript— even aside from the two poems attributed to St. Columba—is also an important consideration; G represents a blending of Celtic and Roman traditions that is found in other devotional manuscripts (as we should expect historically), e.g. *The Book of Cerne*. The additional evidence given below concerning the dating of the two manuscripts, along with the palaeographical and textual data, leads me to conclude that, so far as can be determined, N and G are similar in their blending of Celtic and Anglo-Saxon (Roman) elements, and were originally one manuscript, and henceforth any reference to 'the manuscript' assumes this unity.

There are three conflicting sets of folio numbers in G, two in N (see Appendix B). The series 2–155 has been used for G, since it is the most consistent and was used by Ker; the series 3–13 for N, also because it was used by Ker. These numbers have been given in the left-hand margin at the beginning of each new folio (indicated by / in the text). A note appears at the foot of the page wherever the position of a folio has been changed to restore it to its proper place; as G is presently bound, the following folios are

> reversed: 17, 19, 145, 148, 150;
> out of order: 75, 86, 87, 88, 136;
> reversed and out of order: 146, 147, 149;
> inverted: 73.

Appendix A is a diplomatic transcription of the pages that are too severely damaged to justify their inclusion in the text proper.[12]

---

[12] These are: 134^{r-v}, 135^{r-v}, 136^{r-v}, 138^{r-v}, 139^{r-v}, 142^v, 143^{r-v}, 144^r, 151^v, 152^r, 153^{r-v}, 154^{r-v} and 155^v.

Though almost totally indecipherable, they have been included here in the hope that other liturgists may be able to identify them from the position of the legible words on each page. Folios 136^v, 140^v, 141^v and 155^r have been omitted completely since they are totally illegible, even under ultra-violet light; 64^v, 74^v and 133^r because they are blank.

Script and the Scribes

Since so many different hands are to be found in the manuscript, all that can be said of the script in general is that both late Anglo-Saxon and Anglo-Caroline minuscule are used. Some of the scribes use the insular form of 'g' ($\mathfrak{z}$), others the continental; each text is consistent in its use of one or the other of the forms, never using both. Capitals, more rectangular than 'quadrata', are regularly used for rubrics and initials, and are often done in red ink. There are two slightly decorated capitals, a *D* at the beginning of no. 16 (see plate 4) and a *B* at the beginning of no. 75. That the initial capitals done in red ink were added after the text was finished is apparent from the fact that the scribe failed to insert them in no. 14, lines 88 and 95; this is particularly interesting since both the texts concerned are consecutive verses of an alphabetical poem, where one would expect the scribe, proceeding methodically, to be less likely to skip an initial. Both highly skilled and less well-trained scribes have tried their hand in *G*. At times the script is so poor and/or childishly large (especially ff. 147^r, lines 1–4 and 147^v, lines 1–3), and so plagued by inaccuracies as to make it conceivable that the manuscript was once used as a beginner's or novice's exercise book (see below, pp. xvi–xvii). Some examples of the mistakes (or characteristics) of these 'student scribes' may be given. There are three instances of homoeoteleuton in no. 31 (all three by the same scribe within a short space), and also in nos. 50 and 56; there is homoeotopy in no. 58. In no. 25 (see note 4) it seems as if a gloss in the original may have been incorporated into the text. The words *O reconciliator* (no. 19) have been copied as *ore conciliator*; this kind of spacing, which occurs frequently throughout, may indicate a less than perfect grasp of Latin. This is also suggested by certain texts that have been copied and left to stand in the manuscript although they are at times unintelligible.[13] On two occasions the

---

[13] See the introductory remarks to nos. 7, 8, 20, 21 and 66.

scribe seems to have had trouble deciphering an abbreviation in his exemplar (no. **31**, n. 13, and **54**, n. 6). There are other mistakes as fundamental as not being able to convert a text consistently from the singular to the plural (no. **69**, n. 8). At no. **69**, n. 20, one scribe curiously, and without authority, abbreviates *in evangelium* as *INEŪ GL. Ā*. There are numerous less significant slips in transcription throughout, e.g. *orante* for *oratione* (no. **68**), *pabulo* for *patibulo* (*ibid.*), *asendne* for *arisendne* (*ibid.*—all by one scribe within a short space), and *incipit confessionem* for *incipit confessio* (no. **62**). The following errors suggest a lack of familiarity with Latin vocabulary rather than scribal slips: *terram super aquas* (no. **16**) in a familiar Biblical passage; *est a* for the imperative *esto* (no. **19**); *tue supple* for *te supplex* (no. **23**); *bilidine* for *libidine* (no. **26**); *propiaberis* for *propitiaberis* (no. **28**); and *ascendentem ad inferos* for *descendentem ad inferos* (no. **68**).

Origin and Date

Bishop and Ker agree that internal evidence indicates that the manuscript is from Winchester, and that it was written in the first half of the eleventh century.[14] There is one specific internal reference to Winchester ('Wentana': p. 166), but the text is so badly damaged at that point that more cannot be made of it. The manuscript was written for a religious institution which seems to have housed both men and women since the inflexions in the texts of the prayers—often taken from liturgical settings—indicate use by both sexes. The masculine inflexions are sometimes glossed with feminine forms, and vice versa (e.g. in no. **67**). In other texts masculine and feminine forms occur side by side (e.g. in no. **66**), perhaps indicating that they are hybrid forms produced inadvertently as the texts were recopied. This is interpreted here as evidence that the manuscript was probably used at St. Mary's Convent where, 'Besides the professed nuns and their household the abbey of Nunnaminster supported a certain number of chaplains or canons who had prebendal stalls in the abbey'.[15] The phrase *omnis iura regni mei* (no. **19**) may also be a minute piece of corroborative evidence that the text is from the royal centre at

[14] Bishop, *op. cit.* p. 387 and Ker, *op. cit.* p. 201.
[15] *The Victoria History of the Counties of England: Hampshire and the Isle of Wight*, London, 1973, II. 122.

Winchester, especially since this phrase is not in the analogues, which are from other centres. Many of the texts are related to the regular monastic life: for example, the Calendar and the computational tables, internal references to the 'opus dei' (pp. 68 and 69), the rite of confession for two priests, the processional hymn for use on Sundays and feast days, the prayers for the various 'hours' of the day, and the litanies.

The dating of the manuscript has now been more precisely established. Bishop had concluded that 'this very MS must have been written at the latest at a time not very distant from Ethelred's death (1016) . . . this prayer is the latest indication of the date that I have observed in the volume' (*op. cit.*, p. 389). He was referring to no. **60** (p. 122), a prayer for the soul of the king, who had died on 23 April of that year. The evidence for dating the manuscript more precisely lies in the computational tables at the beginning of both G and N (Bishop, incidentally, had not examined N). These tables have never been deciphered, probably because they are either fragmentary or incomplete and did not seem deserving of attention. They have been identified here, and may be explained thus: the table on p. 15 was intended to give the user of this manuscript all the information needed for making ecclesiastical computations for a nineteen-year lunar cycle running from 1029 to 1047. However, it is defective in places and lacks full information for the last four years. The personal nature of this manuscript, its informal character (see below, p. xvi), is a certain indication that this table would have had to have been functional to have merited being included. Entries may have been made in the manuscript over a longer period, but it was certainly intended for use during this period. This is corroborated by one table from G (no. **10**, p. 28) containing three columns of dates which, because of their incompleteness, are at first obscure. They are parts of more comprehensive tables that have been chosen, once again, for personal reasons (i.e. they contained information useful to the reader of the manuscript): the first column has dates from the sixth to seventh years of the twenty-eight-year solar cursus, appropriate for the years 1034–35; the second is for calculating the 'saltus lunae' for the first year of the nineteen-year lunar cycle, i.e. for the year 1029; the third is from the same table as the first, but is for the complete twelfth year, i.e. 1040. It seems that this, more than any other consideration, but taken in conjunction with them, establishes a firm link between G and N, and suggests that the leaves from N were originally part of G. What has consistently been referred to as a 'Computatio Graecorum de mensibus anni' in the early catalogues (no. **9**, p. 27) is a more elaborate version of the mnemonic 'Thirty days hath September . . .', giving, in addition, the number of days of the nones, ides and calends for each month.

Nothing further is known of the history of the manuscript until it appears in the Cottonian catalogues.

Genre and Structure

I have chosen to refer to this edition as that of a 'pre-Conquest prayer-book', but even this antiseptic generalization would normally suggest a text with a formal structure or a particular type of book. Yet I have suggested in this Introduction that the manuscript is a 'personal' book of 'informal' character, and shall now explain what I mean by this.

The manuscript contains many texts that would have been used in a monastic institution (see above, pp. xiv–xv), and others that were drawn from the liturgy (such as computational charts, litanies, collects, the rite of confession), but which were not necessarily associated with monasticism. Both of these associations underline a connection between the manuscript and the formal worship and rituals of the medieval church. But it is not a *formal* liturgical book like a Benedictional, a Missal, or a Psalter. It is composite and *informal* in that it has no apparent structure other than that the longer prayers are all found in the first half; the second part contains a wide range of shorter texts of various sorts or 'genres' (i.e. collects, recipes, litanies, hymns, etc.) This serves to distance it from the institution that has generated it.

The manuscript was at first a *blank* book. I am not aware of any other manuscript from this early period that was produced in this manner. That it was bound as a set of blank gatherings is clear from the manner in which texts of various lengths were entered without regard for gathering boundaries. Someone in a position of authority must have thought that it would be useful to have such a book at hand for recording texts that might be of general interest within the monastery. This implies its informal nature, but what gives it its personal character? Firstly, the fact that the texts have in many instances been lifted from their formal context, and are recorded in isolation (i.e. out of context). Secondly, although a number of computational tables are included, some of these have been selected from more comprehensive charts covering extended periods (e.g. the 28-year solar cursus); whoever chose them from these larger charts and recorded them in the manuscript did so because they were relevant for him at that time. In doing this, he has made specific for his own use larger computational charts important as a whole for the proper organization of a religious institution. And thirdly, alterations in the inflexions of a number of texts indicate that they were used at one time by a man, and at another by a woman. This too indicates that the book was compiled from various sources for personal or individual use, since no one would have dared alter a formal liturgical book in such an idiosyncratic way.

It was also suggested above (p. xiii) that the manuscript may have been used as an 'exercise' book by those being taught in the monastery. A number of details suggest this: firstly, it was created during the period of reform at the beginning of the eleventh century when concern for improving the standards of education was prevalent (see below, pp. xxiii–xxiv); secondly, the script is often of inferior quality, indicating that the contributors were still not accomplished scribes; thirdly, the Latin is plagued with basic errors of grammar and transcription, and interlinear corrections have been made in many places (e.g. no. 24); and fourthly, the texts chosen for inclusion do not reflect any specific interest or guiding principle. It is not inconceivable that texts like the 'Athanasian Creed' (no. 76), the 'Confiteor' (no. 74) and the 'Benedicite' (no. 212) were read aloud from this manuscript to these same 'students' so that they could repeat them and thereby commit them to memory.[16]

---

[16] Christopher Hohler, directing his attention to the post-reform period, makes two statements of particular interest in light of the observations made here on the low level of linguistic ability displayed in G: 'They [miscellanies from Worcester] look more like fair copies of notes taken by pupils following a course, during which useful items were dictated or circulated for copying, and my instinct is to suggest that that course was held at Winchester. But everything conspires to suggest that the knowledge of Latin among the clergy was almost universally low, and that, except in so far as an insignificant minority of scholars was prepared, as well as able, to provide translations, the Church was cut off from the general cultural heritage of the West.' ('Some Service Books of the Late Saxon Church', p. 74.)

CONTENTS

Language

(a) *Latinity*

A number of aspects of the language in *G* unite to intimidate the classicist: unfamiliar vocabulary, largely neologisms coined by the Christian community; unfamiliar forms, reflecting the greater susceptibility of the 'popular' language to change; non-Classical syntactical formations, such as the use of prepositions with an unexpected case, or the use of the indicative where the subjunctive is expected. None of these in itself would present much difficulty for the classicist, but appearing collectively they give this liturgical Latin an unfamiliar character. This situation is not improved by the presence of a multitude of simple grammatical errors, making consistency in the application of a fixed editorial policy regarding emendation and correction difficult.

Except for occasional and inevitable corrections, the Latin of the manuscript has been left to speak for itself, however inelegantly at times, thus revealing its full medieval character. An example of the type of correction that has been made is the changing of *caput* to *capitis* in the phrase *inuentio capitis Iohannis baptiste* from the Calendar (no. **1**, against 27 February). Left to stand, however, is the indicative *custodies* for the subjunctive after *ut* (no. **24**), since the demise of the subjunctive is an important syntactical feature of medieval Latin.[17]

It is interesting to note that the language of these devotions developed an emotional intensity during the period from the ninth to the eleventh centuries which is realized in certain syntactical features: the use of repetition—*peto et supplico* (no. **16**), *quia scio et credo et confiteor quod tu es pius* (no. **25**); through the yoking of present participles to these same verbs of petitioning—*et gemescens peto et lacrimans obsecro* (no. **21**), or hanging a string of them from a noun—*ut uincam diabolum uigilantem et non dormientem et dimicantem contra me* (no. **17**); and through the liberal employment of superlative and diminutive formations—*precor ut me homunculum quassatum ac miserrimum* (no. **15**, lines 16–17).

---

[17] The study of liturgical Latin is still a much neglected area, but the outline of its development and summary of some of its more important features by Christine Mohrmann in *Annus Festivus* (Brussels, 1938) provides a convenient and succinct introduction. The 'hisperic' Latin of the two poems attributed to St. Columba has been remarked upon in passing in the introduction to the 'Altus prosator' (no. **14**).

Finally, a few words about five particularly problematic texts, nos. **7, 8, 20, 21**, and **66**. The syntax and vocabulary of these are so obscure at times that they have for the most part been left to stand as they appear in the manuscript, and suggestions are given in the notes as to how they might be emended. Another text, the 'Carte dirige gressus' (no. **5**), which also required radical emendation before it would make any sense, has been edited by Lapidge (*op. cit.* pp. 83–93), and his reconstruction and translation of it are given following the text here. The degree of hypothetical reconstruction undertaken by Lapidge goes beyond the scope of the present edition, although the value of such studies is beyond question.

(b) *Old English*

Approximately ten to fifteen per cent of the texts in the manuscript are in Old English; of these, most are either translations of the Latin texts they accompany, or devotional or semi-liturgical texts whose vocabulary and syntax are heavily dependent upon Latin liturgical writings.[18]

(1) The *translations* are not of much interest syntactically since they follow the originals quite closely. When they do not, one of two things happens: they render a Latin word with *two* words: *sciant—wite and ongyte* (no. **12**), *remedium—lacnunge and lœcedome* (no. **68**), *pretioso— halgum and deorwyrð* (no. **68**), *penitentiam—hreowsunge and dœdbote* (*ibid.*); or they add an extra adjective for emphasis; this is done to advantage in no. **12** where the addition of *mihtigu* and *unstrangan* serves to emphasize the contrast between God and the supplicant: *tua manus—seo mihtigu hand*, or *cor meum—mines unstrangan heortan*, and *Ihesu Christi—drihtenes hœlendes Cristes*.

Other than these types of simple amplification, most of the changes are merely stylistic, e.g. *miserere mei* (no. **68**), an imperative, is translated by a *þœt* clause: (*ic gebidde þe*) *þœt ðu gemiltsige me*.

The fact that there *are* translations of certain texts is significant. Liturgical manuscripts from before the year 950 generally do not contain translations, and it may be that their sudden appearance in the last half of the tenth century is directly related to the Benedictine Revival. This is the same period when vernacular poetic explications

---

[18] The following texts do not fall into one of these categories: **13** (a rubric), **34** and **70** (medical recipes), and the fragmentary texts recorded in Appendix A.

of some of the basic articles of the faith—the 'Pater Noster', 'Gloria' and 'Creed'—are first recorded; these texts are also translated and explained in a number of the homilies surviving from the same period.[19] The likelihood that these and other poetic texts were used within the liturgy to instruct the faithful in the vernacular is now generally acknowledged.[20] In light of this, it is not insignificant that one of the texts in *G* is taken from the *Regularis Concordia* itself (no. **68**, the 'Adoro te'—petitions in Latin and Old English). This use of the vernacular for spiritual instruction seems to have been an important aspect of the reform programme of Dunstan, Æthelwold, and Oswold; the *Regularis Concordia* itself was translated, and the so-called *Benedictine Office* was composed in Old English.

This is the period which saw the compilation of the wholly didactic *Exeter Book of Old English Poetry*, the three other major Anglo-Saxon poetic codices, and the secular writings of Byrhtferth of Ramsey, in addition to a large corpus of vernacular homiletic writings. Helmut Gneuss has examined the central role of Æthelwold and his school at Winchester in these developments, dispelling the attractive myth which had prevailed earlier that the establishment of a standard West-Saxon dialect should be credited to the ninth-century Alfredian reform.[21]

(2) As already noted, the vernacular texts that are not direct translations are heavily influenced by Latin liturgical syntax and vocabulary; traditional words have been endowed with Christian significance, and many semantic translations and other new formations have been created to express novel Christian theological concepts. No. **64** is an

---

[19] See *ASPR* III and VI for poetic treatments. Wulfstan's homilies VII and VIIa are examples of explications in prose (D. Bethurum, *The Homilies of Wulfstan*, Oxford, 1957, reprinted 1971). CUL MS. Gg.3.28 (Ker no. 15, Wanley p. 153) contains a number of prayers in Old English including the 'pater noster' and 2 creeds with the rubric, 'Her is geleafa and gebed and bletsung læwedum mannum þe þæt leden ne cunnan' (f. 261ᵛ).

[20] See the discussion of the 'Prone' by Milton McC. Gatch, *Preaching and Theology in Anglo-Saxon England: Ælfric and Wulfstan* (University of Toronto Press, 1977), and by Patrick W. Conner, 'A Contextual Study of the Old English Exeter Book', unpublished Ph.D. dissertation, University of Maryland, 1975. It can readily be seen how wisdom poems such as *Precepts* (*ASPR* 3, pp. 140–43), influenced by Biblical models from the 'Ten Commandments' to the book of 'Proverbs', might have been used within the liturgy at a time set aside for instruction in the vernacular.

[21] 'The Origin of Standard Old English and Æthelwold's School at Winchester', *ASE* 1 (1972) 63–83.

example of this kind of text: It begins with a translation of the
doxology—*In naman þære halgan þrynesse* (note *þrynesse-trinitas*)—
and contains many echoes of common liturgical phrases: *min word and
weorc and mine geþohtas* (cf. the 'Confiteor': *quia peccaui nimis
cogitatione, uerbo et opere*, and nos. **19** and **74**); and *a wesendne and a
wuniendne to widan feore* (or *þu þe leofast and rixast a to worulde*
(no. **66**). In no. **64** there is a series of invocations with the structure
'through your incarnation . . . birth . . . baptism . . . suffering . . .
resurrection . . . ascension . . . return in judgement' which can be
compared with one of the common endings of the litany (see p. 129),
and with the format of the 'Adoro te'-petitions (no. **68**).[22]

The phrase *eallum fiondum gesewenlicum and ungesewenlicum* (no. **64**)
can be compared with *hostes meos uisibiles et inuisibiles* (no. **19**), and
lichomliches oþþe gastlices (no. **64**) with *seculi et . . . spiritale* (no. **24**).
Characteristic of native rhythmical and alliterative prose writing is this
series of balanced phrases:

> min word and weorc . . .
> mine heortan and minne hyge
> min leomu and mine lioðu
> min fell and flæsc
> min blod and ban
> min mod and gemynd (no. **64**)

which may seem stylistically bald and monotonous here, but the same
technique is often used with persuasive rhetorical effect by contemporary homilists, e.g. by Wulfstan in the *Sermo Lupi*.[23]

Finally, something should be said about the 'spirit' or tone of the
texts, with specific reference to the prayers of contrition. Edmund
Bishop once observed that 'in the case of the composer of a prayer for
private use, the familiar words of the liturgy are recalled by memory
as they are held in the heart; they are used almost unconsciously, and
the original is modified or its thought adapted under stress of the
current personal feeling at the moment' (Kuypers, *op. cit.*, p. 234), a

---

[22] This type of catalogue outlining the gradations of Salvation History was a favourite
structural device during the Middle Ages; in the vernacular poetry it was used by
Cynewulf in *Christ II* (ll. 720–43) in a passage based upon a homily by Gregory the
Great (*ASPR* 3, p. xxvii), and in the anonymous *Descent into Hell* (*ASPR* 3, p. 222).
[23] Bethurum, *op. cit.* p. 269, ll. 55–61. R. A. Banks, following A. McIntosh, refers to
this style of rhythmical writing as 'late "debased" Old English verse' (*op. cit.* pp. 209–
10).

remark which stresses the emotive impulse that gives birth to the prayer. Concerning the tone of these prayers, Kuypers noted the contrast between the restraint of those representative of the Roman devotional tradition and the emotional effusiveness of those representing the Celtic (*op. cit.*, p. xxix). Most of the texts edited here represent the former tradition; it is the nature of the latter group, however, that is of greater interest, and that will be illustrated.

In no. **31**, after a long invocation, the confession begins in earnest: the supplicant catalogues the *places where* he has sinned—heaven and earth; then those *before whom* he has sinned—God, the angels and saints; then *which sins* he has committed—the seven deadly sins are almost lost in this extensive list; and, his real *tour de force*, the *parts of the body* with which he has sinned: eyes, ears, nostrils, tongue, throat, neck, chest, heart, thoughts, hands, feet, bones, flesh, marrow, kidneys, spirit, body.[24] And then, he asks forgiveness and to be defended against the darts of attacking devils. No. **26** is another example of this kind of effusive Celtic text.

New Material

As already noted, the most remarkable discoveries in the manuscript are nos. **14** and **15**, the two abecedary poems of Hiberno-Latin origin. The other texts for which there are no known analogues are nos. **5, 7, 8, 13, 20, 21, 32, 60, 62** and **66**.

Notes on the Transcription and Editorial Policy

The following characters have been retained in this edition: insular æ, þ and ð. Runic 'wynn' is normalized to 'w'. Abbreviations have been expanded according to the orthographical practice of the various scribes, and are italicized. The sporadic punctuation of the manuscript has been made regular; accent marks have not been reproduced. Lost or illegible text has been indicated by three asterisks. On several

---

[24] Concerning the background to such texts, K. Hughes remarks: 'The influence of both loricae and [Irish] penitentials is very evident here, for the penitentials are based on the idea that sins must be confessed, and that penance is a spiritual medicine' ('Some Aspects of Irish Influence on Early English Private Prayer', *Studia Celtica* 5 (1970) p. 55).

severely damaged pages the notes indicating the amount of text lost, whether a few letters, words or lines, have been inserted within the text since it was apparent that otherwise at these points the apparatus would have become so complicated as to have discouraged the reader from using it. It seemed desirable to remove as many obstacles as possible for the reader, and to try to illustrate for him the actual state of the manuscript without his having to consult it or a microfilm of it. Several of the texts that are hymns have interlinear musical notation; I have noted where this occurs, but no attempt has been made here to reproduce it.

Plates 5 and 6 will give the reader a fair idea of type of damage the manuscript has sustained, although many folios are in much worse condition. It will be evident that many of the readings that are presented in brackets are tentative, especially when they stretch beyond a word or two. Before supplying a reading I have considered how closely the text in G and the analogue(s) agree overall, and whether the reading chosen would fit realistically into the space available. My intention has been to restore as far as possible the text that was originally written in G (from a close study of analogous material), *not* to try to recreate as pure a version of the texts in G as was possible by collating them with the analogues. In all instances, however, the reconstructed text of G has been edited so that it is readable and logical, even if it is not always the 'best' version of the text concerned; in such instances the 'superior' readings of the analogues have always been noted in the apparatus.[25] The Latin has not been 'corrected' to conform with Classical rules of syntax and spelling, except where there were obvious grammatical errors (as distinct from syntactical features of medieval Latin).

The Analogues

The search for analogues with which to elucidate (and often to reconstruct) the texts in G was an important aspect of this edition, given the extent of the damage sustained by the manuscript in the Ashburnham House fire. As this investigation proceeded, some facts about the different types of collections of devotional texts began to

---

[25] E.g. in no. **26**, note D, G reads *flamma libidens*, which is retained, although the reading of the analogues (*libidinis*) is superior.

emerge; these are summarized at the end of this section.[26] The following works are of inestimable value for anyone working in this area: Pierre Salmon, 'Livrets de prières de l'époque carolingienne', and Helmut Gneuss, 'A Preliminary list of manuscripts written or owned in England up to 1100'.[27]

The following catalogue is in two sections: the first lists the analogues that have been collated in the critical apparatus; the second lists other manuscripts that have been consulted, but not collated. If an analogue is a formal liturgical book like a missal or benedictional, it has not been described in any detail since its general contents will be evident to everyone; it has been noted, however, if one of these formal books contains a collection of devotional material. Information concerning the date and provenance of each item has been given as accurately as possible. The numbers in brackets at the end of each entry indicate the items for which it has been used as an analogue in this edition.

Section I: analogues reported in the critical apparatus

A = BL MS. Harl. 2961. *The Leofric Collectar*, ed. E. S. Dewick, HBS XLV, London, 1914; 11th century, Exeter; (no. **69**).

B = Dublin, RIA MS. 23.P.16 (Leabhar Breac). *The Irish Liber Hymnorum*, edd. J. H. Bernard and R. Atkinson, 2 vols., HBS XIII and XIV, London, 1898; 14th century; (no. **14**).

C = CUL MS. Ll.1.10. *The Prayer Book of Aedeluald the Bishop commonly called The Book of Cerne*, ed. A. B. Kuypers, Cambridge, 1902; 9th century, Mercia. The origin and date of parts of this

---

[26] I say 'facts', but it would perhaps be more prudent to say impressions, since at present scholars are not in agreement concerning the evolution of the prayer-book in England, or about its exact relationship to the continental tradition. Thus this outline reflects my observations to date, though I am very much aware that a great deal of investigation remains to be done. As the discussion will show, I have only had the opportunity to examine manuscripts in London, Cambridge, Oxford, Paris, Orléans and Rouen; there are undoubtedly numerous other manuscripts in other centres which remain to be consulted, but I think that those that are important for a study of the prayer-book in England have all been considered.
[27] Complete bibliographical details for studies cited in this discussion are found below (pp. xxxvii–xl).

manuscript are at present matters of controversy: no one disagrees
with N. R. Ker and T. A. M. Bishop that the manuscript is from the
first quarter of the ninth century, but both Edmund Bishop and
Kuypers thought that it contains material from an earlier collection;
D. Dumville is of the same opinion, but thinks that the whole
collection may have been made earlier, and that *Cerne* 'is no more than
a poor copy (possibly at more than one remove from the exemplar)'.
He concludes, 'The best that can be said of Æðelwald of Lichfield is
that he may have used the work of his namesake [Æðiluald of
Melrose, later bishop of Lindisfarne 721–40] as a nucleus of a
collection of his own'.[28] Hughes, following Sisam, was of the opposite
opinion: 'Dr. Sisam, however, has shown conclusively, arguing from
the spelling of the name, that this Aedelvald cannot be the Bishop of
Lindisfarne. It is almost certain that he is Aethelwald, Bishop of
Lichfield from 818–30'.[29] The arguments by either side concerning
the spelling of the name of the bishop in the acrostic are tenuous, and
the matter may never be resolved fully. What seems to be agreed upon
generally, and what is of most relevance for this discussion of
analogues, is that *Cerne* represents a blending of elements from the
Celtic and the Roman devotional traditions. It contains the Passion
narratives from the four Gospels, prayers and hymns (74 in all), a
defective breviate Psalter, the panegyric piece containing the acrostic,
and the 'Harrowing of Hell' text; (nos. **19, 23, 24, 25, 31**, and **68**).

D = Durham Cathedral Library MS. A.iv.19. *The Durham Ritual*, ed.
T. J. Brown, Copenhagen, 1969; 10th century, Wessex; (no. **54**).

E = Milan, Biblioteca ambrosiana MS. S.Q.N.III.14. *Missale
romanum 1474*, ed. R. Lippe, 2 vols. London, 1899; (no. **69**).

F = Dublin, Library of the Franciscan Convent, Liber Hymnorum.
The Irish Liber Hymnorum (see *B*); 11th century; (no. **14**).

G = BL MS. Cotton Galba A.xiv; *ca.* 1029, Winchester; (no. **6**).

H = Le Havre, Bibliothèque municipale ms. 330. *The Missal of the
New Minster*, ed. D. H. Turner, HBS XCIII, London, 1962; 11th
century, Winchester; (nos. **27, 29, 35, 38, 56, 69, 77, 88, 89, 90, 94**
and **95**).

---

[28] 'Liturgical Drama and Panegyric Responsory from the Eighth Century?', pp. 393
and 399, n. 2.
[29] 'Some Aspects of Irish Influence on Early English Private Prayer', p. 60.

I = *MGH Poetae latini aeui carolini*, vol. iv, ed. P. von Winterfeld, Berlin, 1899; (no. **63**).

J = Rouen, Bibliothèque municipale ms. Y.6. *The Missal of Robert of Jumièges*, ed. H. A. Wilson, HBS XI, London, 1896; post 1044, London; (nos. **10, 71, 73, 77, 81** and **88**).

K = Edinburgh, Faculty of Advocates Library MS. 18.5.19. *The Rosslyn Missal*, ed. H. J. Lawlor, HBS XV, London, 1899; *ca.* 1400—a very late analogue, but no other could be found for this collect from the mass for St. Patrick; (no. **104**).

L = BL MS. Royal 12.D.xvii. *Leechdoms, Wortcunning and Starcraft of Early England*, 3 vols., ed. T. O. Cockayne, Rolls Series, London, 1864–6, rptd. 1961; 10th century; (no. **70**).

M = Westminster Abbey Library MS. 37. *Missale ad usum ecclesie Westmonasteriensis*, 3 vols., ed. J. Wickham Legg, London, 1891–7; 1362 × 1386; (nos. **29, 33, 41, 42, 43, 44, 46, 47, 49, 50, 53, 55, 56, 58, 74, 79, 81, 86, 88, 89, 91, 95, 99,** and **101**).

N = BL MS. Cotton Nero A.ii; *ca.* 1029, Winchester; (no. **11**).

O = BL MS. Harl. 2965. *An Ancient Manuscript of the eighth or ninth century: formerly belonging to St. Mary's Abbey*, ed. W. de Gray Birch, London, 1889. Subsequently this book belonged to Alfred's queen Ealhswith 'who perhaps gave it to the convent at Nunnaminster which she founded at Winchester'.[30] It opens with fragments of the Passion narratives (no Matthew, and only part of Mark), and for the rest is a collection of prayers and hymns. Most of the items are concerned with the life of Christ, and especially his sufferings, and it seems as if this was intended to be the thematic structure of the manuscript; (nos. **24** and **31**).

P = CCCC MS. 391. *The Portiforium of St. Wulstan*, 2 vols., ed. A. Hughes, HBS LXXXIX and XC, London, 1958; *ca.* 1065, Worcester. This book contains a substantial collection of private devotions in both Latin and Old English. (nos. **16, 17, 25, 31, 33, 45, 56, 67, 68, 69, 71, 73, 77, 81, 89, 92** and **95**).

Q = BL MS. Harl. 863 (printed as an Appendix in *A*); 11th century, Exeter; this is a psalter containing a calendar, a hymn, psalms,

---

[30] P. Wormald in *The Anglo-Saxons*, ed. James Campbell, Oxford, 1982, p. 143.

canticles, pater noster, 2 creeds, gloria, a litany. This structure is typical of psalters from the continent at this period. After the litany there is a series of hymns and prayers ('most of which follow closely their carolingian sources'[31]), only one of which, a collect, is identical with an item in *G*; (no. **47**).

R = BL MS. Royal 2.A.xx (printed as an Appendix in *C*); 8th century, Mercia. This text contains glosses and rubrics in Old English added ca. 1000, and some Greek words in Latin characters (cp. no. **63** n. 34); some Latin texts, usually collects, were added in the margins at a later date. It opens with some passages from the Gospels; these are followed by Abgarus' letter, prayers, canticles, hymns (including a long alphabetical poem), a short litany, gloria, creed, and 2 abecedary hymns. Unlike *O*, there does not seem to be a thematic structure to this manuscript, and unlike *G*, none of the prayers is long; (nos. **18**, **22** and **67**).

S = *The Monastic Agreement of the Monks and nuns of the English Nation or Regularis Concordia*, ed. T. Symons, London, 1953; an edition from manuscripts from the tenth and eleventh centuries; (nos. **44**, **47**, **48** and **68**).

T = Dublin, Trinity College Library MS. E.4.2. *The Irish Liber Hymnorum* (see *B*); 11th century; (no. **14**).

U = PL 101. B. *Flacci Albini seu Alcuini Opera Omnia*; (nos. **24**, **25**, **26** and **62**).

V = BL MS. Arundel 155; 11th century, Canterbury. Another 'typical' (see *Q*) psalter; the litany is followed by a series of prayers more like those in *G* in that they are a mixture of long and short texts, a number of them with interlinear glosses in Old English; (nos. **16**, **17**, **19**, **24**, **25**, **26** and **68**).

W = *The Psalter Collects from V–VIth century sources*, ed. Louis Brou, HBS LXXXIII, London, 1949; (no. **28**).

X = Basle MS. A.vii.3; 9th century; this is a Greek psalter with an interlinear Latin version which has at its beginning a few hymns and prayers added in Irish script; (no. **31**).

---

[31] T. H. Bestul, 'St. Anselm and the Continuity of Anglo-Saxon Devotional Traditions', p. 22.

Y = BN ms. lat. 1105. *The Bec Missal*, ed. A. Hughes, HBS XCIV, London, 1963; 13th century, Bec; (nos. **88** and **89**).

Z = BL MS. Harl. 2892. *The Canterbury Benedictional*, HBS LI, ed. R. M. Woolley, London, 1917; late 11th century, Canterbury; (no. **53**).

Þ = *The Gregorian Sacramentary*, ed. H. A. Wilson, HBS XLIX, London, 1915; (no. **81**).

De = *Le sacramentaire grégorien*, ed. J. Deshusses, Fribourg, 1979; (nos. **29, 33, 41, 43, 47, 48, 49, 53, 55, 56, 69, 71, 72, 81, 86** and **89**).

Ma = Ms. Orléans 184 (printed in *De antiquis ecclesiae ritibus*, ed. E. Martène, Antwerp, 1736). This is the 'Fleury' prayer-book, dating from the ninth century, and perhaps originally from Salzburg or Saint Benoît-sur-Loire.[32] This collection of prayers is found among the works of Isidore of Seville (pp. 240–60). This *livret* seems to be a typical Carolingian collection of private devotions. These are found usually in larger compilations, oftentimes of a theological or liturgical nature. They are not always generically related to the other material in the manuscripts, though they are sometimes associated with the author(s) of the other works therein; *Wi* (q.v.) is an edition of four such booklets; (nos. **24, 26, 31** and **67**).

Wi = *Precum libelli quattuor aeui karolini*, ed. A. Wilmart, Rome, 1940. As the title of this edition indicates, *Wi* is an edition of four distinct *livrets* or *libelli*: (i) *libellus Trecensis*, ms. 1742 in the Bibliothèque municipale of Troyes, ff. 52ᵛ–80ʳ; (ii) *Libellus Parisinus*, BN ms. lat. 5596, ff. 119ᵛ–134ᵛ; ca. 815–825; (iii) *Libellus Coloniensis* ms. 106 in the Dombibliothek in Cologne; post 800; (iv) *Libellus Turonensis*, BN ms. lat. 13388; late 9th or early 10th century. In the apparatus, these have been treated under the covering siglum *Wi*; the following information details more specifically the texts for which each has been used as an analogue: (i), nos. **24** and **26**; (ii), nos. **23** and **68**; (iii), no. **26**; (iv), nos. **26** and **69**.

Or = Ms. Orléans 116; *ca.* 850, probably from Saint Benoît-sur-Loire; the *livret* appears on ff. 21ᵛ–28ʳ; for the rest, the manuscript is a collection of miscellaneous liturgical material; (16, 23, 24).

---

[32] As R. Constantinescu observed, 'Les origines du livret de Fleury . . . sont obscures' ('Alcuin et les "Libelli Precum" de l'époque carolingienne', p. 21).

Section II: manuscripts consulted but not reported in the critical apparatus

BN ms. lat. 2731A; 9/10th century; there is a *libellus precum* on ff. 41ᵛ–64ᵛ containing analogues for nos. **26** and **28** in *G*. Wilmart discusses these prayers in *Revue Bénédictine* 48 (1936), 278–95.

BN ms. lat. 2882; 12th century; there is a Carolingian prayer-book on ff. 72ᵛ–91ᵛ, consisting of approximately 60 short prayers (preceded by Anselm's *Monologion* and *Proslogion*). On f. 85ᵛ there is a prayer corresponding loosely to one petition of no. **67**, and on the last folio there is an analogue for the first two lines of no. **26**. Wilmart discusses these prayers in *Auteurs*, pp. 154 sqq.

CUL MS. Ff. 1.23 (the 'Cambridge Psalter'); *c.* 1025; in Latin with an interlinear Old English gloss. The psalter is followed by 2 prayers, the canticles, gloria, pater noster, creeds, a litany, and a large number of short prayers (ff. 276ᵛ–281ᵛ), only one of which corresponds to a text in *G* (277ᵛ = no. **68**). This psalter is structured in the continental style (cp. *Q* and *V* above).

CCCC MS. 272. A psalter with collects; 9th century, Rheims; also contains the canticles, 'Psalter Collects', various responses for the liturgical year, a litany, and some prayers; there are analogues for nos. **17**, **24**, and **28**.

BL MS. Cotton Titus D.xxvi; ante 1035, New Minster, Winchester; a collectar containing prayers, a litany, a calendar, computational tables, devotions to the Cross (prayers and hymns), and Ælfric's *De temporibus anni*. This manuscript is of interest primarily because it has the same date and provenance as *G*, and also because it contains feminine glosses (on ff. 49, 51, 53, 61, 67, 68 and 75).

BL MS. Cotton Titus D.xxvii; described by Ker as a 'commonplace book', its contents are listed in detail in *Cerne* (p. xxxiii). It begins with a calendar and computational tables, followed by the Passion according to John, a full-page painting of the Crucifixion (f. 65ᵛ), devotions to the Cross, and other short prayers including the hymn 'Vexilla regis'. This manuscript, like *O* (q.v.), has the crucifixion as its thematic nucleus.

* * *

The pre-Conquest continental and insular devotional traditions seem to be represented by different kinds of compilations if analogues *Or*, *Wi* and *Ma* are understood to represent the former, and *O*, *C*, and *R* the latter. On the continent, these collections of prayers (*livrets/libelli*) are embedded in manuscripts usually containing theological works, liturgical texts, or some mixture of these. The prayers attributed to a prominent figure like Alcuin (and later Anselm) are included with larger works associated with his name. There are no theological or liturgical texts in the insular prayer-books. Two of the insular books have a central theme, Christ's Passion and Death, governing their structure—*O* and Titus D.xxvii. At a later date, these collections of prayers are commonly found at the end of psalters; they have been referred to here as 'typical' continental manuscripts, but are found in England as well.

There does not seem to be any reason to assume that the insular devotional tradition was dependent on that of the continent except in so far as a number of popular Carolingian texts are found here and there in *later* manuscripts; in fact, it is not inconceivable that the lines of influence were exactly the opposite, and that Alcuin was responsible for the rise in popularity of devotional compilations on the Continent. There is considerable evidence that the devotional tradition developed early and evolved uninterruptedly in England. Both *R* and *C* are regarded as 'private' collections, and both are thought to contain material from different periods in the insular tradition, drawing on devotions representing both the Celtic and Roman streams.[33] Though there are but a handful of witnesses for the English book of private devotions from this early period, the format of *O*, *R*, and *C* suggests that there was some consensus concerning the contents of such books: they began with readings from the gospels, followed by hymns, poems, and prayers of various length. They might contain a litany, antiphons, or a breviate psalter; each book contained some combination of these without specific attention to proportion.[34] Finally, they were self-contained, and were generally longer collections than those on the continent.

[33] In this concluding statement I am combining my own observations with those of K. Hughes (*op. cit*) and D. Dumville (*op. cit.*).

[34] R. Constantinescu describes these books thus: 'Écriture; martyrs et confesseurs: Pères de l'Église; antiennes; litanies, hymnes et poèmes divers; c'est d'ailleurs, le cadre de tous les livres de prière privée compilés en Angleterre au viiie siècle' (*op. cit.*, p. 18); which, though describing the contents accurately, suggests that a large number of books survive.

What then can be said of *G–N*? If Titus D.xxvi is rightly described by Ker as a commonplace book (and it seems to be), then *G–N* must be called a miscellany, or better, a collection of miscellaneous private devotions. It contains many of the items characteristic of the 'traditional' insular compilations, but lacks the structural principle associated with them. Earlier in the Introduction it was suggested that this is because it was first produced as a blank book, and so reflects the ideas of a number of contributors as to what ought to be recorded in such a collection. The large proportion of 'monastic' texts included in it indicates its institutional affiliations; the presence of texts in translation reflects the influence of the Benedictine Revival of the late tenth and early eleventh centuries.

The Plates

Several reproductions of folios from *G* have been included at the end
of the present volume to give the reader an idea of the severity of the
damage to some of the folios, and of the relatively good condition of
many others. All the folios in *G* have suffered either fire or water
damage, often both.

Plates 1–3: 20^{r-v}, 21^r. These are three of the most well-preserved
folios; they are especially interesting since they contain the newly
discovered copy of the poem 'Altus prosator'. Note the stress marks.

Plate 4: 28^v. Note the initial decorated with interlace, the stress
marks, and the punctuation at the end of the third last line.

Plates 5–6: 103^{r-v}. This folio has sustained an 'average' amount of
damage, i.e. both fire and water damage to all margins, with long slits
into them where the folio has ripped; parts of the text not lost are
illegible because the ink has been washed away. Note the short lines in
double columns with interlinear musical notation.

Plates 7–8: 111^{r-v}. This folio has suffered severe damage to the outer
margin. The rectangular patches down this margin are strips of badly
discoloured tape which were used to prevent further deterioration
originally, but now, unfortunately, serve only to obliterate part of the
text. The text is in Old English. The photographs were taken with the
aid of ultra-violet light.

BIBLIOGRAPHY

Banks, R. A. 'Some Anglo-Saxon Prayers from BM Cotton Galba A. xiv', *N&Q* 210 (1965) 207–13.

Bestul, T. H. 'St. Anselm and the Continuity of Anglo-Saxon Devotional Traditions', *Annuale Mediaevale* 18 (1977) 20–41.

Bignami-Odier, J. et al. *Bibliographie sommaire des travaux du père André Wilmart O.S.B. 1876–1941*, Sussidi Eruditi 5, Rome, 1953.

Birch, W. de Gray. *An Ancient Manuscript*, London, 1889.

——. *Cartularium Saxonicum*, 3 vols., London, 1885–93.

Bishop, E. *Liturgica Historica*, Oxford, 1918.

Bishop, E. and F. A. Gasquet. *The Bosworth Psalter*, London, 1908.

Braekmann, W. 'Some Minor Old English Texts', *Archiv* 202 (1966) 271–76.

Brou, L. *The Psalter Collects from V–VIth century Sources*, HBS LXXXIII, London, 1949 (edited from the papers of A. Wilmart).

Brown, T. J. et al. *The Durham Ritual*, EEMF 16, Copenhagen, 1969.

Bruckmann, J. 'Latin Manuscript Pontificals and Benedictionals in England and Wales', *Traditio* 29 (1973) 391–458.

Bullough, D. A. 'The Continental Background of the Reform', in *Tenth Century Studies*, ed. D. Parsons, London, 1975, 20–36.

——. 'Alcuin and the Kingdom of Heaven; Liturgy, Theology, and the Carolingian Age', in *Carolingian Essays*, ed. U. Blumenthal, Washington, 1983, 1–70.

Chevalier, U. *Repertorium Hymnologicum*, 6 vols., Louvain, 1892–1920.

Cockayne, T. O. *Leechdoms, Wortcunnings and Starcraft of Early England*, 3 vols., London, 1864–66, repr. 1961.

Constantinescu, R. 'Alcuin et les "Libelli Precum" de l'époque carolingienne', *RHS* 50 (1974) 17–56.

Denzinger, H. and A. Schönmetzer. *Enchiridion Symbolorum Definitionum Declarationum*, Freiburg, 1965.

Deshusses, J. *Le sacramentaire grégorien*, 2nd ed., Fribourg-en-Suisse, 1979.

Dewick, E. S. *The Leofric Collectar*, HBS XLV, London, 1914.

Dumville, D. N. 'Liturgical Drama and Panegyric Responsory from the Eighth Century? A Re-Examination of the Origin and Contents of the Ninth-Century Section of the Book of Cerne', *JTS* N.S. 23 (1972) 374–406.

———. 'Biblical Apocrypha and the Early Irish; A Preliminary Investigation', *RIA Proceedings* 73 (1973) 299–338.

Gamber, K. *Codices Liturgici Latini Antiquiores*, 2 vols., Freiburg, 1968.

Gatch, M. 'Old English Literature and the Liturgy: Problems and Potential', *ASE* 6 (1977) 237–48.

Gjerløw, L. 'Notes on the Book of Cerne and on MS Uppsala C 222', *Nordisk Tidskrift för Bok- och Biblioteksväsen* 47 (1960) 1–29.

———. *Adoratio Crucis*, Oslo, 1961.

Gneuss, H. 'The Origin of Standard Old English and Æthelwold's School at Winchester', *ASE* 1 (1972) 63–83.

———. 'A Preliminary List of Manuscripts written or owned in England up to 1100', *ASE* 9 (1981) 1–60.

Hohler, C. 'Some Service Books of the Late Saxon Church', in *Tenth Century Studies*, ed. D. Parsons, London, 1975, 60–83.

Holthausen, F. 'Altenglische Interlinearversione lateinischen Gebete und Beichten', *Anglia* 65 (1941) 230–54.

Hughes, A. *The Portiforium of Saint Wulstan*, vol. 2, HBS XC, London, 1960.

Hughes, K. 'Some Aspects of Irish Influence on Early English Private Prayer', *Studia Celtica* 5 (1970) 48–61.

Jones, C. W. *Bedae opera de temporibus*, Cambridge, Mass., 1943.

Jungmann, J. A. *Die lateinischen Bussriten in ihren geschichtlichen Entwicklung*, Innsbruck, 1932.

———. *The Mass of the Roman Rite (Missarum Sollemnia)*, trans. F. A. Brunner, New York, 1951.

Ker, N. R. *A Catalogue of Manuscripts containing Anglo-Saxon*, Oxford, 1957.

Kuypers, A. B. *The Prayer Book of Aedeluald the Bishop, commonly called the Book of Cerne*, Cambridge, 1902.

Lapidge, M. 'Some Latin Poems as Evidence for the Reign of Athelstan', *ASE* 9 (1981) 61–98.

Lawlor, H. J. *The Rosslyn Missal*, HBS XV, London, 1899.

Legg, J. W. *Missale ad usum Ecclesie Westmonasteriensis*, 3 vols., HBS I, V and XII, London, 1891–97.

Levison, W. 'Alchfrid the Anchorite and the Book of Cerne', in *England and the Continent in the Eighth Century*, Oxford, 1946, 295–302.

Logeman, H. 'Anglo-Saxonica Minora', *Anglia* 11 (1889) 97–120.

Martène, E. *De antiquis ecclesiae ritibus*, Antwerp, 1736.

Mohrmann, C. *Annus Festivus*, Brussels, 1938.

Muir, B. J. 'Two Latin Poems by Colum Cille (St. Columba)', *Revue du moyen age latin* 39 (1983) 205–16.

Parsons, D., ed. *Tenth Century Studies*, London 1975.

Salmon, P. 'Livrets de prières de l'époque carolingienne', *Revue Bénédictine* 96 (1976) 218–34.

Smith, T. *Catalogus librorum manuscriptorum Bibliothecae Cottonianae*, Oxford, 1696, repr. ed. C. G. C. Tite, Cambridge, 1984.

Stevenson, W. H. 'A Latin Poem addressed to King Athelstan', *EHR* 26 (1911) 482–7.

Symons, T. *The Monastic Agreement of the Monks and Nuns of the English Nation or Regularis Concordia*, London, 1953.

———. 'Regularis Concordia: History and Derivation', in *Tenth Century Studies*, ed. D. Parsons, London, 1975, 37–59.

Szövérffy, J. *Die Annalen der lateinischen Hymnendichtung*, 2 vols., Berlin, 1964–65.

Tolhurst, J. B. L. *The Monastic Breviary of Hyde Abbey, Winchester*, 6 vols., HBS LXIX, LXX, LXXI, LXXVI, LXXVIII and LXXX, London, 1932–42.

Turner, D. H. 'The Prayer-Book of Archbishop Arnulph II of Milan', *Revue Bénédictine* 70 (1960) 360–92.

———. *The Missal of the New Minster*, HBS XCIII, London, 1962.

Ure, J. M. *The Benedictine Office*, Edinburgh, 1957.

Wanley, J. *Librorum veterum septentrionalium catalogus*, repr. Scolar Press, 1971.

Wilmart, A. 'Prières médiévales pour l'adoration de la croix', *Ephemerides liturgicae* 46 (1932) 22–65.

———. *Precum libelli quattuor aeui karolini*, Rome, 1940.

———. *Auteurs spirituels et textes dévots du moyen âge latin*, Paris, 1932, repr. 1971.

Wilson, H. A. *The Benedictional of Archbishop Robert*, HBS XXIV, London, 1903.

———. *The Missal of Robert of Jumièges*, HBS XI, London, 1896.

Winterfeld, P. von. *MGH Poetae latini aeui carolini*, vol. IV, Berlin, 1899.

Wordsworth, C. and H. Littlehales. *The Old Service-Books of the English Church*, London, 1904.

Wormald, F. *English Kalendars before A.D. 1100*, HBS LXXII, London, 1934.

Zupitza, J. 'Kreuzandacht, Kreuzzauber', *Archiv* 87 (1892) 361–64.

NOTE ON EDITORIAL PROCEDURE

All abbreviations have been expanded (with the exception of a few in the computational tables whose significance is obvious), and are in italics; they have been expanded in accordance with the orthographical practice of the various scribes. Punctuation and capitalization are editorial; stress marks and the interlinear musical notation have not been reproduced. The use of coloured ink has not been noted unless it seemed of interest.

The critical apparatus is in English. There are three registers of notes on most pages: the top set (keyed with lower-case letters) contains textual notes, usually indicating where the manuscript was damaged in the fire; the middle set (keyed with upper-case letters) contains the variant readings drawn from the analogues upon which the reconstruction has been based; the bottom set (numbered) contains all the notes which do not fall into one of the two categories just mentioned. Square brackets indicate words to be deleted from the text; angle brackets, material added editorially; and three asterisks, damaged and, at this stage, irrecoverable sections of the text. A dagger on either side of a word indicates a *locus desperandus*; this has been used sparingly.

Abbreviations

add.   added / Additional
Archiv   Archiv für das Studium der neueren Sprachen und Literaturen
art.   article
ASE   Anglo-Saxon England
ASPR   Anglo-Saxon Poetic Records
BL   British Library
BN   Bibliothèque Nationale
CCCC   Corpus Christi College, Cambridge
col.   column
cont.   continues

corr.   corrected
Cot.   Cotton
CUL   Cambridge University Library
EEMF   Early English Manuscripts in Facsimile
EHR   English Historical Review
f(f).   folio(s)
Harl.   Harleian
HBS   Henry Bradshaw Society Publications
ILH   Irish Liber Hymnorum
interl.   interlinear / -ly
JTL   Journal of Theological Studies
l(l).   line(s)
lt   letter / -s
marg.   margin
MGH   Monumenta Germaniae Historica
MS(S).   manuscript(s)
mun.   municipale
N&Q   Notes and Queries
no(s).   number(s)
nt.   note
om.   omit / -s
oppos.   opposite
PL   Patrologia Latina
r   recto
RHS   Revue d'histoire de la spiritualité
RIA   Royal Irish Academy
sq(q).   and following
sup.   above
Tib.   Tiberius
trans.   transactions
v   verso / verse
vis.   visible
vol(s).   volume(s)
wd   word / -s

Sigla

For further annotations and bibliographical data on these manuscripts and editions, see pp. xxvii–xxxi.

A = BL MS. Harl. 2961
B = Dublin, RIA MS. 23.P.16
C = CUL MS. 2139
D = Durham Cathedral Library MS. A.iv.19
E = Milan, Biblioteca ambrosiana ms. S.Q.N.III.14
F = Library of the Franciscan Convent, Dublin, *Liber Hymnorum*
G = BL MS. Cotton Galba A. xiv
H = Le Havre, Bibliothèque mun. ms. 330
I = *MGH Poetae latini aeui carolini*
J = Rouen, Bibliothèque mun. ms. Y.6
K = Edinburgh, Faculty of Advocates Library MS. 18.5.19
L = BL MS. Royal 12.D.xvii
M = Westminster Abbey Library MS. 37
N = BL MS. Cotton Nero A. ii
O = BL MS. Harl. 2965
P = CCCC MS. 391
Q = BL MS. Harl. 863
R = BL MS. Royal 2.A.xx
S = *Regularis Concordia*
T = Dublin, Trinity College Library MS. E.4.2
U = *PL* 101
V = BL MS. Arundel 155
W = *The Psalter Collects*
X = Basle MS. A.vii.3
Y = BN ms. lat. 1105
Z = BL MS. Harl. 2892
P̵ = *The Gregorian Sacramentary*
De = *Le sacramentaire grégorien*
Ma = Ms. Orléans 184
Wi = *Precum libelli quattuor aeui karolini*
Or = Ms. Orléans 116

British Library, Cotton Nero A.ii,
ff. 3–13

[1] This calendar has been printed previously by: (1) F. Wormald, *English Kalendars before A.D. 1100, vol. 1*, HBS LXXII, London, 1934, pp. 28–41, with a plate of f. 7ᵛ facing p. 29; and (2) F. A. Gasquet and E. Bishop, *The Bosworth Psalter*, London, 1908, pp. 165–71. Folio 10ᵛ has been reproduced by F. Rose-Troup, 'The Ancient Monastery of St Mary and St Peter at Exeter', *Transactions of the Devonshire Association* 63, p. 179. Wormald remarks that this calendar represents 'the early type of English Kalendar containing many martyrological entries (*op. cit.*, p. ui)'. He prints four other calendars from in or around Winchester: nos. 9 (1023–35), 10 (1025), 11 (1060) and 12 (1060).

2

1

⟨Calendar⟩[1]

⟨January⟩

f. 3^r

1] iii	a	*Kalendae* Ianu*arii* : Circumcisio D*omi*ni.
2]	b	iiii N. : Isidori, Ep*iscopi*.
3] xi	c	iii N. : Genosese, U*irginis*.
4]	d	ii N.
5] xix	e	N*onae*.
6] uiii	f	uiii Id. : Epiphania D*omi*ni.
7]	g	uii Id.
8] xiii	a	ui Id.
9] u	b	u Id. : *Sancti* Æþelmodi, C*onfessoris*.
10]	c	iiii Id.
11] xiii	d	iii Id.
12] ii	e	ii Id. : Benedicti, Abb*atis*.
13]	f	Id*us* : Oct*aba* Epiphanie.
14] x	g	xix k. Febr*uarii* : Felicis, Ep*iscopi*.
15]	a	xuiii k. : Calesti, Pape *et* Mauri, Abb*atis*.
16] xuiii	b	xuii k. : Marcelli, Pape.
17] uiii	c	xui k. : Antoni, Monachi.
18]	d	xu k. : Prisce, U*irginis*.
19] xii	e	xiiii k. : Marie et Marthe.
20] iiii	f	xiii k. : Sabastiani *et* Fabiani.
21]	g	xii k. : Agne, U*irginis*.
22] xii	a	xi k. : Uincentii, M*artyris*.
23] i	b	x k. : Emerentiane, U*irginis et* M*artyris*.
24]	c	ix k. : Babilli, Ep*iscopi et* M*artyris*.
25] ix	d	uiii k. : Conuertio Pauli.
26]	e	uii k. : Policarpi, M*artyris*.
27] xuii	f	ui k. : Saturnini cum xxxu Mar*tyribus*.
28] ui	g	u k. : Sabine, U*irginis et* Agnetis, U*irginis*.
29]	a	iiii k. : Gylde, C*onfessoris*.
30] xiiii	b	iii k. : Balthildis, Regine.
31] iii	c	ii k.

5] Nonae: *an abbreviation sign is wanting*   13] *MS*. epiphania
28] et Agnetis Uirginis: *added by another hand*

3

‹February›

f. 3ᵛ

1]		d	Kal*endae* Febru*arii* : Brigide, U*irginis*.
2]	xi	e	iiii N. : Purificatio S*ancte* Marie.
3]	xix	f	iii N. : Wærburge, U*irginis*.
4]	uiii	g	ii N.
5]		a	N*onae* : Agathe, U*irginis*.
6]	xui	b	uiii Id. : i incens*io* lu*ne* i*n*itii.
7]	u	c	uii Id. : Uer oritur, habe*t* xcii.
8]		d	ui Id. : Pri*mus* di*es* initii. Cuþmanni, C*onfessoris*.
9]	xiii	e	u Id. : Alaxandri.
10]	ii	f	iiii Id. : Scolastice, U*irginis*.
11]		g	iii Id. : Eulalie, U*irginis*.
12]	x	a	ii Id. : Castrenensis, M*artyris*.
13]		b	Id*us* : Iuliani, M*artyris*.
14]	xuiii	c	xui K. Martii : Ualentini, M*artyris*.
15]	uii	d	xu K. : Sol in pisces. Iouite, U*irginis*.
16]		e	xiiii K. : Iuliane, U*irginis et* Uitalis, M*artyris*.
17]	xu	f	xiii K. : Donati, M*artyris*.
18]	iiii	g	xii K. : Martialis.
19]		a	xi K. : Pollicarpi, Ep*iscop*i *et* M*artyris*.
20]	xii	b	x K. : Calesti, Pape *et* Gagii, Ep*iscop*i.
21]	i	c	ix K. : Uictoris, M*artyris*.
22]		d	uiii K. : Cathedra Petri.
23]	ix	e	uii K. : Milburge, U*irginis*.
24]		f	ui K. : Mathie, Ap*ostol*i. Locus bissextus.
25]	xuii	g	u K. : Inuentio capitis Pauli.
26]	ui	a	iiii K. : Cipriani *et* Alaxandri.
27]		b	iii K. : Inuentio capitis Ioh*annis* Bap*tiste*.
28]	xiiii	c	ii K.

2] *MS*. purificatione   4] *Something has been erased after this date*
5] Nonae: *an abbreviation sign is missing*   7] *MS*. uerus   14] xuiii : *the second*
'i' has been added interlinearly   15] *MS*. piscem   24] Mathie: *this has been*
corrected from '-ii'   27] *MS*. caput

⟨March⟩

f. 4^r	1]	d	*Kalendae* Mar*tii* : Donati, Ep*iscop*i, M*artyris* et Deawig, Ep*iscop*i.

f. 4^r

1]   d *Kalendae* Mar*tii* : Donati, Ep*iscop*i, M*artyris* et Deawig, Ep*iscop*i.

2]   e ui N. : Adriani, M*artyris*.

3] xi   f u N. : Albini, Ep*iscop*i *et* Felicis.

4]   g iiii N. : Uictoris cu*m* dccc Mar*tyribus*.

5] xix a iii N. : Eusebii *et* Saturnini.

6] uiii b ii N. : Ultima ii lu*ne* initii.

7]   c Nonae : i incen*sio* xiiii lu*ne* pas*chalis*.

8] xui d uiii Id. : Candide, U*irginis*.

9] u   e uii Id. : xl militu*m*.

10]   f ui Id. : Martiani *et* Gorgoni, M*artyris*.

11] xiii g u Id.

12] ii   a iiii Id. : Gregorii, Pape.

13]   b iii Id.

14] x   c ii Id.

15]   d Id*us*.

16] xuiiii e xuii Kl. Aprilis : Eugenie, U*irginis*.

17] uiii f xui Kl. : Patrici, Ep*iscop*i.

18]   g xu Kl. : Eadweardi, M*artyris*.

19] xu a xiiii Kl. : Theodoli, Ep*iscop*i.

20] iiii b xiii Kl. : Cuþberhti, Ep*iscop*i.

21]   c xii Kl. : Benedicti, Abb*atis*.

22] xii d xi Kl.

23] i   e x Kl.

24]   f ix Kl.

25] ix g uiii Kl. : Adnuntiatio S*anct*e Mar⟨ie⟩.

26]   a uii Kl. : Eulalie, U*irginis*.

27] xuii b ui Kl.

28] ui   c u Kl.

29]   d iiii Kl.

30] xiiii e iii Kl.

31] iii   f ii Kl.

6] *MS. initi*   7] Nonae: *an abbreviation sign is missing*
8] uiii: *MS.* uii   12] iiii: *MS.* iii   25] Marie: *MS. damaged*

⟨April⟩

f. 4ᵛ

1]		g	*Kalendae* Aprilis : Ualentini, *Confessoris.*
2]	i	a	iiii N.
3]		b	iii N. : Theodocie, U*irginis.*
4]	ix	c	ii N. : Ambrosi, Ep*iscop*i *et* C*onfessoris.*
5]	u	d	Nonae : Ultima incens*io* xiiii *lune* pas*chalis.*
6]	ui	e	uiii Id. : Prima incens*io lune* rog*ationum* xxi.
7]	i	f	uii Id.
8]		g	ui Id. : Machari, P*resbiteri.*
9]	ii	a	u Id. : uii Uirginu*m.*
10]	i	b	iiii Id. Theodori, *Confessoris.*
11]		c	iii Id. Cuthlaci, *Confessoris et* Leonis *et* Hilari.
12]		d	ii Id.
13]		e	Id*us* : Eufemie, U*irginis.*
14]	ii	f	xuiii Kl. Maii : Tiburti *et* Ualeriani, M*artyrum.*
15]	ii	g	xuii Kl.
16]		a	xui Kl.
17]	i	b	xu Kl. : Sol in tauru*m.*
18]	ii	c	xiiii Kl. : Ultima xiiii lu*ne* pas*chalis.*
19]		d	xiii Kl.
20]	i	e	xii Kl.
21]		f	xi Kl.
22]	★	g	x Kl.
23]	★	a	ix Kl. : Georgi, M*artyris.*
24]		b	uiii Kl. : Melliti, Ep*iscop*i *et* Wilfridi, Ep*iscop*i.
25]	i	c	uii Kl. : Letania maiore. Marci, Eu*angeliste.*
26]		d	ui Kl.
27]		e	u Kl. : Anastasi, Ep*iscop*i.
28]	i	f	iiii Kl. : Uitalis, M*artyris et* Cristofori, M*artyris.*
29]		g	iii Kl.
30]		a	ii Kl. : Erconwaldi, Ep*iscop*i.

2, 4, etc.] *The left-hand margin has been trimmed, leaving all of the Golden Numbers defective*   5] Nonae: *an abbreviation sign is missing*   17] taurum: *first 'u' added interlinearly*

6

⟨May⟩

f. 5^r

Hora iii		*et* ix : pedes ix; H⟨ora ui : pedes ★★★⟩²
1]	xi	b *K*alendae Ma*ii* : Philippi *et* Iacobi.
2]		c ui N. : [Inue].
3]	xix	d u N. : Inuentio *Sancte* Crucis.
4]	uiii	e iiii N. : Ultima incen*sio lune* xx *r*ogationum.
5]		f iii N. : i ⟨incensio lune⟩ pen*tecostes* i ascensio.
6]	xui	g ii N. : Ioh*annis* Apos*t*oli ante porta*m* lati⟨nam⟩.
7]	u	a N*onae* : Ioh*annis*, Ep*iscop*i.
8]		b uiii Id. : Uictoris, *M*artyris.
9]	xiii	c uii Id. : Æstas orit*ur*. Transla*tio* And⟨reæ⟩.
10]	ii	d ui Id. : Gordiani *et* Epimathi, *M*artyrum.
11]		e u Id. : Mamerti, Ep*iscop*i.
12]	x	f iiii Id. : Nerei *et* Achilei *et* Pancrati, *M*artyrum.
13]		g iii Id.
14]	xuiii	a ii Id. : Machuti cu*m* cccciiii Mar*tyribus*.
15]	uii	b Id*us* : i Pen*tecostes*.
16]		c xuii K. Iun*ii* : Eugenie, U*irginis*.
17]	xu	d xui K.
18]	iiii	e xu K.
19]		f xiiii K. : Potentiane, U*irginis et* Dunstani.
20]	xii	g xiii K. : Æþelbrihti, *M*artyris *et* Nicodemis.
21]	i	a xii K.
22]		b xi K. : Helene, U*irginis*.
23]	ix	c x K. : Petrocii, *C*onfessoris.
24]		d ix K. : Ultima xxi *lune* roga*tionum*. Estas ori*tur*.
25]	xuii	e uiii K. : Urbani, *M*artyris *et* Hæmma, Abb*atis*.
26]	ui	f uii K. : Augustini, Ep*iscop*i *et* Bede, Presbi*teri*.
27]		g ui K. : Germani, Ep*iscop*i.
28]	xiiii	a u K.
29]	iii	b iiii K. : Felicis, *M*artyris *et* Pape.
30]		c iii K. : Felicitatis, *M*artyris.
31]	xi	d ii K. : Petronelle, filia Petri.

1] *The rest of the line was lost when the page was trimmed*   3] *The scribe accidentally started the entry for l. 3 here and stopped*   5] incensio lune: *MS. faded*
6, 9] *The ends of these lines were lost when the page was trimmed*
7] Nonae: *an abbreviation sign is missing*

² This line has been misinterpreted in the past by lexicographers who have understood *pedes* as somehow being a unit of time since it is coupled with the word *hora*. In fact, these figures, which also appear for June, July, August, September and December in this text, give the length of the shadow at three different times of the day, 9 a.m., noon and 3 p.m. For a more complete table, see T. O. Cockayne, *Leechdoms, Wortcunning and Starcraft of Early England*, III, pp. 162–7.

⟨June⟩

f. 5ᵛ Hora iii   *et* ix : p*edes* uiii; H*ora* ui : p*edes* ii.

1]	e	K*alendae* Iun*ii* : Nicomedis, M*artyris*.
2] xix	f	iiii N. : Marcelli *et* Petri *et* Erasmi, M*artyrum*.
3] uiii	g	iii N. : Ultima incent*io* iiii *lune* Pentecostes.
4] xui	a	ii N. Ultimo ascens*io* Domini.
5] u	b	N*onae* : Bonefatii, M*artyris et* Pape.
		Apollonaris, M*artyris*.
6]	c	uiii Id. : Furtuna *et* Audomari.
7] xiii	d	uii Id. : Pauli *et* Fursei.
8] ii	e	ui Id. : Medardi *et* Gildardi.
9]	f	u Id. : P*rimi et* Feliciani *et* Collu*m*cylle, C*onfessoris*.
10] x	g	iiii Id.
11]	a	iii Id. : Barnabe, Ap*ostoli*.
12] xuiii	b	ii Id. : Basilidis, Cirini, Naboris, Nazari, M*artyrum*.
13] uii	c	Id*us* : Ultima Pen*tecostes*.
14]	d	xuiii K. Iul*ii* : Aniani, Ep*iscopi*.
15] xu	e	xuii K. : Uiti, Modesti *et* Crescente, M*artyrum*.
16] iiii	f	xui K. : Ciriaci *et* Iuliani cum xl milia.
17]	g	xu K. : Sol in cancrum. Botulfi, Ep*iscopi*.
18] xii	a	xiiii K. : Marci *et* Marcelliani, Mar*tyrum*.
19] i	b	xiii K. : Geruasi *et* Protasi, M*artyrum*.
20]	c	xii K. : Solstitiu*m* s*ecundu*m Grecos.
21] ix	d	xi K. : Leodfriþi, Ep*iscopi et* C*onfessoris*.
22]	e	x K.
23] xuii	f	ix K. : Uig*i*lia Ioh*ann*is. Æþeldryþe, U*irginis*.
24] ui	g	uiii K. : Natiuitas Ioh*ann*is. Solstitiu*m* s*ecundum*
		Romanos.
25]	a	uii K.
26] xiiii	b	ui K. : Ioh*ann*is *et* Pauli *et* Salui.
27] iii	c	u K. : Simforose cu*m* uii filiis.
28]	d	iiii K. : Uig*i*lia. *Et* Leonis, Pape.
29] xi	e	iii K. : Petri *et* Pauli.
30]	f	ii K. : Pauli.

1] Iunii: *added interlinearly*   4] xui: *a second 'i' has been scratched away*
5] Nonae: *an abbreviation sign is missing*   martyris: *added interlinearly*
12] xuiii: *second 'i' added above*   Nazari Martyrum: *written interlinearly above from '-ri'*
24] Romanos: *'-anos' written above*

8

⟨July⟩

f. 6ʳ Hora iii   *et* ix : *pedes* uiii; H*ora* ui : *pedes* ui.

1] xix   g K*alendae* Iul*ii* : Timothei *et* Agapiti. Oc*taua* Ioh*annis*.
2] uiii   a ui N. : Processi *et* Martiniani, C*onfessorum*.
3]   b u N.
4] xui   c iiii N. : Tra*nslatio* S*ancti* Martini.
5] u   d iii N.
6]   e ii N. : Oc*taua* Ap*ostolorum et* Sexburge, U*irginis*.
7] xiii   f N*onae* : Marine, U*irginis et* S*ancti* Ercenwaldi.
8] ii   g uiii Id. : Grimbaldi, C*onfessoris et* Quintini.
9]   a uii Id. : Anatholie, U*irginis*.
10] x   b ui Id. : uii fr*atum et* Felicitatis, M*artyrum*.
11]   c u Id. : Benedicti, Abb*atis*.
12] xuiii   d iiii Id.
13] uii   e iii Id. : Mildryþe, U*irginis et* Margarete, ⟨U*irginis*⟩.
14]   f ii Id. : Dies caniculares 1.
15] xu   g Id*us* : Cirici pueri *et* Iulite matris eius.
16] iiii   a xuii K. A*ugusti*.
17]   b xui K. : Kenelmi, M*artyris*.
18] xii   c xu K. : Sol in leone.
19] i   d xiiii K.
20]   e xiii K.
21] ix   f xii K.
22]   g xi K.
23] xuii   a x K.
24] ui   b ix K.
25]   c uiii K. : Iacobi, Ap*ostoli*.
26] xiiii   d uii K.
27] iii   e ui K. : uii dormientiu*m*.
28]   f u K. : Saturnini, Ep*iscopi et* M*artyris*.
29] ui   g iiii K. Felicis *et* Simplici.
30]   a iii K. : Abdon *et* Senen, M*artyrum*.
31] xix   b ii K. : S*ancti* Germani, Ep*iscopi* et S*ancti* Neoti,
   Presb*iteri*.

7] Nonae: *an abbreviation sign is missing*   13] uirginis: *The abbreviation sign was lost when the page was trimmed*   14] *MS.* canculares   27] *MS.* domientium
31] Sancti Germani . . . presbiteri: *added later by another hand*

9

⟨August⟩

f. 6ᵛ Hora iii   *et* ix : p*edes* ix; ⟨Hora ui : pedes ★★★⟩.ᵃ
  1] uiii   c K*alendae* A*ugusti* : Machabeor*um* uii.
  2] xui   d iiii N. : Stephani, Ep*iscopi et* M*artyris.*
  3] u   e iii N. : Inuentio corporis Stephani.
  4]   f ii N.
  5] xiii   g N*onae* : Oswaldi, Regis *et* M*artyris.*
  6] ii   a uiii Id. : Sixti, Ep*iscopi et* M*artyris.*
  7]   b uii Id. : Autumnus orit*ur;* h*abet* d*ies* xcii.
  8] x   c ui Id.
  9]   d u Id. : Uig*ilia.*
  10] xuiii   e iiii Id. : S*ancti* Laurenti, M*artyris.*
  11] uiii   f iii Id.
  12]   g ii Id. : Eupli, M*artyris.*
  13] xu   a Id*us* : Ypoliti, M*artyris.*
  14] iiii   b xix K. : Uig*ilia* Sep*tembris.*
  15]   c xuiii K. : Assumtio S*ancte* Marie.
  16] xii   d xuii K.
  17] i   e xui K. : Oc*taua* Laur⟨entii⟩.
  18]   f xu K. : Sol in uirgine.
  19] ix   g xiiii K. : Magni, M*artyris et* Helene, U*irginis.*
  20]   a xiii K. : Ualentini *et* Maximiani.
  21] xuii   b xii K. : Iulii *et* Iuliani; Simforiani.
  22] ui   c xi K.
  23]   d x K. ★★★
  24] xiiii   e ix K.
  25] iii   f uiii K. : Bartholomei, Ap*ostoli.*
  26]   g uii K.
  27] xi   a ui K.
  28]   b u K.
  29] xix   c iiii K. : Decolatio Ioh*annis* Bap*tiste.*
  30] uiii   d iii K.
  31]   e ii K.

ᵃ *Part of this line was lost when the page was trimmed*   3] *MS.* corpus
5] Nonae: *an abbreviation sign is missing*   7] *MS.* autunus
15] *MS.* assumtione   17] Laurentii: *part of this word has faded or been erased*
18] *MS.* uigine   23] *The entry has been erased*

‹September›

f. 7ʳ Hora iii   et ix : pedes xi; Hora ui : pedes u.

1] xui   f Kalendae Septembris : Prisce, Uirginis et Martyris.
2] u   g iiii N. : Iustini, Episcopi.
3]   a iii N. : Bonefacii, Episcopi et Martyris et Marcelli et Birini.
4] xiii   b ii N.
5] ii   c Nonae : Berhtini, Abbatis; hic finiunt dies c‹ani›cu-
             la‹res›.
6]   d uiii Id.
7] x   e uii Id.
8]   f ui Id. : Natiuitas Sancte Marie.
9] xuiii g u Id. : Gorgoni, Martyris.
10] uii   a iiii Id.
11]   b iii Id. : Proti et Iacincti, Martyrum.
12] xu   c ii Id.
13] iiii d Idus.
14]   e xuiii K. Octobris : Exultatio Sancte Crucis.
15] xii   f xuii K. : Nicomedis, Martyris et Iuliani.
16] i   g xui K. : Eufemie, Uirginis et Martyris et Lucie, Uirginis.
17]   a xu K. : Sol in libram; et Landberhti, E‹piscopi›.
18] ix   b xiiii K. : Meliti, Episcopi.
19]   c xiii K. : Theodori, Episcopi.
20] xuii d xii K. : Uigilia.
21] ui   e xi K. : Mathei, Apostoli et Euangeliste; Equinoctium.
22]   f x K. : Maurici cum ui, dclxui Martyribus.
23] xiiii g ix K. : Tecle, Uirginis et Martyris.
24] iii   a uiii K. : Conceptio Iohannis.
25]   b uii K. : Sancti Firmini, Martyris et Sancti Ceolfridi,
             Abbatis.
26] xi   c ui K. : Cipriani et Iustine, Uirginis.
27]   d u K. : Cosme et Damiani, Martyrum.
28] xix   e iiii K. : Gylde, Confessoris.
29] uiii f iii K. : Dedicatio Ecclesie Michaelis.
30]   g ii K. : Germani, Episcopi et Confessoris.

3] et Birini: *added above*   5] Nonae: *an abbreviation sign is missing.*
caniculares] MS. *illegible.* -cula- *added above line*   17] *MS. illegible*
25] *MS.* Sceollfridi

11

⟨October⟩

f. 7ᵛ

1] xui	a	*Kalendae* Octobris : Remegi *et* Uedasti.
2] u	b	ui N. : Leodgari, Epi*scopi*.
3] xiii	c	u N. : Marci *et* Marcelliani.
4] ii	d	iiii N.
5]	e	iii N. : Cristine, U*irginis*.
6] x	f	ii N.
7]	g	N*onae* : Marci, Pape *et* Marcelli.
8] xuiii	a	uiii Id. : Richari, C*onfessoris et* Faustini, *et* Iwi, C*onfessoris*.
9] uiii	b	uiii Id. : Dionisi, Rustici *et* Eleutheri, M*artyrum*.
10]	c	ui Id. : Paulini, Epi*scopi et* C*onfessoris*.
11] xu	d	u Id. : Æþelburge, U*irginis et* Firmini, Epi*scopi*.
12] iiii	e	iiii Id.
13]	f	iii Id. : Anastati, Epi*scopi*.
14] xii	g	ii Id. : Calesti, Epi*scopi et* M*artyris et* Furtunati, Epi*scopi*.
15] i	a	Id*us*.
16]	b	xuii K. Nou*embris* : Luciani *et* Maximiani.
17] xi	c	xui K. : Æþeldryþe, U*irginis*.
18]	d	xu K. : Luce, Eu*angeliste*.
19] xuii	e	xiiii K.
20] ui	f	xiii K. : Neoti, Presbi*teri*.
21]	g	xii K. : Hilarionis, C*onfessoris*.
22] xiiii	a	xi K. : Flauiani et Filippi.
23] iii	b	x K. : Thodorici, M*artyris*.
24]	c	ix K. : Felicis *et* Audacti, M*artyrum*.
25] xi	d	uiii K. : Crispini *et* Crispiniani, M*artyrum*.
26]	e	uii K. : S*ancti* Eadfridi, C*onfessoris*.
27] xix	f	ui K. : Uig*i*lia.
28] uiii	g	u K. : Simonis *et* Iude.
29]	a	iiii K. : S*ancti* Iacincti, M*artyris*.
30] xui	b	iii K. : Maximiani.
31] u	c	ii K. : Quintini, M*artyris*; Uig*i*lia.

1] *The unusual abbreviations for October (OCB̄) and November (NOB̄) found here occur also in G, f. 2ᵛ*   7] Nonae: *an abbreviation sign is missing*
9] Martyrum: *added above interlinearly*   22] Filippi: *altered from Pilippi*

12

‹November›

1] uiii   d *Kalendae* No*uembris* : Omniu*m* San*ctorum.*
2] xui   e iiii N. : Eustachi, M*artyris.*
3] ii   f iii N. : Rumwaldi *et* Germani, Ep‹iscopi›.
4]   g ii N. : P*er*petue, U*irginis.*
5] x   a N*onae* : Felicis *et* Eusebi.
6]   b uiii Id. : Winnoci, Ep*iscopi.*
7] xuiii c uii Id. : Hiems orit*ur*; habet dies ‹x›cii.
8] uiii d ui Id. : iiii Coronato*rum.*
9]   e u Id. : Theodori, M*artyris.*
10] xu   f iiii Id. : Iusti, Ep*iscopi.*
11] iiii   g iii Id. : Martini, Ep*iscopi et* Menne, M*artyris.*
12]   a ii Id.
13] xii   b Id*us* : Bricii, Ep*iscopi*; Initiu*m* xl hel.
14] i   c xuiii K. De*cembris.*
15]   d xuii K. : Machuti, Ep*iscopi et* C*onfessoris.*
16] ix   e xui K.
17]   f xu K. : Sol in sagitario; *et* Ania‹ni›.
18] xiiii g xiiii K. : Romani *et* Barali, pueri, M*artyrum.*
19] ui   a xiii K.
20]   b xii K.
21] xiiii c xi K. : Colu*m*bani, C*onfessoris.*
22] iii   d x K. : Cecilie, U*irginis.*
23]   e ix K. : Clementis, Pape *et* M*artyris.*
24] xi   f uiii K. Grisogori,[3] M*artyris.*
25]   g uii K.
26] xix a ui K. : Lini, Pape.
27] uiii b u K. : Primus aduent*us* D*o*mini.
28]   c iiii K.
29] xui d iii K. : Saturnini, M*artyris*; Uig‹ilia›.
30] u   e ii K. : Passio Andree, Ap*ostoli.*

3, 7] *MS. illegible where emended*   5] Nonae: *an abbreviation sign is missing*
17, 29] *MS. illegible where emended*

---

³ *Grisogori* This is perhaps a misreading of *Crisogoni.*

13

⟨December⟩

f. 8ᵛ Hora iii *et* ix : p*edes* xuii; Hora ui^a : p*edes* xi.
　1] xiii　f K*alendae* Dec*embris* : Candide, U*irginis.*
　2] ii　　g iiii N.
　3]　　　a iii N. : Birini, Ep*iscop*i.
　4] x　　b ii N. : Tr*anslatio* Benedicti, Abb*atis.*
　5]　　　c N*onae.*
　6] xuiii　d uiii Id. : Nicolai, Archiep*iscop*i *et* C*onfessoris.*
　7] uii　　e uii Id. : Oc*taua* Andree.
　8]　　　f ui Id.
　9] xu　　g u Id.
　10] iiii　a iiii Id. : Eulalie, U*irginis.*
　11]　　　b iii Id. : Damasi, Ep*iscop*i *et* C*onfessoris.*
　12] xii　c ii Id. : Donati, Ep*iscop*i *et* C*onfessoris.*
　13] i　　d Id*us* : Lucie, U*irginis et* Iudoci.
　14]　　　e xix K. Ian*uarii* : Uictoris *et* Uictorie, M*artyrum.*
　15] ix　　f xuiii K. : Maximiani, Ep*iscop*i.
　16]　　　g xuii K.
　17] xuii　a xui K. : Ignati, Ep*iscop*i *et* M*artyris.*
　18] ui　　b xu K. : Sol in capricornum.
　19]　　　c xiiii K.
　20] xiii　d xiii K. : Iuliani *et* Bassilisce, U*irginis.*
　21] iii　　e xii K. : Thomas; Solstitiu*m.*
　22]　　　f xi K.
　23] xi　　g x K.
　24]　　　a ix K. : Uigilia.
　25] xix　b uiii K. : Natiuitas D*omi*ni.
　26] uiii　c uii K. : Stephani, M*artyris.*
　27]　　　d ui K. : Ioh*anni*s, Eu*angeliste.*
　28] xui　e u K. : Innocentiu*m.*
　29] u　　f iiii K.
　30]　　　g iii K.
　31] xiii　a ii K. : Siluest*ri*, Pape *et* Sanc*ti* Eguini, Ep*iscop*i.

5] Nonae: *an abbreviation sign is missing*　6] archi-: *added interlinearly*
11] Damasi: *a letter (e?) has been erased before the 'i'*　14] Martyrum: *added interlinearly*
24] Uigilia: *added later*　31] et . . . episcopi: *added later*

14

2

⟨Table of Computation I⟩[1]

f. 9r	epac.	conc.	xiiii ł.	dies pas.	ł ipsius diei
xxix	iii	ii	iiii N. Ap.	uiii Id. Ap.	xuiii
xxx	xiiii	iii	xi K. Ap.	iiii K. Ap.	xxi
xxxi	xxu	iiii	iiii Id. Ap.	iii Id. Ap.	xu
5 xxxii	ui	ui	iii K. Ap.	iiii N. Ap.	xuii
xxxiii	xuii	uii	xiiii K. Mai.	x K. Mai.	xuiii
xxxiiii	xxuiii	i	uii Id. Ap.	xuiii K. Mai.	xxi
xxxu	uiiii	ii	ui K. Ap.	iii K. Ap.	xuii
xxxui	xx	iu	xuii K. Mai.	xiiii K. Ma.	xuiii
10 xxxuii	i	u	ii N. Ap.	iiii Id. Ap.	xx
xxxuiii	xii	ui	ix K. Ap.	uii K. Ap.	xui
xxxix	xxiii	uii	iii Id. Ap.	⟨xuii K. Mai.⟩	xuii
xl	iiii	ii	K. Ap.	uiii Id. Ap.	xix
xli	xu	iii	xii K. Ap.	xi K. Ap.	xu
15 xlii	xxui	iiii	u Id. Ap.	iii Id. Ap.	xui
xliii	uii	u	iiii K. Ap.	iii N. Ap.	xix
xliiii	xuiii	uii	xu K. Mai.	x K. Mai.	xix
xlu	⟨null.	i	N. Ap.	uii Id. Ap.	xui⟩
xlui	⟨xi	ii	uiii K. Ap.	iii K. Ap.	xix⟩

20 ccxxxu lunares sunt in decenouenali circulo; luna i *et* iii *et* u *et* ix *et* xi *et* xu : q*ui* inciderit in eis cito morietur.

4] xxu: *MS.* xxiiii   5] (epac.)ui: *MS.* xxui   xuii: *MS.* xuiii
7] uii: *MS.* ui   8] uiiii: *MS.* xxuiiii   9] xuiii: *MS.* xuii
11] xxxuiii: *first 'i' added interlinearly*   12] xuii K. Mai: *om. MS*   xuii: *MS.* xui
13] uiiii: *MS.* iii   14] xii K. Ap.: *MS. omits 'K'*   (xi K.)Ap.: *MS.* Mai
18, 19] *MS. omits supplied details*   20] decenouenali: *'-na-' added interlinearly*

---

[1] This table is discussed in the Introduction, p. xv.

3

⟨Instructions for Computing Concurrences⟩

f. 9ᵛ Si uis scire quot concurrentes in anno sunt, scito in qua feria ix Kalendas Aprilis euenerit, uerbi gratia, iᵃ, iiᵃ, iii, iu, u, ui, uii, quam plus non crescunt tot concurrentes sunt illo anno et ratio numquam fallit. Nam Kalendas Aprilis dicitur esse locus concurrentium quia quot ferias ibi transactas inueneris ex tunc presenti ebdomada tot concurrentes in ipso anno concurere.

Scito xi Kalendas Aprilis dicitur esse sedes epactarum quia quantos dies etatis lune illic euenerit tot epactas habebis in illo anno; ᵃqualis luna in xi Kalendas Aprilis euenerit talem epactam habebis omni tempore sine dubioᵃ, quia Greci epactam xi Kalendas Aprilis ponunt eo quod lumen primatum noctis iubente domino tenent.

ᵃ ... ᵃ qualis ... dubio: MS. twice

16

4

⟨Instructions for computing the age of the moon⟩

10ʳ   Hee sunt septem etates lune tam initio quam in Pas*cha* nisi salt*us et* bisext*us*. Singulis singule respondent hoc m*odo* sec*un*dum Dionitiu*m et* de die d*omi*nico celebrant*ur*. Quando iiiᵃ lu*na est* init*ii* sec*un*dum Grecos in Pas*cha* xu erit; *et* q*u*ando erit iiiiᵃ lu*na* i*n*it*ii* in Pas*cha* xui est; i*n*itio uᵃ Pas*cha* xuiii; initio uiᵃ in Pas*cha* xuiiii; Initio *septem* in Pas*cha* xix; initio *octo* in Pas*cha* xx; initio ix in Pas*cha* xxi habeb*i*s. Ite*m*, si pas*chalis* lu*na* xu fuerit in sabbato accensa *est*; si xui in uiᵃ fer*ia* accensa *est*; si xuiiᵃ in uᵃ fer*ia* accen*sa est*; si xuiiiᵃ iiiiᵃ fer*ia* ac*c*ensa *est*; si xixᵃ iiiᵃ fer*ia* ac*c*ensa; si xxᵃ fer*ia* accensa *est*; si xxiᵃ in iᵃ fer*ia* accensa *est*.

5

⟨'Carte dirige' : A Poem from the Reign of King Æþelstan⟩[1]

f. 10ᵛ

Carta dirige gressus
per maris et nauium
telluris que spatium
ad reges palatum.

5 Regem primum salute
reginem et clitanum
clarus quoque commitis
militis armieros.

Quorum regem cum Æþelstanum ista
10 perfecta saxonia
uiuit rex Æþelstanum

f. 11ʳ

perfecta / gloriosa.

---

[1] This text was described by W. de Gray Birch as a 'curious ungrammatical translation of an Anglo-Saxon poem' found in MS. Cot. Tib. B.iv's version of the *Anglo-Saxon Chronicle* for the year 926 (*Cartularium Saxonicum*, London, 1887, II. 331). In 1909, C. H. Turner reported the discovery of a fragment of the same text in a form more corrupt than that preserved here (if that seems possible) in Durham MS. A.II.17 in the lower margin of f. 31ᵛ; this manuscript is a Gospel Book of the eighth century. The addition was made either in the late tenth or early eleventh century when the manuscript is known to have been at Chester-le-Street (see M. Lapidge, 'Some Latin Poems as Evidence for the Reign of Athelstan', *ASE* 9 (1981) especially pp. 83–93 and n. 108). The following is the text from the Durham MS.:

> Quarta dine gressus per maria navigans
> stellarumque spacium ad regem spalacium/
> Regem primum salutem regem aditu ne
> clerum quoque conditum armites milierum/
> Illic Sitric defuncto armatura prelio sex
> annum excersitum uiuit rex Adelstanum/
> Constantine. (*JTS* 10 (1908–09) p. 537)

W. H. Stevenson noted in an early article that the Nero poem seemed to be inspired by a Carolingian poem that begins 'Carta, Christo comite, per telluris spatium', and through comparison with that text tried to recover what the poet of the Nero text had originally written; some of his basic assumptions have been shown to have been incorrect, but his reconstructed text did eventually appear in *The Oxford Book of Medieval Latin Verse* (cf. Lapidge, *op. cit.* p. 83 and nn. 105 and 106).

Instead of undertaking yet another reconstruction of this poem here, M. Lapidge's reconstruction and translation have been given following the text from *N* (which is presented in unemended form) since it seemed unlikely that much improvement could be made upon his work, which shows great resourcefulness and imagination; it is taken from p. 98 of the above-mentioned article.

Ille Sictric defunctum
armatum in prelia
15 Saxonum exercitum
per totum Bryttanium.

Constantinus rex Scottorum
et uelum Brytannium
saluando regis Saxonum
20 fideles seruitia.

Dixit rex Æþelstanus
per Petri preconia
sint sani sint longe in
11ᵛ   salua- / toris gratia.

Lapidge's reconstruction:

Carta, dirige gressus	Letter, direct your steps
per maria nauigans	sailing across the seas
tellurisque spacium	and an expanse of land,
ad regis palacium.	to the king's burh.
Rege primum salutem	Direct first of all your best wishes
ad reginam, clitonem,	to the queen, the prince,
claros quoque comites,	the distinguished ealdormenn as well,
armigeros milites.	the arm-bearing thegns.
Quos iam regit cum ista	Whom he now rules with this
perfecta Saxonia:	England [now] made whole:
uiuit rex Æþelstanus	King Athelstan lives
per facta gloriosus!	glorious through his deeds!
Ille, Sictric defuncto,	He, with Sictric having died,
armat tum in prelio	in such circumstances arms for battle
Saxonum exercitum	the army of the English
per totum Bryttanium.	throughout all Britain.
Constantinus rex Scottorum	Constantine, king of the Scots,
aduolat Bryttanium:	hastens to Britain:
Saxonum regem saluando,	by supporting the king of the English
fidelis seruitio.	[he is] loyal in his service.

19

Dixit rex Æþelstanus
per Petri preconia:
sint sani, sint longeui
saluatoris gratia!

King Athelstan said [these things]
through the announcements of Peter:
may they be well, live long,
through the Saviour's grace!

6

⟨'Domine deus omnipotens rex regum' : A Prayer to God the Father⟩[1]

Domine deus omnipotens,[2] rex regum et dominus dominantium, in cuius manu omnis uictoria consistit et omne bellum conteritur, concede mihi ut tua manus cor meum corroboret ut in uirtute tua in manibus uiribusque meis bene pugnare[A] uiri- / literque agere ualeam ut inimici mei in conspectu meo cadent et corruant sicut corruit Golias ante faciem pueri tui Dauid,[3] et sicut populus Pharaonis[4] coram Moysi in mare rubro,[5] et sicut Philistini coram populo Israhel[6] cecidi sunt,[B] et Amalech coram Moysi et Cha- / nanei[7] coram Iesu corruerunt sic cadant inimici mei[8] sub pedibus meis et per uiam unam[9] conueniant aduersum me et per septem fugiant a me;[10] et conteret deus arma eorum et confringet[C] framea eorum,[11] et liquescent[D] in conspectu meo sicut cera a facie ignis ut sciant[a] omnes populi terre quia inuocatum est nomen domini nostri Ihesu[E] super me [b]et magnificetur nomen tuum, domine, in aduersariis meis, domine deus Israhel.[b]/

12[r]

12[v]

---

[a] sciant: *There is ligature between the 'n' and 't' the lower margin* [b]. . .[b] et . . . Israhel: *squeezed into*

[A] pugnare: dignare *G* [B] ceciderunt *G* [C] confringit *G*
[D] eliquisce *N* [E] Ihesu: *G adds* Christi

---

[1] The analogue for this prayer, showing few variants, appears in *G* (ff. 3[r]–4[v]) where it is followed by an Old English translation (ff. 4[v]–6[r]).
[2] Ap. 19: 16.
[3] *inimici . . . Dauid.* Cp. BL MS. Harl. 7653, f. 2, ll. 13–17: 'Omnes inimici mei et aduersarii fugiant ante conspectum maiestatis tue et per istos angelos conruant sicut conruit Goliat ante conspectum pueri tui Dauid'.
[4] 1 Rg. 17: 49–50.
[5] Ex. 14: 23–25.
[6] 1 Rg. 7: 9–14.
[7] Ex. 7: 8–16; Act. 7: 45.
[8] Ps. 17: 39.
[9] Dt. 28: 7.
[10] Ps. 45: 10.
[11] Ps. 67: 3.

7

⟨'O inclite confessor': A Prayer to St. Dunstan⟩[1]

f. 13ʳ   O inclite confessor Chri*sti*, O candelabra doctorq*ue* angligena gente, O
bone pastor Dunstane, altorq*ue* totius Albionis, qui es sanator
diuersorum debilium tuo tumulo uisitantium, te nunc flagitamus p*er*
illa s*anct*a merita que te ab altithrono concesse sunt ut tuis s*anct*is[a]
precibus deo flagitas ut hanc patriam ab hostibus eruat nosq*ue* a nexu
criminis soluat atq*ue* ad eternam uitam p*er*ducat.[b]/

---

[a] sanctis: *added interlinearly*   [b] perducat: *the prefix is separated from the root in the
MS. in order to accommodate extended interlinear musical notation*

---

[1] There is no analogue for this text which has a few syntactical peculiarities; compare
the style of nos. **8, 20, 21** and **66** below, and see the discussion of 'Language' in the
Introduction. A few suggestions for improving the text are: (1) *candelabra* is usually
neuter; (2) *angligena gente* would be better read as *angligene gentis*; (3) *te* for the
expected *tibi* after *concesse*; and (4) *concesse* should read *concessa*.

8

⟨'Inclite martir': A Poem to Æthelberht the Martyr⟩[1]

13ᵛ Inclite martir ouans te plebs uenerator in oda
Æþelberhte tiro die per quem fraudem secarat
angelicus cetus sed apostolicusque coronant
ordo simul procerunt Christi confesio sacra
5 et diadema ueunt sortitum sceptra beata,
plaudet et omnis solum recolens certamina palme.

1–6] *there is interlinear musical notation*

---

[1] The editor finds this short text so plagued by syntactical and lexical peculiarities as to be virtually indecipherable (although what is intended is quite straightforward); compare the style with nos. 7, 20, 21 and 66. Some of the problems are: 1) *ueuerator* should probably read *ueneratur*; 2) *tiro* does not seem to mean 'recruit' here, and is probably a misconstruing of *tertio*; 3) *secarat* and *procerunt* are obscure unless completely altered; 4) *ueunt* read *uehunt*. See the discussion of 'Language' in the Introduction.

23

British Library, Cotton Galba A.xiv

9

⟨'Computatio Grecorum': Table of Computation II⟩

2ʳ Incipit[1] computatio Grecorum de mensibus anni : Ianuarius, Augustus
et December iiiiᵃ nonas habent, xix kalendas post idus et di⟨es⟩ᵇ xxxi;
Martius, Maius, Iulius et October ui nonas habent, xuii kalendas post
idus et dies xxxi; Aprilis, Iunius, September et Nouember iiii nonas
habent, xuiii kalendas post idus et dies xxx. Februarius uero iiiiᵃ nonas
habet, xui kalendas post idus et dies xxuiii; et si bisextus fuerit, habet
dies xxix. Omnes uero menses octo idus habent./

ᵃ *MS.* iiiiᵃ   ᵇ dies: *MS. damaged*

---

[1] This entire page has been written in red ink which is best preserved in the first five
lines. Most of the text had been obscured through water damage and has been
recovered with the aid of an ultra-violet lamp.

10

⟨Table of Computation III⟩

f. 2v	Mar. u	Ian. ix	Ian. ii
	Apl. i	Feb. x	Feb. u
	Mai. iii	Mar. ix	Mar. u
	Iun. ui	Apl. x	Apl. i
5	Iul. i	Mai. xi	Mai. iii
	Ags. iiii	Iun. xii	Iun. ui
	Sep. uii	Iul. xiii	Iul. i
	Ocb. ii	Ags. xiiii	Ags. iiii
	Nob. u	Sep. xui	Sep. uii
10	Dec. uii	Ocb. xui	Ocb. ii
	Ian. iii	Nou. xuiii	Nob. u
	Feb. ui	Dec. xuiii	Dec. uii
	Sep. u		
	Ocb. u		
15	Nob. ui		
	Decb. iii /		

1–12 These charts are selected parts of larger ones used to determine the 'saltus lune' and the 'cursus solaris'. Column one has dates from the sixth and seventh years of the twenty-eight-year solar cursus, applicable to the years 1034–35; the second is for calculating the saltus lune for the first year of the nineteen-year lunar cycle, i.e., for the year 1029; and the third is from the same chart as the first, but is for the complete twelfth year, i.e., 1040. These have been identified through comparison with similar charts in *J*.

13–16 This fragment has not been identified yet.

11

⟨'Domine deus omnipotens rex regum' : A Prayer to God the Father⟩[1]

3ʳ Domine deus omnipotens,[2] rex regum et dominus dominantium, in
cuius manu omnis uictoria consistit et omne bellum conteritur,
concede mihi ut tua manus cor meum corroboret ut[a] in uirtute tua in
manibus uiribusque meis bene dignare[A] uiriliterque agere ualeam ut
3ᵛ inimici mei in conspectu meo ca- / -dent et corruant sicut corruit
Golias ante faciem pueri tui Dauid,[3] et sicut populus Pharaonis[4]
coram Moysi in mare rubro,[5] et sicut Philistini coram populo Israhel[6]
cecidi sunt,[B] et Amalech coram Moysi et Chananei[7] coram Iesu
4ʳ corruerunt, sic cadant ini- / mici mei[8] sub pedibus meis, et per uiam
unam[9] conueniant aduersum me et per septem fugiant a me;[10] et
conteret deus arma eorum et confringet[C] framea eorum,[11] et
liquescent[bD] in conspectu meo sicut cera a facie ignis ut sciant omnes
4ᵛ populi terre quia inuocatum est nomen / domini nostri Ihesu Christi[E]
super me et magnificetur nomen tuum domine, in aduersariis meis,
domine deus Israhel.

---

[a] ut: *add. by another hand*   [b] liquescent: *altered from* liquiscent

---

[A] dignare] pugnare *N*   [B] ceciderunt *G*   [C] confringit *G*   [D] eliquisce *N*
[E] Christi: *om. N*

---

[1] This text and the Old English translation of it which follows (no. **12**) have been
published previously by W. de Gray Birch, *Cartularium Saxonicum* (London, 1887)
as no. 656, where it is collated with the version in *N* (no. **6** above) — and no. 657,
respectively.
[2] Ap. 19: 16.
[3] *inimici . . . Dauid* see no. **6**, n. 3.
[4] 1 Rg. 17: 49–50.
[5] Ex. 14: 23–25.
[6] 1 Rg. 7: 9–14.
[7] Ex. 7: 8–16; Act. 7: 45.
[8] Ps. 17: 39.
[9] Dt. 28: 7.
[10] Ps. 45: 10.
[11] Ps. 67: 3.

12

⟨'Æla þu drihten' : a translation of no. 11⟩[1]

Æla þu drihten,[2] æla þu ælmihtiga god, æla cing ealra cynynga, hlaford ealra waldendra on þæs mihta[3] wunaþ ælc sige *and* ælc gewin

f. 5ʳ   weorþ tobryt, forgif me, drihten, þæt þin seo mihtigu / hand mines unstrangan heortan gestrangie, *and* þæt ic þurh þine þa miclan mihte mid handum minu*m and* mihte stranglice *and* werlice ongan mine fynd winnan mæge, swa þæt hy on minre gesihþe feallan[4] *and* gereosan swa swa gereas Golias ætforan Dauides ansyne þines cnihtes, *and* swa swa gereas *and* wearþ besenct Faraones folc[5] on þære Readan Sæ ætforan

f. 5ᵛ   Moyses ansene, *and* swa swa / feollan Filistei beforan Israela[a] folce,[6] *and* swa swa gereas Amalech ætforan Moisen, *and* Chananei[7] ætforan Iesu Naue, swa feallan *and* gereosan mine fynd[8] under minu*m* fotu*m and* hy ealle samod þurh ænne weg ongæn me cumen[9] *and* þurh seofan wegas hie fram me gewitan.[10] Forbryt, drihten, heora wapna *and* heora sweord tobrec;[11] *and* do, drihten, þæt hy formeltan on ⟨mi⟩nre[b] gesihþe

f. 6ʳ   swa swa weax / mylt fram fyres ansyne þæt eall eorþan folc wite *and* ongyte þæt ofer me is geciged noma ures drihtenes hælendes Cristes, *and* þæt þin noma, drihten, sy geweorþad on minu*m* wiþerwinu*m*, þu þe eart drihten Isræla god.[12]

---

[a] Israela: '-a' is a gloss on an earlier '-e'   [b] MS. damaged

---

[1] This translation is very accurate, differing notably at only four points: the adjective *mihtigu* modifies *hand* (Latin *tua manus*); *unstrangan* modifies *heortan* (Latin *cor meum*); *wite and ongyte* expands the Latin *sciant*; and *hælendes* replaces *Ihesu* of the Latin. This is Wanley's Art. I (*op. cit.* p. 231).

[2] Ap. 19: 16.

[3] *on þæs mihta.* The Latin is *in cuius manu.*

[4] 1 Rg. 17: 49–50.

[5] Ex. 14: 23–25.

[6] Rg. 7: 9–14.

[7] Ex. 7: 8–16; Act. 7: 45.

[8] Ps. 17: 39.

[9] Dt. 28: 7.

[10] Ps. 45: 10.

[11] Ps. 67: 3.

[12] Wanley quotes this desinit and further remarks, 'Notandum est, quod versus finem hujusce MS. invenire licet Maledictiones gravissimas Latine scriptas, contra Regem inimicum. Sic autem incip. "Dominus disrumpet regnum tuum N. excutiet d*ominus* pulverem potestatis tuæ"' (*op. cit.* p. 230). The text he refers to here is now lost.

13

⟨'Suscipe sancta trinitas' : An Oblations Prayer⟩

Ðis gebed man sceal singan æt offrunga for hine sylfne *ond* for his brodore *ond* for his geswysterna *ond* for ealle þ⟨am⟩[a] þe he on gebed ræden ne biþ *ond* for eal Cristen folc.[1]/

Suscipe *sancta* trinitas has oblationes quas tibi ego peccatrix offero p*ro* me peccatrice et pro omni populo Chr*isti*ano, pro fratrib*us* quoq*ue* et sororibus n*os*tris, et p*ro* his qui nobis[b] memoriam in suis continuis habent orationib*us* ut in hoc p*re*senti *se*c*ulo* remissionem omni*um* peccator*um* n*os*tror*um* recipere mereamur, et in futuro requie[c] consequi mereamur et*er*na p*er* te, Ih*esu* Chr*iste*, redemptor mundi[d] q*ui* c*um* patre et sp*iritu* s*ancto*[e] ★★★s in s*ecula* sec*ulorum*. Am*en*./

[a] þam: *MS. damaged tops of 'mun-' are visible*   [b] *MS.* nostris   [c] *MS.* requei   [d] mundi: *only the*   [e] *The last line, which has been squeezed into the lower margin by another hand, is damaged at the beginning. As the line is formulaic, the missing words are probably 'uiuis et regna-'*

[1] This is a rubric. Wanley lists two others for this prayer (*op. cit.* p. 231) which are now lost.

31

14

⟨'Altus prosator' : An Abecedary Poem attributed to Colum Cille (St. Columba)⟩

f. 7ʳ   **A**ltus prosator uetus dierum et ingenitus
erat absq*ue* origine primordii et crepidine,
est *et* erit in secula seculor*um* infinita;
cui est unigenitus Chri*stu*s et sanc*tus* sp*iritu*s
5 coeternus in gloria deitatis p*er*petua.

f. 7ᵛ   Non tres deos depromimus, sed unum / deum dicimus
salue fide in p*er*sonis tribus gloriosissimis.

1] uetustus *TFB*

1] The evidence supporting the attribution of this poem and the next, the 'Adiutor laborantium', to Colum Cille has been reviewed in a recent edition of them by me, 'Two Latin Hymns by Colum Cille (St. Columba)', *Revue du moyen âge latin* 39 (1983) 205–16. While the present edition was in progress, it was believed that a new full critical edition and study of the 'Altus' was being prepared by Michael Herren, to appear in *Hisperica Famina II*; it now seems that this project has been abandoned, so that the outdated edition from the seven previously known witnesses for the text remains the best and most accessible one: J. H. Bernard and R. Atkinson, *The Irish Liber Hymnorum*, HBS XIII and XIV, London, 1898, I. 62–83 (text and apparatus) and II. 140–69 (notes and translation). There is a second edition: C. Blume, *Analecta hymnica medii aeui*, vol. 51, Leipzig, 1908, pp. 275–83; and the most recent translation of the 'Altus' is by H. Isbell, *The Last Poets of Imperial Rome*, Harmondsworth, reprinted 1982, pp. 268–77.

The new witness is complete, having twenty-four verses and a refrain. Of the seven other witnesses, only the 'Irish' group (*BFT*) has been collated here; of these, *F* alone is complete; *T* lacks the O-X verses, and *B* has only those for A-H. The readings in *G*, though sometimes inferior, have been left to stand wherever possible.

There is an extensive, and severely damaged, marginal note on folio 7ʳ⁻ᵛ which is discussed in Appendix A.

uetus Cp. Dn. 7: 9. The Vulgate reads *aspiciebam donec throni positi sunt et antiquus dierum sedit. uetus* (or *uetustus*) is from the Old Latin Bible (see *ILH* II. 144–45 for a discussion of the type of Bible used by St. Columba). The text in *G* is not a direct descendant of any of the other witnesses; its readings are closest to those of *F*. See *ILH* II. 146–49 for a discussion of the relationship between this poem and the 'Aeterne rerum conditor' of Hrabanus Maurus.

2–7] Compare this with the opening of the *Athanasian Creed* (no. **76**, below).

℞   Quis potest deo placere nouissimo in tempore
           exceptis contemptoribus mundi præsentis istius
10   u⟨a⟩riatis insignibus ueritatis ordinibus?

           Bonos creauit angelos ordines et archangelos
f. 8ʳ   principatum ac sedium, po- / testatum, uirtutum,
           uti non esset bonitas otiosa ac maiestas
           trinitatis in omnibus largitatis muneribus,
15   sed haberet, cælestia in quibus priuilegia
           ostenderet magnopere possibili fatimine.

℞   Quis potest deo placere? (ut supra)

f. 8ᵛ   **C**æli de regni apice sta- / tionis angelice
           clari⟨tate⟩ pro fulgoris, uenu⟨sta⟩t⟨e sp⟩eciminis
20   superbiendo ruerat Lucifer, quem formauerat,
           apos⟨tate⟩que angeli eodem lapsu lugubri
           auctoris cæn⟨o⟩doxiae, peruicacis inuidie,
           ceteris remanentibus in suis pri⟨nci⟩patus.

℞   Quis potest deo placere? (ut supra) /

f. 9ʳ, 25   **D**⟨ra⟩co magnus, teterri⟨m⟩us, terribilis ⟨et⟩ antiquus,
           qui fuit serpens lubricus, sapientior omnibus
           bestiis et animantibus terre ferocioribus,
           tertiam partem siderum traxit secum in barathrum
           loco⟨r⟩um infernalium diuersorumque carcerum
f. 9ᵛ, 30   refugas ueri luminis pa- / rasito precipites.

10] uariatis: *MS. damaged*   12] *MS.* pricipatum   19, 21–23] *MS. damaged*
20] *Something has been erased before* formauerat   22] *MS.* auctores, per uicaces
25, 29, 37] *MS. damaged*   26] serpens: '*ser-*' *added interlinearly in another hand*

9] ex gentis *G*   15] preuigilia *T*: preuilegia *F*   16] fatimini *B*
19] præfulgoris *TF*   apostotaque *B*   25] deterrimus *T*   27] et: *om. F*
30] refuga *T*: refugax *F*

9–10] These two lines are in the opposite order in *TFB*.
11–12] Cf. Col. 1: 16.
23] Cp. Iu. 6.
25] Ap. 12: 7–12.
26] Gn. 3: 1.
28] Ap. 12: 4.
30] The Old Latin version reads, 'et praecipitatus est in terram', whereas the Vulgate
    has 'proiectus est' (Ap. 12: 9).

℞   Quis potest deo placere?

      Excelsus mundi machinam prouidens et armoniam,
      cælum et terram fecerat, mare et aquas condidit,
      herbarum quoque germina, uirgultorum arbuscula,
35   solem, lunam ac sidera, ignem ac necessaria,
f.10ʳ aues, pisces et pecora, bes- / tias, animalia,
      hominem ⟨de⟩mum regere protoplastum presagmine.

℞   Quis potest deo placere? (ut supra)

      Factis simul sideribus, aetheris luminaribus,
40   conlaudauerunt angeli factura pro mirabili
      inmense molis dominum, opificem celestium,
      preconio laudabili, debito et inmobili
f. 10ᵛ con- / centuque eg⟨regio grates⟩ egerunt d⟨omino
      amore et arb⟩itrio, ⟨non⟩ na⟨tu⟩re donar⟨io⟩.

℞   45 Quis potest deo placere? (ut ⟨supra⟩)

      Grassatis primis duobus seductisque parentibus
      secundo ruit zabulus cum suis ⟨sa⟩tellitibus,
      quorum horrore uultum sonoque uolitantium
f. 11ʳ consternerent⟨ur⟩ homines metu territi fra- / giles
50   ⟨non ua⟩lentes carnali⟨b⟩us hec intue⟨ri⟩ uisibus,
      qui ⟨n⟩unc ligantur fascibus, ergastulorum nexibus.

℞   Quis potest deo placere? (ut supra)

      Hic sublatus a medio deiectus est a domino,
      cuius aeris spatium constipatur satellitum
55   globo inuisibilium turbido perduellium,

34] *MS.* heribarum   43, 44, 45, 47, 49–51] *MS. damaged*   46] grassatis: *first*
'*s*' *added interlinearly*   47] zabulus: '*z*' *over* '*di*' (*erased*)
49] consternerentur: '-*ner*-' *corrected from* '-*nar*-'

32] præuidens *T*   35] ac: *om. B*   36] pecora: apeccora *B*
36] bestias: *T adds* et   41] celetium *B*   42] laudabile, immobile *T*
49] consternarentur *T*

39–40] The Old Latin version of Ib. 38: 7 reads, 'quando facta sunt simul sidera,
    laudauerunt me uoce magna omnes angeli mei', whereas the Vulgate has,
    'cum me laudarent simul astra matutina . . .'.

f. 11^v ne malis exemplaribus imbuti ac sceleribus /
nullis umquam tegentibus septis ac parietibus
fornicarentur homines palam omni*um* oculis.

℞ Quis potest d*e*o placere? (ut sup⟨ra⟩)

60 Inuehunt nubes pontias ex fontibus brumalias
tribus profundioribus oceani dodrantib*us*
maris, celi climatibus, ceruleis turbinib*us*
profuturas segitibus, uineis et germinibus,
f. 12^r agitate flaminibus thesauris emer- / ⟨g⟩entibus,
65 quiq*ue* paludes marinas euacuant reciprocas.

℞ ⟨Qu⟩is potest d*e*o placere? (ut sup*ra*)

Kaduca ac tyrannica mundi⟨que⟩ momentanea
regum p*re*sentis gloria nutu dei deposita;
ecce, gygantes gemere sub aquis magno ulcere
70 comprobantur, incendio aduri ac supplicio
Coccitiq*ue* Caribdibus strangulati turgentib*us*,
f. 12^v Scylleis / obtecti fluctibus elid⟨untur⟩ et scrupibus.

℞ Quis potest d*e*o placere? (ut sup*ra*)

Ligatas aquas nubibus frequenter crebrat d*ominus*,
75 ut ne erumpant protinus simul ruptis obicibus,
quarum uberioribus uenis uelut uberibus
pedetemptim natantibus teli per tractus istius
f. 13^r gelidis ac feruentibus / diuersis in temporibus
us⟨qu⟩am influunt flumina numquam deficientia.

℞ 80 Quis potest d*e*o placere? (ut sup*ra*)

Magni dei uirtutibus appenditur dialibus
globus terre et circulus abysso magno indutus
suffulta dei, iduma omnipotentis ualida,

59, 64, 66] *MS. damaged*   65] quique: *from this point, final 'ue' of '-que' has been
erased and replaced by the abbreviation sign ';'*   67, 72, 79] *MS. damaged*
77] teli: *for* telli tractus: *corrected interlinearly*

58] oculis: *B ends here*   79] usquam: unquam *T*   82] abyssi magnæ *T*
83] suffultu *T*

35

f. 13ᵛ   columnis uelut uectibus eundem sustentantib*us*, /
  85   promuntoriis et rupibus solidis fundaminibus
       ue⟨lut⟩ quibusdam bassibus firmatis immobilibus.

℞   Quis potest d*e*o placere? (ut sup*ra*)

      ⟨**N**⟩ulli uidetur dubium in imis esse infernum,
      ubi habentur tenebre, uermes et dire bestiæ,
  90   ubi ignis sulfureus ardens flammis edacibus,
f. 14ʳ   ubi rugitus homi- / num fletus et stridor dentium,
      ubi gehenne gemitus terribilis et antiquus,
      ubi ardor flammaticus, sitis famisque horridus.

℞   Quis potest d*e*o placere? (ut sup*ra*)

  95   ⟨**O**⟩rbem infra, ut legimus, incolas esse nouimus,
      quor*um* genu precario frequenter flectit d*omi*no,
f. 14ᵛ   quibusque inpossibile librum scriptum / reuoluere
      obsigna⟨tum⟩ si⟨g⟩naculis ⟨sep⟩tem de Chr*is*ti m⟨o⟩nitis,
      quem idem resignauerat, postquam ⟨uic⟩to⟨r⟩ exstiterat
 100   explens sui pr⟨e⟩sagmina aduentus prophetalia.

      Plantatum a prochemio paradisum a d*omi*no
      legimus in primordio Genesis nobilissimo,
f. 15ʳ   cuius ex fonte flu- / ⟨mina quattuor⟩ sunt manan⟨tia,

---

86] *MS. damaged*   88] nulli: *the rubricator has failed to add the capital initial*
95] orbem: *the rubricator has failed to add the capital initial*   96] flectit: *a later hand seems to have added an abbreviation sign (for final '-ur')*
98–100, 103–106] *MS. damaged*   98] *MS.* Christo   101] *MS.* prochemi

---

85] solis *T*   86] firmatus *TF*   95] orbem: *T omits from this verse to the beginning of the 'Y' verse below*   98] Christo *F*

86] The reading of *TF* is superior.
89] Cp. Ecli. 10: 13.
91] Mt. 8: 12.
95–100] Cp. Ap. 5.
97] *reuoluere* This reading is from the Old Latin version of Ap. 5: 4; the Vulgate has 'aperire'.
100] The reference to the refrain is omitted after this verse.
101–106] Cp. Gn. 2: 8–14.

cuius etiam⟩ floridor*um* ⟨lignum uite in medio⟩,
105 cuius ⟨non cadunt⟩ folia gentibus ⟨salutifera,
cuius in⟩e⟨narrabiles delicie⟩ ac fertiles.

℞ Quis potest d*e*o placere? (ut sup*ra*)

Quis ad condictum d*omi*ni montem conscendit Sinai;
f. 15ᵛ quis audiuit tonitrua ultra modum sonantia;/
110 quis clangorem perstr⟨epe⟩re inormitatis bucine;
quis quoq*ue* uidit fulgura in gyro coruscantia;
quis lampades et iacula saxaq*ue* conlidentia
praeter Israhelitici Moysen iudicem populi?

℞ Quis potest d*e*o placere? (ut sup*ra*)

115 **R**egis regum rectissimi prope est dies d*omi*ni,
f. 16ʳ dies ire et uin- / dicte, tenebrarum et nebule
diesq*ue* mirabilium tonitruor*um* fortium,
dies quoq*ue* angustie, meroris ac tristitie,
in quo cessabit mulierum amor ac desiderium
120 hominumq*ue* contentio mundi huius et cupido.

℞ Quis potest d*e*o placere? (ut sup*ra*)

Stantes erimus pauidi ante tribunal d*omi*ni
f. 16ᵛ redemusq*ue* / de omnibus rationem affectibus,
uidentes quoq*ue* posita ante obtutus crimina
125 librosq*ue* conscientie patefactos in facie;
in fletus amarissimos ac singultus erumpemus
subtracta necessaria operandi materia.

106] inenarrabiles: *the 'e' legible in the text might have been added interlinearly*
108] *MS.* monte   110] *MS. damaged*   113] *MS.* propter   125] *MS.* facie

104] etiam floridorum: et tua florido *F*   in: est *F*   108] ascendit *F*
109] ultra: supra *F*   123] effectibus *F*

108–13] Cf. Ex. 19: 3–23; the reading in *F*, *ascendit*, is from the Vulgate.
116] Is. 34: 8.
125] Cf. Dn. 7: 10, Ap. 10 and Ap. 20: 12.

℞ Quis potest d*e*o placere? (ut sup*ra*)

  Tuba primi archangeli strepente admirabili
f. 17ᵛ, 130 eru*m*- / pent munitissima claustra ac poliandria,
  mundi presentis frifola hominum liquescentia
  undique conglobantibus ad compagines ossibus,
  animabus aetralibus eisdem obeuntibus
  rursumq*ue* redeuntibus debitis mansionib*us*.

℞ 135 Quis potest d*e*o placere? (ut sup*ra*)

  Vagatur ex clymactere Orion celi cardine
f. 17ʳ derelicto Ver- / gilio, astrorum splendidissimo,
  per metas Thetis ignoti orientalis circuli;
  girans certis ambagibus redit priscis reditibus,
  140 Oriens post biennium Vesperugo in uesperum;
  sumpta in problesmatibus tropicis intellectibus.

℞ Quis potest d*e*o placere? (ut sup*ra*)

  Xr*is*to de celis d*omi*no descendente celsissimo
f. 18ʳ prefulgebit cla- / rissimum signum crucis et uexillum,
  145 tectisq*ue* luminaribus duobus principalibus
  cadent in terram sidera ut fructus de friculnea,
  eritq*ue* mundi spatium et fornacis incendium;
  tunc in montium specubus abscondent se exercitus.

131] frifola: *altered interlinearly* 133] *MS*. aetralib *with an interlinear 'i' added over*
'-ra-' 139] *MS*. piscis 141] *MS*. sumpto 151, 157] *MS. damaged*
164] *MS. damaged* 167] ut: *this is an interlinear correction of original* in

---

131] frigora *F* 138] tithis *F* 146] ficulnea *F*

129–34] Cf. Ez. 38: 7–12; Ap. 8: 7.
130] Folio 17 is mounted backwards in the MS.
132] Ez. 37: 7. The Vulgate reads, 'ad iuncturam suam'; the Old Latin version used
by St. Ambrose has 'unumquodque ad suam compaginem'.
137] Cf. Ib. 9: 9. The Vulgate reads, 'qui facit Arcturum et Oriona'; the Old Latin
version has, 'qui facit uirgilias et uesperum'.
143–48] Cf. Ap. 19: 11–16 and Ap. 6: 12–17.
146] *friculnea* The Vulgate reads 'sicut ficus emittit grossos suos' for Ap. 6: 13; the
Old Latin version has 'sicut ficulnea deicit grossos suos'.
147] Cf. 2 Pt. 3: 10

℞   Quis potest deo? (ut supra)

150   **Y**mnorum cantationibus sedulo tinnientibus
f. 18ᵛ   tripudis / sanctis milibus angelorum ⟨uer⟩nantibus
         quattuorque plenissimis animalibus oculis
         cum uiginti felicibus quattuor senioribus,
         coronas submittentibus agni dei sub pedibus,
155   laudatur tribus uicibus trinitas æternalibus.

℞   Quis potest deo placere? (ut supra)

f. 19ᵛ   **Z**elus ignis furibundos con- / ⟨su⟩met aduersarios
         nolentes Christum credere deo a patre uenisse.
         Nos uero euolabimus obuiam ei protinus
160   et sic cum ipso erimus in diuersis ordinibus
         dignitatum pro meritis premiorum perpetuis
         permansuri in gloria a seculis in secula.

℞   Quis potest deo placere? (ut supra)

f. 19ʳ   ⟨**D**eu⟩m patrem / ingenitum, celi ac terre dominum,
165   ab eodemque filium secula ante progenitum
         deumque spiritum sanctum, uerum, unum, altissimum,
         inuoco ut auxilium mihi oportunissimum
         minimo prestet omnium sibi deseruientium,
         quem angelorum milibus consociabit dominus./

150] cantionibus *T*   151] tropodis *T*: tripodiis *F*   154] admittentibus *TF*
162] secula: gloria *T*   165] primogenitum *T*: genitum *F*   169] consociauit *F*

150] *T* resumes here.
152–54] Ap. 4: 4–11.
157] Cf. Heb. 10: 27. Folio 19 is mounted backwards in the MS.
160] Cf. Ap. 22: 3–5 and I Cor. 15: 41–42.
164] This collect is found only in the 'Irish Group', and is designated for use at the ceremony 'pedilauium' on Maunday Thursday (see *ILH* II. 168 note). It is also in *A* (p. 226) and *J* (p. 275).
165] Col. 1: 15.

39

15

⟨'Adiutor laborantium' : An Abecedary Poem attributed to Colum
Cille (St. Columba)⟩

f. 20^r   Adiutor laborantium,
bonorum rector omnium,
custos ad propugnaculum
defensorque credentium,
5 exaltator humilium,
fractor superbientium,
gubernator fidelium,
hostis inpoenitentium,
iudex cunctorum iudic[i]um,
10 Castigator errantium,
Casta uita uiuentium,

f. 20^v   Lumen et pater / luminum,
Magna luce lucentium,
Nulli negans sperantium
15 Opem atque auxilium,
Precor ut me homunculum
Quassatum ac miserrimum
Remigantem per tumultum
Seculi istius infinitum

3] *MS.* pro pugnabulum   5] *MS.* exaltatur   18] *MS.* tumulum

---

1] As indicated in the introductory note to the 'Altus prosator' (no. **14**), the evidence supporting the attribution of this poem to St. Columba has been reviewed by me in a recent article. Summarizing briefly, until now it was thought that the hymn composed by the saint on the way to the mill which is referred to in the prefaces of the *BFT* versions of the 'Altus', and which was said to have begun with the words *Adiutor laborantium*, was the 'In te Christe credentium', the refrain of which begins *Deus in adiutorium / Intende laborantium*. The verbal echoes made the identification seem at least possible. It is now clear that the 'Adiutor', placed side by side with the 'Altus' in *G*, is the poem referred to in those prefaces.

The 'Adiutor', as presented here, has twenty-five verses and a closing liturgical formula. It is an alphabetical poem, but curiously, there are two verses for 'k' (written each time with a 'c'); the 'z' verse is two lines long instead of the usual one. Each line originally had eight syllables, and the text has been emended in one instance to restore the pattern. All of the verses ended in -(*i*)*um*, and the text has been emended once to restore this pattern also. A two-syllable word has been omitted in line twenty-two. I am indebted to M. Lapidge for some suggestions concerning the metrical pattern of the poem.

19] *seculi* This should be read as two syllables (*secli*) if the metre is to work out.

40

20 Trahat post se ad supernum
Uite portum pulcherrimum.
Xristus ★★★ infinitum
Ymnum sanctum in seculum

f. 21^r Zelo / subtrahas hostium

25 Paradisi in gaudium.
Per te, Christe Ihesu, qui uiuis et regnas.

23] *MS.* secula

26] *ihesu* The abbreviation was read as *domine* originally (*op. cit.* p. 210), but upon re-examination with ultra-violet light proved to be *ihu*, not *dne*; it has been obscured by water damage.

16

⟨'Domine exaudi orationem' : A Prayer for Reconciliation as Death
Approaches⟩

Domine[1] exaudi orationem[A] quia iam cognosco quod[B] tempus meu*m*
pro*pe* est;[C] presta mihi, d*omine*, sapientiam et intellectu*m*, et inlumina

f. 21ᵛ   cor meu*m* ut cognoscam te sem*per* omnibus diebus uite / mee,[2] quia tu
es d*eus* et no⟨n⟩[a] est alius preter te[D] solum qui descendisti de celo et
inluminasti[3] Mariam[b] de sp*iri*tu s*an*cto;[c] te ergo deprecor,[E] d*omine*,
humiliter[F] ut[G] inlumines cor meu*m* quia peccata mea innumerabilia

f. 22ʳ   sunt ualde. Presta mihi, d*omine*, queso[H] / ⟨u⟩t[d] illa merear deflere[I] p*er*
fidem et ueritate*m* et p*er* tuu*m* nomen[e] mirabile. Adiuro te[J] ut[K] in
quacu*m*que die inuocauero te uelociter exaudire[fL] me digneris, sicut[M]
exaudisti Tobiam[4] et Sarra*m*; effunde mihi[N] lacrimas cordis[O] sicut

f. 22ᵛ   fundasti aquas[5] sup*er* terra*m*,[gP] quia obduratum est cor meum[6] / quasi

---

ᵃ *MS. damaged*   ᵇ Mariam: *followed by an erasure*   ᶜ sancto: *followed by a space*
ᵈ *MS. damaged*   ᵉ nomen: *followed by a space*
ᶠ exaudire: *'-au-' added interlinearly*   ᵍ *MS.* terram super aquas

---

ᴬ orationem: *P adds* meam   ᴮ quod: *om.* PV   ᶜ esse *V*
ᴰ te: *PV cont.* nisi tu solus (qui)   ᴱ ego precor *P*: (ergo) precor *V*
ᶠ humiliter: *om.* PV   ᴳ ut: et *P*   ᴴ queso: *om.* PV   ᴵ deflere: delere *PV*
ᴶ adiuro te: *om.* PV   ᴷ ut: et *V*   ᴸ exaudi *P*: me exaudire *V*   ᴹ sic *P*
ᴺ mihi: *V adds* domine   ᴼ cordis: *om.* PV   ᴾ terram super aquas *V*

---

[1] The analogues for this text are *V* (ff. 174ʳ–175ᵛ), *P* (II. 12–14) and *Or* (ff. 23–24—
not collated here). *P* has this rubric: 'Incipit oratio Sancti Gregorii. Quicumque hanc
orationem in die cantauerit sicut ipse Sanctus Gregorius dixit quod nec malus homo
nec diabolus numquam nocere poterit, nec ad animam nec ad corpus.' *V* has the
same rubric except that it omits the initial 'incipit' and the concluding 'nec ad
animam nec ad corpus'. *G* has the same attributive paragraph for the prayer
'Domine Ihesu Christe qui in hunc mundum' (no. **24**, p. 87), which is also in *PV*.
Such attributive passages, which endowed a prayer with some prestige, were popular
throughout the Middle Ages, but their authenticity is questionable in many
instances. None of the three versions collated here seems to be a direct descendant of
one of the others. When there is a variant reading, however, *P* and *V* oftentimes
agree against *G*.
[2] Dt. 4: 35.
[3] Lc. 1: 35.
[4] Cf. Tb. 8.
[5] Cf. Gn. 1: 9–10.
[6] Cf. Dt. 15: 7–8.

pe*t*ra. Peccaui,[h] do*mine*,[Q] peccaui nimis in uita mea; omnes iniquitates[7] meas ego cognosco.[R] Te dep*r*ecor, do*mine*,[i] *et*[S] ad te clamo;[8] tu porrige mihi dexter*am* tua*m* et libera me de aduersario meo sicut liberasti tres pueros de camino ignis ardentis, Sidrac, Misaac et Abdenago.[9] Ergo
23[r] deprecor[j] te,[T] deus / rex celestis,[k] p*r*esta mihi patientiam[l] et continentiam, caritatem[U] et humilitem, fidem et ueritatem ut merear perseuerare in bonis operibus,[V] sicut cor meu*m* desiderat. Quicquid[W] inique[mX] locutus fui aut cogitaui aut feci ⟨a⟩[n] iuuentute mea[Y] dimitte
23[v] mihi. Te deprecor,[Z] do*mine*,[o] ad te clamo clamore / magno in[A] toto corde meo.[B] Te laudo, te[C] magnifico cum[10] tuis s*ancti*s ap*osto*lis et martyribus[pD] ut in[E] auxiliu*m* meu*m*[q] mittere digneris[F] angelo⟨s⟩[r] tuos et apostolos, martyres,[s] confessores, uirgines[11] et[t] ★★★[r] (2 ll.) eu⟨an⟩gelistas; precor te, s*anct*a Maria, ★★★[r] (1 wd) de*um* ut omnes
24[r] sanctas / uirgines[u] ut me exaudiant. Peto[v] et supplico te p*er* s*anct*os et electos tuos ut exaudias me ★★★[r] (1–2 wd) mihi ad uiam ueritatis peruenire.

---

[h] peccaui: *'-ui' added above by another hand*   [i] domine: *added interlinearly, another hand*   mihi: *added interlinearly, another hand*   [j] deprecor: *'de-' added interlinearly, another hand*   [k] celestis: *there is an erasure after this*
[l] patientiam: *added interlinearly*   [m] inique: *added interlinearly, another hand*
[n] a: *hiatus in MS.*   [o] dimitte . . . domine: *added with a finer pen*
[p] martyribus: *there is a blank space before this*   [q] in auxilium meum: *added interlinearly, finer pen*   [r] *MS. damaged*   [s] martyres . . . uirgines *added later, finer pen*
[t] et: *from here the text has been expuncted and the page washed clean*   [u] uirgines . . . exaudiant: *expuncted*   [v] peto . . . me: *written interlinearly, a cramped hand*

[Q] domine: *PV cont.* et nimis peccaui   [R] agnosco *PV*   [S] et: *om. V.*
[T] te: *PV add* domine   [U] caritatem: *om. P:* caritatem et humilitatem: *om. V*
[V] operibus bonis *PV*   [W] quicquid: *V cont.* domine cogitaui uel (locutus)
[X] inique: *om. P*   [Y] mea: *V adds* tu piissimus   [Z] te deprecor: nunc *V*
[A] in: ex *V*   [B] meo: *V adds* et   [C] te *om. V*   [D] cum . . . martyribus: cum sanctis tuis martyribus *P*   [E] in . . . digneris: mittere digneris in auxilium meum *P*
[F] *P adds* sanctos (angelos)

---

[7] Cf. Ps. 50: 5.
[8] Cf. Ib. 30: 20.
[9] Dn. 3: 93–94.
[10] *cum . . . peruenire. V* reads : 'et omni deuotione obsecro ut mittere digneris sanctos angelos tuos in auxilium meum. Peto et supplico omnes sanctos apostolos et iiii euangelistas atque martyres confessores uirgines ac omnes sanctos et electos tuos ut me exaudiant et pro me peccatore apud te intercedant et prestent mihi ad uiam ueritatis uenire. Amen.'
[11] *et . . . peruenire. P* reads : 'apostolos et confessores et prophetas et quattuor euangelistas. Peto et supplico te dominum nostrum Ihesum Christum et omnes sanctos electos tuos ut me exaudiant et prestent mihi ad uitam ueritatis peruenire. Amen.'

43

17

⟨A Prayer of Confession⟩

Peccaui,[1] d*omi*ne, et[A] nimis peccaui[B] in homine quanto magis in te,
d*eus*[C] meus,[D] ut non est numerus[E] operum maloru*m*[F] que operatus
sum a iuuentute mea usque[G] ★★★[a] (1–2 wd) et tu,[H] d*eus* meus, rex

f. 24[v]   eterne glorie[b] qui me dignatus es[I] redimere[J] / pretioso sanguine tuo, et
posuisti[K] te in ligno pro[L] me indigno p⟨ec⟩catore.[a] Non pro meis
meritis, sed[2] ⟨pro[cM]mag⟩na[a] mis*eri*cor*di*a, non pro mea ueritate, sed
pro tua magna pietate[N] ita[O] eripere me digneris[dP] ut non intrem in
illum locum pessimum quod[eQ] se*mper* est sine refrigerio et ⟨sine⟩[a]

f. 24[r]   splendore et[fR] sine / dulcedine et erit sine fine.[S] In inferno autem[T] quis
⟨c⟩onfitebitur[a] tibi?[3] Neq*ue*[g] mors laudabit te. Miserere mihi, d*omi*ne,
et exaudi me miseru*m*[U] te[V] deprecante*m*, sicut exaudisti Mariam et
Martham rogantes te ut ires ad monumentum[h] suscitare[W] Lazarum et

f. 25[v]   resuscitatus[i] est.[4] / Ita precor[X] te,[Y] d*omi*ne, ut me resuscites[Z] de

---

[a] *MS. damaged*   [b] rex . . . glorie: *added with finer pen*   [c] pro . . . sed: *added
with finer pen*   [d] ita . . . digneris: *added with finer pen*   [e] *MS.* qui
[f] et: *added interlinearly, and later erased*   [g] neque: *'-ue' erased; cf. no.* **46,** *line 65, app.*
[h] monumentum: *'-tum' added interlinearly*   [i] resuscitatus: *'re-' added interlinearly*

[A] et: *om. V*   [B] peccaui: *om. V*   [C] deum meum *V*   [D] meus: *P adds* ita
[E] numerus: *PV cont.* de operibus malis   [F] malorum: *V adds* meis
[G] usque *(and portion lost): om. PV*   [H] tu: *PV add* domine   [I] fuisti *P*
[J] redimere: *PV cont.* de (*V om.*) tuo sancto sanguine   [K] posuisti . . . ligno: te in
ligno promisisti crucifigi *V*   [L] pro . . . peccatore: *om. V*   [M] pro: *P adds* tua
[N] *om. P*   [O] *P adds* deprecor ut (ita)   [P] digneris: *P adds* pro tua misericordia
non pro meis meritis   [Q] qui *PV*   [R] et: ac *V*   [S] fine: *PV add* quia
[T] autem: *om. P*   [U] miserrimum *V*
[V] te: *om. P*: deprecantem te *V*   [W] resuscitare *V*   [X] deprecor *PV*
[Y] te: *om. V*   [Z] resuscites me *V*

---

[1] The analogues for this text are *V* (ff. 175[r–v]), *P* (II. 13–14) and *Or* (f. 24, not
collated here).
[2] *pro . . . digneris* The text of *V* is superior to that of *G* or *P*; it reads: 'pro tua magna
misericordia ut me saluares. Te deprecor domine ut pro tua pietate me digneris
eripere. . .'.
[3] Cf. Is. 38: 18.
[4] Io. ll: 1–30.

morte[j] ★★★[a] (1 wd) quo ★★★[a] (1 wd) cum[k] his q*ui* ★★★[a] (1 wd) dexteris
tuis[5] et audire uocem tua*m* dicentem,[A] Venite, benedicti patris mei,
percipite[6] regnum quod[lB] uobis paratum est ab origine mundi; et ut[mC]
sis mihi mitis sicut fuisti mulieri[n] meretrici in domo Symonis./

26[r]   E⟨ff⟩unde[aD] oculis meis la⟨c⟩rimas[a] sicut suadasti[8] ei ⟨q⟩uando[a] pedes
tuos lauit quasi[E] pillis suis[o] tersit, et dimisisti eam in[F] pace. Te
deprecor, d*omi*ne de*us* om*nipoten*s, ut dimittas mihi omnia peccata
mea antequam moriar[q] ut non gaudeat[r] inimi⟨cus⟩[a] meus de me.[9]/ Et

26[v]   te deprecor, s*an*c*t*e Petre,[G] tenens[s] claues regni celor*um*[10] ut me
saluas[H] sup*er* terram. Et[I] da mihi, d*omi*ne Ih*esu* Chri*ste*, fortitudinem
de celo ut uincam diabolum uigilantem et non dormientem[J] et
dimicantem contra me ne[tK] trahat me ad foueam tenebrar⟨um⟩.[a]
Precor[u] s*an*c*t*os ang*el*os *et* archangelos tuos, precor om*nes*[L] patriarchas
et om*nes* prophetas tuos[M] et[v] s*an*c*t*os ap*osto*los tuos, precor om*nes*[N]

27[r]   martyres tuos,[w] confessores[x] *et* uirgines ut / ⟨in⟩tercedant[a] ⟨pro⟩[a] me,
domine, misero pecca⟨tore⟩;[aO] inuoco illos qui ante d*eu*m[Q] non
cessant clamore[yR] dicentes, ⟨Sanctus⟩,[a] s*an*c*tu*s, s*an*c*tu*s d*omi*nu*s* de*us*

---

[j] morte: *what followed this was erased*   [k] cum . . . dexteris: *added with a finer pen*
[l] quod . . . mundi: *expuncted*   [m] ut: *added interlinearly*   [n] *MS.* mulier
[o] suis: *followed by a space*   [q] moriar: *a word* (morte?) *has been erased before this*
[r] gaudeat: *followed by an erasure*   [s] *MS.* tenes   [t] ne . . . tenebrarum: *added*
interlinearly, finer pen   [u] precor . . . tuos: *added interlinearly, finer pen*
[v] et sanctos apostolos tuos: *added interlinearly*   [w] omnes, tuos: *expuncted*
[x] confessores et uirgines: *added interlinearly later*   [y] clamore: *added interlinearly*

[A] dicentem: *P adds* mihi   [B] quod . . . et (. . . mundi: *V om.*) : *om. P*
[C] ut: *om. V*   [D] effunde: *V adds* domine suasisti: infudisti *PV*   [E] quasi . . .
suis: et crine *PV*   [F] in: cum *PV*   [G] Petre: *PV cont.* qui tenes
[H] saluas: soluas *PV, with V gl.* alyse   [I] et: *V om.*   [J] et non dormientem: *om. PV*
[K] ne: ut non *PV*   [L] omnes: sanctos *V: P adds* sanctos
[M] *P reads:* (prophetas) precor omnes sanctos apostolos et martyres et confessores et
omnes sanctas uirgines et omnes sanctos electos tuos ut dignenter intercedere pro me
misero (peccatore)   [N] *V reads:* (precor) et sanctos martyres precor sanctos
confessores et uirgines atque omnes sanctos et electos tuos ut dignentur intercedere pro
me misero et (peccatore)   [O] peccatore: *P adds* et inuoco: *V adds* et
[Q] *PV add* die ac nocte   [R] clamare *PV*

---

[5] *morte . . . tuis. VP* read: '(morte) mea ut merear esse ad dexteram tuam'; cf. Ps.
  109:1.
[6] Mt. 25: 34 reads, '. . . possidete paratum uobis regnum a constitutione mundi'.
[7] Cf. Lc. 7: 37:50.
[8] *suadasti: for* suasisti.
[9] Cf. Ps. 40: 12.
[10] Mt. 16: 19.

45

sabaoth'. Hos^{zS} omnes humiliter obsecro^{b5} ut orent pro me peccatore^T quo^U merear superare omnes iniquitates meas quascumque^V commisi ab infantia mea usque in presentem diem. Nunc exoro^X dominum

f. 27^v nostrum Ihesum / Christum ut ill⟨e⟩^{a} misericors audiat preces meas, saluator mundi qui uiuis et regnas in secula seculorum. Am⟨en⟩.^{a}

---

^{z} hos . . . obsecro: *expuncted* ^{a} *MS. damaged* ^{b} obsecro: *glossed* ic halsige

---

^{S} hos . . . obsecro: *om. PV* ^{T} *om. PV* ^{U} ut *PV* ^{V} quas *PV*
^{W} a iuuentute *PV* ^{X} *P reads*: (exoro) te domine ihesu christe qui es misericors et miserator tribue omnibus qui inuocant te in ueritate bonam fidem et bonam perseuerantiam. Et te domine precor ut exaudias deprecationem meam qui cum patre et spiritu sancto uiuis et regnas deus per omnia secula seculorum. Amen. *V reads*: (exoro) te domine ihesu christe qui es miserator et misericors tribue omnibus qui inuocant te in ueritate bonam fidem et bonam perseuerantiam ac felicem in tua uoluntate consummationem. Item te rogo domine et supplico ut exaudias deprecationem meam et meum desiderium secundum gratiam tuam in beneplacito tuo omni tempore perficias ut ad tuam misericordiam cum sanctis fidelibus tuis peruenire ualeam qui cum patre et spiritu sancto uiuis et regnas deus, per.

18

⟨Our Lord's Letter to Abgarus, Toparch of Edessa⟩

Incipit epistola[1] saluatoris domini nostri Ihesu Christi ad Abagarum regem quam dominus manu sua^A scripsit^a et dixit, Beatus es qui^B non uidisti et credidisti in me;[2] scriptum est enim^C quia hii qui uiderunt^D me non credent in me, et qui me non ui- / derunt^E ipsi^b credent^F et uiuent.^{c3} De eo autem quod scripsisti mihi, ut uenirem ad te, oportet me omnia propter que^d missus sum hic explere et posteaquam compleuero tempus^G recipi me^H a quo missus sum.[4] Cum ergo fuero adsumptus,[5] mittam tibi aliquem[6] ex discipulis meis ut curet egritudinem tuam, et uitam tibi atque^I/ his qui tecu⟨m sunt⟩^{e} prestet saluus eris, sicut scriptum est,^{J7} qui credit^K saluus erit.[8]

28^r

28^v

---

^{a} MS. sripsit ^{b} MS. ipsium ^{c} uiuent: '-n-' add. interl.
^{d} que: MS. quem ^{e} MS. damaged

---

^{A} sua: om. R ^{B} qui: R adds me ^{C} enim: R adds de me
^{D} uident R ^{E} uident R ^{F} credent: R adds in me
^{G} tempus: om. R ^{H} me: R adds ad eum ^{I} R at with illegible interl. addition
prestet: R adds et ^{J} est: om. R ^{K} credit: R adds in me

---

[1] This is a Latin version of the earliest Greek apocryphal epistle which has survived. It was first recorded by Eusebius in his *Ecclesiastical History* (I.13). The Greek text of Eusebius was translated into Latin and condensed to two books by Rufinus *c.* 402 (*PL* 21.463–540). J. D. A. Ogilvy interprets Colman's phrase, 'ut ecclesiastica docet historia', in Bede's *Ecclesiastical History of the English People* (III. 25) as a reference to Rufinus's text (*Books Known to the English 597–1066*, Camb. Mass., 1967, p. 236). Since it was generally accepted that the text recorded the actual words of Christ, it became very popular, circulating widely, independent of the rest of the *History*, and was believed to have curative powers. For further historical background and bibliographical data, see W. Schneemelcher (ed.), *New Testament Apocrypha*, trans. A. J. B. Higgins et al., English version ed. R. McL. Wilson (Philadelphia, 1963–66) pp. 437–44. The analogue used here is *R* (f. 12^{r-v}); there is an edition of this text from several manuscripts in *ILH* I. 93–95.

[2] Cf. Io. 20: 29.

[3] Cf. Mt. 13: 14.

[4] Cf. Io. 16: 5; the Vulgate reads, 'uado ad eum qui misit me'.

[5] Cf. Ac. 1: 2, 11, 22.

[6] *aliquem* The apostle Thaddeus or Addai.

[7] Mr. 16: 6.

[8] *R* has a postscript (about 75 words) that illustrates the type of salutary or curative powers this text was believed to have had.

19

⟨'Domine Ihesu Christe qui dedisti potestatem':
A Prayer to Christ and the Twelve Apostles⟩

Domine[a1] Ihesu Christe, qui dedisti potestatem apostolis tuis infirmos curare,[2] mortuos suscitare, leprosos mundare, demones eicere,[A] da
f. 29[r] mihi ueram humilitatem[3] et fidem firmam et[B] patien- / tiam in tribulationibus[4] meis[C] et[D] salutem mentis et corporis et[E] corde meo constitue cogitationes sanctas; et dirige pedes meos[F] in uiam pacis ut habeam in conuersatione iustitiam,[5] in moribus disciplinam et in omnibus initium semper sapientie[G] timorem tuum.[6] O reconciliator[b]
f. 29[v] humani / generis, obsecro[H] propter nomen tuum et[I] per orationes[c] apostolorum tuorum, exaudi me, deus et sanctus Israhel, et omnium uitiorum meorum ⟨mala⟩[dK] multitudinem[L] misericordie[M] tuæ[N] mortifica;[7] meque donis tuis interius exteriusque restaura et tenebras[e]
f. 30[r] cordis mei lumine caritatis[O] tue inlustra per- / enius.[P] Et[Q] per auxilium[R] apostolorum tuorum fidelissimum[fS] confirma fragilitatem nostram,[T] et mihi contra mundi pericula prebe firmamentum et custodi me[g] contra hostes meos uisibiles et inuisibiles. O rex glorie,[U]

---

[a] 1 domine: *the 'd' is the first letter decorated with simple interlace in G*
[b] *MS*. ore conciliator   [c] *MS*. perorationes   [d] *MS. damaged*
[e] *MS*. tenebris   [f] *MS*. fidelissimo   [g] custodi me: *MS*. custodia

---

[A] eicere: effugere *V*   [B] et . . . meis: *om. V*   [C] meis: *om. C*   [D] et: ac *V*
[E] et: *C cont.* constitue in cordē meo: inspira domine cordi meo *V*
[F] pedes meos: me *V*   [G] sapientie: *V adds* id est   [H] obsecro: *V adds* te
[I] et: *om. C*   [J] omnium: omnem *V*   [K] mala: *om. V*   [L] multitudine *C*
[M] misericordie tuæ: *om. V*   [N] tuæ: *om. C*   [O] claritatis tuae *V*: tuae claritatis *C*
[P] perenne: *C om. V*   [Q] et: ac *V*   [R] auxilia *CV*: *after* auxilium *C adds* beatorum
[S] fidelissima *CV*   [T] meam *CV*   [U] glorie: *CV add* et

---

[1] The analogues for this text are *C* (no. 30, pp. 127–30) and *V* (f. 184[r] sqq.); a version of it also appears in a fifteenth-century English MS., BL Harl. 2445 (ff. 44[r]–48[v]) which is not collated here, but whose text bears significant readings which are discussed below.
[2] Cf. Mr. 3: 15.
[3] Cf. Mt. 10: 8.
[4] Cf. Rm. 12: 12.
[5] Lc. 1: 79.
[6] Ps. 110: 10.
[7] Cf. Ps. 5: 8.

30^v do*m*ine uirtutum,[8] in primis quidem^V pieta- / tem^h tuam peto. Per
merita beati Petri apostoli tui, da mihi prudentiam iustitiam diligere^W
et odire iniquitatem[9] in uerbis, in factis,^{X} in cogitationibus.^{Y} Et^Z per
merita beati Pauli apostoli tui,^{A} da mihi fidei, spei^B et caritatis
31^r augmentum ut te cre- / dam,^{C} cognoscam et^D diligam ex omnibus
uiribus meis.[10] Et per merita beati Andree apostoli tui, da mihi^E
uirtutem et fortitudinem^F om*n*es inimicos meos^G sup*e*rare^H s*an*c*t*e
trinitatis protectione.^{I} Et per merita s*an*c*t*i^J Iacobi apostoli tui,^{K} da
31^v mihi^L uic- / toriam^M sup*er* aduersarios meos^N in uirtute tua, filii dei
uiui, deprecor. Et per merita beati^O Iohannis ap*osto*li tui^P et
euuangelistæ, multiplica^Q gratiam tuam in me, miseratus,^{R} ut
uoluntarie^{iS} uigeam ⟨et⟩^{jT} proficiam in uolunte tua.^{U} / Et per merita
32^r s*an*c*t*i^V Thome ap*osto*li tui, da mihi^W spiritalem intellectum et
scientiam ut tibi uiuere^k ualeam et in uiis tuis[11] ambulem et^X in te
permaneam. Et per merita beati Iacobi ap*osto*li tui, pretende^Y mihi
dexteram celestis auxilii sup*er*^{Z} om*n*es habitantes in habitaculis meis,[12]
32^v et propi- / tius esto^l nobis.^{A} Amen.^{B} Et per merita s*an*c*t*i Philippi

---

^{h} pietatem: *followed by a space* ^{i} *MS.* uoluntauie ^{j} et: *add. ed.*
^{k} uiuere: *added interlinearly* ^{l} *MS.* est a

---

^{V} quidem: *om. V* ^{W} diligere iustitiam *C* ^{X} factis: *V adds* et
^{Y} cogitationibus: *C adds* meis ^{Z} et: *om. C* ^{A} tui: *V adds* domine
^{B} speique *C* ^{C} credam: *V adds* te ^{D} et: *C cont.* ex omnibus uiribus meis
diligere ^{E} mihi: *V adds* domine ^{F} fortitudinem: *V adds* ut
^{G} meos: *V cont.* ualeam superare cum ^{H} superare: *C adds* cum tua
^{I} protectione trinitatis *C* ^{J} beati *C* ^{K} tui: *om. C* ^{L} mihi: *V adds* domine
^{M} uictoriam: *C adds* semper: *V cont.* contra hostes uisibiles et inuisibles ^{N} super
aduersarios meos: *om. V* ^{O} sancti *CV* ^{P} tui: *om. C* ^{Q} multiplica: *V*
adds domine ^{R} miserator *C* ^{S} uoluntate *C* ^{T} et: *V cont.* tuam in
omnibus uoluntem proficiam ^{U} uoluntatem tuam *C* ^{V} beati *CV*
^{W} mihi: *V adds* domine ^{X} et: *V adds* iugiter ^{Y} pretende: *V adds* domine
^{Z} super . . . meis: *om. V* ^{A} mihi *V* ^{B} amen: *om. V*

---

[8] Ps. 23: 10.
[9] Ps. 44: 8.
[10] Lc. 10: 27.
[11] Ps. 127: 1.
[12] Cp. Eph. 1: 20.

apostoli tui,^{C} concede mihi pacem et^D tranquillitatem in^E temporibus meis. Et per merita beati Bartholomei apostoli tui, te deprecor^F ut omnia^G iura^H regni^I mei[13] et memet ipsum in felicitate et incolomitate

f. 33^r custodias. / Et per merita sancti Mathei apostoli tui ⟨et⟩^{m} euuangeliste, presta mihi, piissime pater,^{J} ut^K ego^L per inspirationem^M sancti spiritus a morte anime resurgere merear. Et per merita sanctorum apostolorum^N Simonis et Tathei, da mihi^O potestatem^{nP} ut per merita

f. 33^v omnium bonorum operum^Q inferni tene- / bras et inmortales uerm⟨es⟩^{o} euadere, et eterne premia promereri ualeam^R ⟨per⟩^{P} te, Ihesu Christe. Tu^S dixisti discipulis tuis, 'Petite[14] et dabitur uobis, querite et inuenietis, pulsate^T et aperietur uobis'.^{U} Ego^V peto in nomine tuo,

f. 34^r Ihesu Christe^W redemptor,^{X}/ ut^Y tu deum patrem petas, et donetur mihi indulgen⟨t⟩ia.^{oZ} Vultum tuum, domine,[15] requiram;^{A} adiuua me^B ut inueniam, exaudi^C me ut uideam. Ego pulso precibus;[16] aures misericordie^D tue^E aperi mihi et^F portas paradisi post obitum meum /

---

^{m} et: *add. ed.* ^{n} potestatem: *corrected* ^{o} *MS. damaged*
^{p} per: *add. ed.*

---

^{C} tui: *V adds* domine ^{D} et: *om. V* ^{E} in . . . meis: *V has* et salutem ut ea que tibi placita sunt omni dilectione perficiam ^{F} deprecor: *V adds* domine
^{G} omnia . . . custodias: *V reads* (ut) me et omnia que ad me tua largitione pertinent longa felicitate et incolomitate secundum tuam misericordiam (custodias)
^{H} omnia iura: omnes actos meos *C* ^{I} regni mei: *om. C*
^{J} pater: *om. C*: domine *V* ^{K} ut: *C adds* et ^{L} ego: *om. V*
^{M} inspirationem: *C adds* tui ^{N} apostolorum: *C adds* tuorum
^{O} mihi: *V adds* domine ^{P} potestatem . . . Christe: *V reads:* (mihi) gratiam et misericordiam tuam ut inferni tenebras ualeam euadere et ad aeterna premia te annuente peruenire ^{Q} ut . . . operum: *om. C* ^{R} ualeam: *om. C*
^{S} tu: *V adds* domine ^{T} pulsate . . . uobis: *om. V* ^{U} uobis: *V adds* ecce
^{V} ego . . . tuo: ego in nomine tuo peto *C* ^{W} Christe: *om. CV*
^{X} redemptor: *V adds* pie ^{Y} ut . . . indulgentia: *om. V*
^{Z} indulgentia: *V adds* et ^{A} requiro *V* ^{B} me: *V adds* domine
^{C} exaudi . . . uideam: et uideam: *C* et optineam quicquid ad bonum tota deuotione exposco *V* ^{D} tue misericordie *V* ^{E} tue: *V adds* deus: *C adds* domine deus
^{F} et: *om. CV*

---

[13] *omnia iura regni mei* This interesting phrase is not in the contemporary analogues *CV*; however, it is also found in BL MS. Harl. 2445 (f. 46^v). In addition, although *C* is incomplete and *V* has a different conclusion from *G* (see below), the Harleian MS. agrees completely with *G*. Thus there is a possibility that these two belong to a common MS. tradition, the other members of which are lost or yet undiscovered. The phrase may also offer corroborative evidence that *G* was written at Winchester.
[14] Mt. 7: 7.
[15] Ps. 26: 8.
[16] Cf. Ap. 3: 20.

34[v] ut in electorum tuorum numero requiescere[G] liceat[H] mihi coram te, Christe, cum[I] ⟨an⟩gelis[q] tuis.[J] Exaudi me,[K] adiuua me.[17] Trahe me: post te curremus in odorem ungue⟨n⟩torum[q] tuorum.[18] Deus meus, in auxilium meum respice.[19] Ne dereliquas me, domine, quem ad

35[r] imaginem et[L] similitudinem tuam condidisti.[20] Neque / dispicias[21] me quem pretiosissima[M] pignore[r] tui sacrosancti[22] sanguinis tui[N] in cruce comparasti, qui clamasti celitus[O] ad patrem tuum omnipotentem pro apostolis tuis supplicans,[P] et[Q] pro omnibus[R] sanctis[S] dicens, non pro his[T] tantum rogo,[U] sed pro eis qui credituri[23] sunt[V] per uerbum

35[v] eorum in me, ut omnes / unum sint, sicut tu pater in me et ego in te, ut et ipsi in nobis unum sint, ut mundus credat quia tu me misisti. Credo, domine deus Israhel,[W] adiuua incredulitatem[s] meam.[24] Ego credidi et uere scio quia tu es Christe[X] filius dei uiui qui in[Y] mundum

36[r] uenisti saluare quod perierat; parce pecca- / ⟨t⟩is[t] nostris[Z] quia innumerabilia sunt, et libera nos[A] propter nomen tuum.[B] Per merita beatorum apostolorum tuorum munda[uC] me,[D] salua[v] me et protege[w] me, qui cum patre et spiritu sancto uiuis et regnas, deus unus et trinus, omnipotens, eternus, tibi honor et gloria in secula seculorum. Amen. /

---

[q] *MS. damaged*   [r] *MS.* pignorum
[s] incredulitatem: '*in-*' *erased, it seems*   [t] *MS. damaged*   [u] munda: *gl.* geclænsa
[v] salua: *gl.* gehæl   [w] protege: *gl.* gescyld

[G] requiescere . . . coram: mihi requiescere liceat coram *C*   [H] mihi liceat *V*
[I] cum: et coram *CV*   [J] tuis: *V adds* amen   [K] me *V adds* Christe
[L] et . . . condidisti: tuam et similitudinem condidisti *C*
[M] pretiosa: *C* pretiosissimo *V*   [N] tui: *om. CV*   [O] celitus: *om. V*
[P] supplicando *V*   [Q] et . . . sanctis: *om. V*   [R] pro omnibus: *om. C*
[S] sanctis: *C adds* ita   [T] his: *C adds* autem   [U] rogo: *V adds* pater
[V] sunt: *C ends here*   [W] deus Israhel: *om. V*   [X] Christus *V*
[Y] in: *V adds* hunc   [Z] meis *V, adds* domine   [A] me *V, adds* domine
[B] tuum: *V adds* et   [C] emunda *V*   [D] *V reads* (me) in presenti uita et perduc me ad aeternam uitam ubi cum omnibus sanctis tuis perfruar gloria uisionis tue domine in secula seculorum (Amen)

---

[17] Cn. 1: 3.
[18] Ps. 70: 12.
[19] Ps. 26: 9.
[20] Gn. 1: 26.
[21] Ps. 26: 9.
[22] Cf. 1 Pt. 1: 19.
[23] Io. 17: 20–21.
[24] Mr. 9: 23.

20

⟨A Prayer to St. John the Baptist⟩

f. 36ᵛ Oratio¹ sancti Iohanis baptist⟨e⟩ᵃ. Sancte Iohannis baptista, qui spiritu et uirtute² Helie fuis⟨ti⟩ᵃ a patre donatus dominice aduentus baptimsi et predicatio, fidelissime precursor,³ cui inter natos mulierum nemo surrexit maior ipso adtestante redemtorem quem ostenderis
f. 37ʳ baptizando po- / pulo agnum peccata mundi tollentem,⁴ intercede pro me ut salutaris lauacr⟨o⟩ᵃ redemptionem cum mundis et inmaculas accipere merear in futuro. Amen.

ᵃ MS. damaged

---

¹ There is no analogue for this text which is noteworthy for the peculiarities of its syntax; compare the style of nos. **7, 8, 21** and **66**, and see the discussion of 'Language' in the Introduction. Some of the problems in the text are: (1) *cui*, should be *quo* with *maior*; (2) *redemtorem*, should be in the ablative; (3) *salutaris* should perhaps be in the ablative (*salutari*), 'by means of a saving bath' (i.e. baptism); (4) *inmaculas* should be in the ablative as *mundis* is.
² Lc. 1: 17.
³ Lc. 7: 28.
⁴ Io. 1: 29.

21

⟨A Prayer to St. Peter⟩

Sanctus[1] Petrus, princeps ap*ostolorum*, miserere mihi[2] quia arbitriu*m*[a] tuu*m* reliquit d*eus* ce⟨lum⟩[b] et terra*m*, ideo dona mihi ut / tibi adscribar[c] ⟨q⟩ui[b] es regni celestis quia eius clauicularius es, intercede p*ro* me ut donet mihi d*eus* requiem in aula celesti, et ne umquam dimittas anima*m* mea*m* in interitu; sed obsecro te ut suscipias eam in die nouissimo, et gemescens peto et lacrimans[d] obsecro ut uenies ad auxiliandu*m* me et tunc me a⟨d a⟩liquam[b] paste*m*[3] colloca ut / tibi possim tue p*re*clare[4] uisione fruere[5] et d*omi*ni asspectu, ut ibi leto uideam purissima*m*[e] diuinitate*m*.

37ᵛ

38ʳ

---

[a] arbitrium: *corrected*   [b] *MS. damaged*   [c] adscribar: '*c*' *added interlinearly*
[d] *MS.* lacrimas   [e] purissimam: *2nd* '*s*' *added above*

---

[1] This text, for which there is no analogue, is noteworthy for the peculiarities of its syntax; compare the style of nos. **7, 8, 20** and **66**, and see the discussion of 'Language' in the Introduction.

[2] *mihi.* More correctly, *mei.*

[3] *pastem.* This form is unrecorded elsewhere; it may be related to *pasco*, and mean 'pasture' or something similar. Alternatively, it could be an error for *partem.*

[4] *tue preclare.* More correctly, *tua preclara.*

[5] *fruere.* Usually the passive *frui.*

22

⟨A Prayer to Christ for Spiritual Direction⟩

Domine[1] Ihesu Christe,[A] qui de hoc mundo transisti ad patrem,[2] et dilexisti eos[B] qui erant in mundo, fac me mente[C] de terrestribus transire[D] ad superna, cuncta labentia contemnere et sola celestia desiderare flammigeroque igne[a] amoris tui[E] flagrare.[F] Et tu, deus,[G]

f. 38ᵛ qui sanctorum apostolorum tuorum[3] / sacrosanctis manibus[H] pedes lauar⟨e⟩[b] dignatus es,[I] et cor meum iubar spiritus[J] sancti[C] infundendo purifica,[K] ut in omnibus et super omnia[d] diligere ualeam te, dominum nostrum Ihesum Christum. Amen.

ᵃ *MS.* ignem   ᵇ *MS. damaged*   ᶜ *MS.* sanctus   ᵈ *MS.* omia

---

ᴬ Christi *R*   ᴮ tuos *R*   ᶜ mente: *R adds* et anima
ᴰ transire de terrestribus *R*   ᴱ tui: *R adds* suauiter   ᶠ flagrare: *R adds* et anhelando iugiter redundare   ᴳ tu deus: *om. R*   ᴴ manibus: *R adds* tuis
ᴵ es: *R adds* cogitationes meas   ᴶ sancti spiritus *R*   ᴷ purifica: *R ends here*

---

[1] The analogue for this text is *R* (f. 24v), where it has the rubric 'Oratio sancti Augustini episcopi'; see the introductory note to no. **16** above.
[2] Io. 13: 1.
[3] Io. 13: 5–11.

23

⟨A Prayer to St. Peter⟩

S*ancte*[1] Petre apostole, te supplex[a] queso ut mihi idigno adiuues tuis
orationib*us*, tibique flecto genua pr*o*pter mea scelera.[b] Tu pio se*mper*
animo digneris me recipere; agnoscoque mea crimina. D*eus*,[c][A] peto
5 ueniam; te oro ut mihi . . .[2] /

---

[a] *MS.* tue supple   [b] *MS.* mei sceleri   [c] *MS.* deum

---

[A] deum *C*

---

[1] The analogue for this text, the ending of which is lost, is *C* (no. 63, pp. 158–59); see
also *Wi* (p. 41) and *Or* (ff. 25^v–26^n).
[2] *mihi. C* continues, 'adiuues iacenti in periculo; hostis iniquus inuigilat ut me fraude
decipiat. Sed tua sancta oratio eius excludat aditum. Sis mihi in auxilium aduersus
eius impetum. Ne mens praerepta ab impio recedat a proposito ille ut ledat inuigilat
et tu orando adiuues. Ne possit aduersarius tuo nocere famulo; perfidus ille doleat et
tu laetus congaudeas. Repulsa aduersarium tuis orationibus. Gloria tibi altissime qui
es benignus in sanctis et regnas in perpetuo in trinitate dominus. Amen.'

55

24

⟨A Prayer to the Patriarchs and Prophets for Intercession⟩

f. 39[r] Oratio[1] ad patriarchas[a] et prophetas:[b] Dominator domine[A] deus omnipotens, qui es trinitas una,[B] pater in filio et[C] filius in patre cum sancto[D] spiritu, qui es semper in omnibus et eras ante omnia et[E] eris per omnia deus benedictus in secula,[2] commendo animam meam

f. 39[v] in manus potentie tue[3] ut custodies eam diebus ac noctibus / horis atque momentis; miserere mei, deus angelorum, dirige me, rex archangelorum, custodi me[c] per orationes patriarcharum, per merita prophetarum, per suffragia apostolorum, per uictoriam[dF] martyrum, per[eG] fidem confessorum, per castitatem[H] uirginum et omnium sanctorum qui tibi placuerunt[I] ab initio[J] mundi.[K4] Oret[L] pro me

f. 40[r] sanctus Michael archangelus Christi cum omnibus sanctis agminibus angelorum et archangelorum. Oret[M] pro me sanctus Abel,[5] qui primus coronatus[N] martyrio.[O] Oret pro me sanctus Enoch,[6] qui ambulauit cum deo[P] et translatus est a[Q] mundo. Oret pro me sanctus[R] Noe,

---

[a] *MS.* patriarchis   [b] *MS.* prophete   [c] me: *added interlinearly*
[d] uictoriam: *corrected, finer pen*   [e] per . . . sanctorum: *added above, finer pen*

[A] dominus *CO*   [B] unus *P*   [C] et: *om. U*   [D] spiritu sancto *CPOU*
[E] et . . . omnia: *om. P*   [F] uictorias *CPOU*   [G] per . . . sanctorum: *om. CPO*
[H] castitatem . . . et: intercessionem *U*   [I] placuerunt tibi *CO*   [J] origine *U*
[K] mundi: *U adds* usque ad consummationem sæculi
[L] oret . . . archangelorum: *om. CPOU*   [M] oret . . . martyrio: *relocated by Kuypers in C*   [N] coronatus: *CPOU add* est (*P* est†), *P adds* in
[O] martyrio: *U adds* oret pro me sanctus Seth qui primus coepit inuocare nomen domini
[P] cum deo: coram domino *P*   [Q] a: de *U*   [R] beatus *P*

---

[1] The analogues for this text are *C* (no. 15, pp. 103–06), *P* (II. 15–17), *O* (ff. 16v–18v) and *U* (101.589–91). André Wilmart has published an edition of this prayer from two continental MSS. (from Zürich and Verdun) in an appendix to his *Auteurs spirituels et textes dévots du moyen âge latin* (Paris, 1932), pp. 571–77; the prayer is attributed to St. Augustine there. In *C*, *O* and *U* it is attributed to St. Gregory the Great; there are no attributive phrases in *P* (see the introductory note to no. **16** above). See also *Ma* (col. 674), *Or* (ff. 21ᵛ–23ʳ) and *Wi* (pp. 11–13).
[2] Rm. 9: 5.
[3] Ps. 30: 6; Lc. 23: 46.
[4] Sap. 9: 19.
[5] Cf. Gn. 4: 8.
[6] Gn. 5: 22; Heb. 11: 5.

40ᵛ quem d*ominu*s seruauit in diluuio[7] / *propter* iustitiam.ˢ Roget pro me
fidelis Abraham, qui primus credidit d*e*o,ᵀ cui reputataᵁ estⱽ fidesᵂ
ad iustitiam.[8] Intercedatˣ *pro* me iustus Isaac,[9] q*ui* fuit obediens patri
usq*ue* ad mortem in exemplum d*omi*ni n*os*tri Ih*es*u Chri*sti*, q*ui* oblatus
41ʳ estʸ *pro*ᶠ salute mundi. Postu- / let *pro* me felix Iacob,[10] q*ui* uidit
angelosᶻ deiᴬ uenientesᴮ in auxilium sibi.ᶜ Oret *pro* me beatusᴰ
Moyses[11] cum quoᴱ locutus est d*ominu*sᶠ facie ad faciem.ᴳ Subueniat
mihi s*anctu*s Dauid,[12] quemᴴ elegisti regemᵍᴵ secu*ndu*m cor tuum,
d*omi*ne. Deprecetur *pro* me Heliasᴶ s*anctu*s propheta,[13] quem eleuasti
41ᵛ in / curru igneo usq*ue* ad celum. Oretᴷ *pro* me s*anctu*sᴸ Heliseus,[14]
qui suscitauit mortuumᴹ post mortem.ᴺ Oret *pro* me s*anctu*sᴼ Isaias[15]
cuius mundataʰ sunt labiaᴾ igneᵠ celesti. Adsitᴿ mihi beatusⁱˢ
Hieremias[16] propheta,ᵀ quem s*ancti*ficasti in utero matris sue.ʲᵁ Oret
42ʳ *pro* me s*anctu*s Ezechielⱽ[17] propheta,ᵂ / q*ui* uidit uisiones mirabiles

---

ᶠ pro: *the letters* pam *are in the margin beside this*
ᵍ regem: *partially erased though visible*   ʰ *MS.* mundate
ⁱ beatus: *added interlinearly*   ʲ sue: *added above, finer pen*

ˢ iustitiam: *U adds* oret pro me Melchisedech rex justus qui obviavit Abrahæ et
benedixit ei   ᵀ deo: *om. U*   ᵁ reputatum: *C* reputatus *P*
ⱽ est: *P adds* ei   ᵂ fides: *om. P*   ˣ intercedet *O*
ʸ est: *CP add* patri: *OU add* deo patri   ᶻ angelum *P*
ᴬ dei: *U adds* et domini   ᴮ uenientem sibi *P*   ᶜ *U reads* (Oret pro me beatus)
Joseph qui soluit somnia regis et interpretatus est et liberatus est de carcere. Oret pro
me sanctus Job magnus et potiens qui nihil peccauit in labiis suis in omnibus quae
acciderunt illi   ᴰ sanctus *CO*   ᴱ cum quo: ad quem *P*   ᶠ deus *U*
ᴳ *U reads* (faciem) Oret pro me Hiessus filius Nun quem elegisti domine post Moysen
famulum tuum. Oret pro me sanctus Samuel propheta qui benedixit et unxit reges
super Israel   ᴴ qui *P*   ᴵ regem: *om. CPO*   ᴶ sanctus Helias *COU*
ᴷ oret . . . mortem: *om. U*   ᴸ sanctus: *O twice*   ᴹ mortem *P*
ᴺ mortem: *P adds* suam   ᴼ beatus *PU*   ᴾ labia mundata sunt *CO*
ᵠ igni *O*   ᴿ adsistat *P*   ˢ sanctus *P*   ᵀ propheta: *om. CPOU*
ᵁ sue: *om. CO*   ⱽ Ezechiel sanctus *P*   ᵂ propheta: *om. CO*

---

[7] Cf. Gn. 6: 9.
[8] Rm. 4: 9.
[9] Ph. 2: 8.
[10] Gn. 28: 12, Ps. 120: 1.
[11] Ex. 33: 11.
[12] 1 Rg. 13: 14.
[13] Cf. 4 Rg. 2: 11.
[14] Cf. 4 Rg. 13: 20–21.
[15] Cf. Is. 6: 6–7.
[16] Cf. Ir. 1: 5.
[17] Cf. Ez. 1: 1.

dei.[k][X] Deprecetur *pro* me electus Danihel,[118] desiderabilis dei, qui soluit somnia regis et interpretatus[m] est,[19] et bis[n][Y] liberatus *est* de lacu leonu*m*.[20] Orent[o] *pro* me[Z] tres pueri quos liberasti[A] ab igne,[B] Annanias,[CD] Azarias,[P] Misahel,[q][E] et. xiiii.[r][FG] *prophete*, Osee, Amos,

f. 42[v] Miche*am*, Iohel, / Abdiam, Abbacuc, Iona, Naum, Soffonia, Aggeum, Zachariam, Malachiam, Hesdram *et* Samuhel.[s][H] Oret[I] *pro* me *sancta*[J] Maria,[t] uirgo et mat*er* d*omi*ni n*ost*ri Ih*esu* Chri*sti*, cum omnib*us* s*an*c*ti*s uirginibus et uiduis. Adiuuet[K] me *sanctus* Ioh*ann*es baptista cum exercitu omnium s*anctorum*. Obsecro te s*ancta* crux p*er*

f. 43[r] uirtutem / tuam et signum dominice passionis ut eripias me[u] de inimicis meis.[21] Libera me, d*omi*ne d*eus* Isr*ah*el, ex omnibus tribulationibus meis. Hos om*nes* inuoco in auxilium meum; adsistant mihi[L] om*nes* s*an*c*ti* ap*osto*li d*omi*ni n*ost*ri Ih*esu* Chri*sti*,[M] Petrus,[N] Paulus, Andreas,[v][O] Ioh*ann*es, Iacobus,[P] Philippus,[Q] Bartholomeus, Matheus,[R]

---

[k] dei: *added above*   [l] danihel: '*-h-*' *added above*   [m] interpretatus: '*-ter-*' *added in margin*   [n] bis: *added above*   [o] orent pro me: *added above, over an erasure*   [p] Azarias: *a letter erased after 1st 'a'*   [q] Misahel: '*-h-*' *added above*   [r] xiiii: *altered interlinearly from earlier* xii   [s] et Samuhel: *added above, finer pen*   [t] Maria: *followed by an erasure*   [u] ut eripias me: *added above, another hand*   [v] Andreas: et *erased after this*

[X] dei: *om. P*: *U adds* et prophetavit resurrectionem mortuorum
[Y] bis: *om. U*   [Z] orent pro me: et *CO*: subueniat mihi *P*
[A] quos liberasti: liberati *CPO*   [B] igni *CO*   [C] Annanias . . . Misahel: *om. P*
[D] Annanias . . . et: *om. CO*   [E] Misahel: *U adds* liberati ab igne
[F] *P reads* (et) uiginti duo prophetae samuel dauid nathan helias heliseus esaias hieremas ezechiel daniel oseae iohel amos abdias ionas michias naus abbacuc soffonias aggeus zacharias malachias iohannes   [G] xii *COU*   [H] et Samuhel: *om. CO*: Esras, Tobias et Machabæi U *and adds* hos et omnes sanctos Veteris Testamenti invoco in auxilium meum   [I] oret . . . meis: *om. CO*: *P reads* (Samuhel) Hos omnes inuoco in auxilium meum. Adsistant mihi omnes apostoli domine mei ihesu christi petrus paulus andreas iacobus iohannes thomas philippus bartholomeus matheus simon iudas mathias iacobus et omnes martires tui et omnes sancti tui intercedant pro me
[J] sancta . . . uiduis: sancta uirgo Maria mater salvatoris *U*   [K] adiuuet . . . mihi: et sanctus Ioannes baptista precursor domini et *U*   [L] mihi: *U adds* et
[M] Christi: *C adds* et sanctissima Maria genetrix domini dei nostri Iesu Christi cum sanctis uirginibus ora pro nobis sanctus   [N] Petrus: *COU add* et
[O] Andreas: *U adds* et: *CO* Iohannes et Andreas   [P] Iacobus: tres Iacobi *COU*
[Q] Philippus: *COU add* et   [R] Thomas et Matheus *COU*

---

[18] Cf. Dn. 9: 23; cf. Dn. 4.
[19] Dn. 6, 14.
[20] Dn. 3.
[21] Cf. Ps. 58: 2; Ps. 142: 9; Ps. 24: 22.

58

43^v et^w Thomas, / Simon^S et Taddeus, Barnabas^x et Mathias et^T omn*es*
s*ancti*^{U} martyres tui.^{yV} Repelle^W a me, d*omine*, concupiscentiam gule
et da mihi^X uirtute*m* abstinentie; fuga^Y a me sp*iritum* fornicationis, et
da mihi ardore*m*^{Z} castitatis;^{A} extingue in^B me cupiditate*m*, et da mihi
44^r uoluntariam pau*per*tate*m*; coibe^C iracundiam meam, et accende / in
me nimiam suauitatem^z et caritate*m* d*e*i et p⟨ro⟩ximi;^{a} abscide^D a me,
d*omine*,^{b} tristitiam s*e*c*u*li,^{22} et^E auge mihi gaudiu*m* spiritale;^{F} expelle^G
a me^H iactantiam mentis, et^I tribue mihi conpunctione*m* cordis;
minue su*per*biam meam,^{c} et^J p*er*fice in me humilitatem ueram.
44^v Indignus^K ego sum et infelix^d homo;^{23} quis me / liberabit^{L24} de
corpore mortis^M huius peccati^N nisi gratia^O d*omini* mei,^{P} Ih*e*su Chr*ist*i?^{25}
Quia ego peccator sum, et innumerabilia sunt^Q delicta mea; et non
sum dignus uocari seruus tuus,^{26} d*omine*.^{eR} Suscita in me fletum
penitentie,^{fS} et mollifica cor meum durum^{27} et lapideu*m*, et^g accende
45^r in me ignem timoris tui, d*omine*,^{T} quia ego^U su*m* cinis^{28} et^V /

---

^{w} et: *add. above, another hand*
^{x} *MS.* Barnab ^{y} tui: *add. above, another hand* ^{z} *MS.* suauitate
^{a} *MS. damaged* ^{b} domine: *added above* ^{c} meam: *added above*
^{d} infelix: '*in-*' *added above* ^{e} domine: *add. above*
^{f} penitentie et: *add. above* ^{g} et . . . et: *add. above by another hand*

---

^{S} Simon et Taddeus: *om. CO*: Tathæus Simon *U* ^{T} et . . . tui: *U adds* Marcus
Lucas Stephanus; per horum ergo cæterorum omnium sanctorum Novi Testamenti merita
^{U} sancti: *om. CO* ^{V} tui: *C has textual problems here* ^{W} depelle *COU*
^{X} mihi: *P adds* ardorem ^{Y} effuge *P* ^{Z} amorem *O*
^{A} castitatis . . . proximi: *P reads* (castitatis) Tolle domine a me iracundiam abscide a me
anime suauitatem Abscide a me domine seculi huius cupiditatem. Da mihi uoluntariam
paupertatem. Expelle a me iactantiam mentis et tribuit mihi conpunctionem cordis.
Abscide a me domine tristitiam seculi. Auge mihi gaudium spiriale ^{B} in: a *CO*
^{C} coibe: *U adds* a me ^{D} abscinde *U* ^{E} et: *om. PU* ^{F} spiritalem *O*
^{G} depelle *O* ^{H} me: *C adds* domine ^{I} et tribue mihi: timorem tuum et
amorem *U* ^{J} et: *om. P* ^{K} indignus: *P adds* quidem ^{L} liberauit *CPO*
^{M} mortis: *om. P* ^{N} peccati huius *P* ^{O} gratia: *U adds* tua, *and cont.* domine
Iesu Christe ^{P} nostri *COP* ^{Q} sunt: *om. PU* ^{R} domine: *om. CPOU*
^{S} penitentie et: *om. OU* ^{T} domine: *om. CPOU* ^{U} ego: *om. U* ^{V} et:
om. CPOU

---

^{22} Cf. Ecli. 30: 24.
^{23} Rm. 7: 24–25.
^{24} *liberabit*. This is the reading of the Vulgate.
^{25} Lc. 5: 8.
^{26} Cf. Lc. 15: 18–19.
^{27} Ez. 11: 19; 36: 26.
^{28} Cf. Gn. 18: 27.

mortuus.[h] Libera a⟨ni⟩mam[i] meam, domine,[jW] ab omnibus[jX] insidiis inimici,[29] et conserua me in tua uoluntate;[Y] doce me facere uoluntatem tuam[Z] quia deus meus es tu.[A] Tibi[30] honor et gloria per omnia[k] secula seculor⟨um⟩.[iB]

---

[h] mortuus: '*mor-*' *add. above*   [i] *MS. damaged*   [j] domine, omnibus: *add. above*
[k] omnia: *add. above*

[W] domine *om. CPOU*   [X] omnibus: *om. U*   [Y] uoluntate: *PC add* et
[Z] tuam: *P adds* sanctam   [A] tu: *P reads* (tu) Spiritus tuus bonus deducet me in terram rectam propter nomen tuum domine uiuificabis me in aequitate tua. Educes de tribulatione animam meam et in misericordia tua disperdes inimicos tuos. Et perdes omnes qui tribulant animam meam quoniam ego seruus tuus sum. Tibi est honor et gloria et potestas et imperium in aeternum in secula seculorum. Amen.
[B] seculorum: *COU add* amen

---

[29] Cf. Ps. 142: 9–10.
[30] Cf. Rm. 16: 27.

25

⟨'Domine Ihesu Christe qui in hunc mundum' :
A Prayer of Contrition⟩

In[1] quacumqu*e* die cantauerit hom⟨o⟩[a] hanc orationem nec diabolus
nec ullus homo inpedime*ntum* ei facere poterit, et quod petierit
dabitur[b] ei.

5ᵛ Domine Ihesu Christe[c] qui in hunc mundum propter nos[A] peccato- /
res de sinu[d] patris aduenisti[2] ut[B] de Ade[C] peccato nos redimires,[D]
quia scio et credo et confiteor[E] non propter iustos, sed p*ropter*
peccatores in terra habitare uoluisti.[3] Audi[F] et exaudi me, d*omine* d*eus*
m*eus*,[G] peccatorem[H] et culpabilem,[I] indignum[J] et neglegentem[K]
atqu*e*ᵉᴸ obnoxium.[M] Tibi, domine,ᶠᴺ confiteor omnia[O] peccata mea[P]
et omnia mala mea qu*e*ᵍQᴿ gressi[S] *et* que[T] in hoc *seculo* proprioʰᵁⱽ u*el*

6ʳ alieno[W4] reatu et instinctu[X] commisi, in[Y] delicto, / ⟨i⟩niᴬ uerbo,[ZB] inᴬ

---

[a] *MS. damaged*   [b] dabitur ei: *add. below: there are a few illegible letters before this*
[c] *MS.* Christe   [d] sinu: 'i' *corr. from earlier* 'e' *(?)*   [e] atque: *added by another hand*
[f] domine: *expuncted*   [g] que gressi et: *added above*   [h] proprio . . . instinctu:
added interlinearly above   [i] *MS. damaged*

[A] nos: *om. CU*   [B] ut nos de *CU*   [C] Ade: eodem *U*   [D] redimeres *V*
[E] et confiteor: *om. CPVU: V adds* quod   [F] audi et: *om. CVU*   [G] meus:
om. CU   [H] peccatricem *C gl.* peccatorem   [I] culpabilem: *CPU add* et
[J] indigna *C*   [K] neglegentem atque: *om. V:* neglegentia *C*   [L] atque: et *CPU*
[M] obnoxium: *V adds* et in mandatis tuis neglegentem; benignus reuoca ad penitentiam
[N] domine: *om. CPU:* domine deo *V*   [O] omnia peccata mea et: *om. CU*
[P] mea: *V cont.* quecumque cogitatione locutione uel opere commisi
[Q] que . . . et: *om. P*   [R] que . . . seculo: quidquid in hoc seculo gessi *U*
[S] gressi: egi *C*   [T] et que: *om. CU*   [U] proprio . . . in: *om. U*
[V] proprio . . . delicto: *om. C*   [W] uel alieno: *om. P*
[X] et instinctu: *om. P*   [Y] in: *om. P*   [Z] de dicto de facto *C*
[A] in: *om. P*.   [B] uerbo: *U adds* meo

---

[1] The analogues for this text are *C* (no. 18, pp. 111–14), *P* (II. 3–5), *V* (ff. 175 sqq.)
 and *U* (101.476 sqq.). The attributive phrase is discussed in the introductory note to
 no. **16**.
[2] Cf. Io. 1: 18.
[3] Mt. 9: 13, Mr. 2: 17, Lc. 5: 32 and 1 Tm. 1: 15.
[4] *uel alieno* and *et instinctu*. These are perhaps earlier glosses that have been incorporated into the text by the scribe of *G*.

facto^C siue in^D iniquis^E cogitationib*us*.^{F} De omnib*us* ueniam peto; peccaui,^{G} erraui^H tam*en* non te^j negaui nec^I dere ★★★^{i} (2–3 1t) a as

---

^{j} te: *there is an interlinear addition* tamen *above this*

---

^{C} facto: actu *U* ^{D} in: de: *C om. PU* ^{E} iniquis: *om. C*
^{F} cogitationibus: *V adds* et; *from here V reads* (cogitationibus) et de omnibus his humiliter a te ueniam peto. Peccaui domine tamen te non negaui quia tu pius es et misericors et miserationes tue super omnia opera tua. Te dominum laudo. Te glorifico. Te in diuinitate sancte trinitatis supplex adoro. Tibique in omnibus infirmitatibus meis gratias ago quia non in alio spem habeo nisi in te deum creatorem omnium. Ad portam aecclesie tue domine ihesu christe confugio et ad pignora sanctorum tuorum prostratus indulgentiam peto. Domine pro tua magna misericordia concede mihi peccatori omnium delictorum meorum perfectam remissionem. Precor te domine et supplico ut in omni uita mea me conseruare et adiuuare digneris et in illa hora tremenda quando anima mea de corpore erit assumptura. Rogo domine ut mihi peccatori concedas rectum sensum ueram fidem et perfectam peccatorum remissionem. Domine deus omnipotens libera animam meam ex inferno inferiori. Domine deus libera me de igne inextinguibile. Domine deus libera me de omni tribulatione et angustia. Domine deus libera me de omnibus malis, et ab insidiis omnium inimicorum meorum uisibilium et inuisibilium. Rogo xxiiii^{or} seniores et omnes angelos sanctos deprecor omnesque patriarchas et prophetas dei supplico omnes quosque apostolos martyres confessores uirgines inuoco atque omnes sanctos et electos dei in auxilium mihi rogo et obsecro ut in cunctis necessitatibus meis mihi adsistent et iugiter uitam meam ab omnibus maculis incontaminatam conseruent. Simulque orationibus assiduis a deo mihi peccatorum omnium indulgentiam deposcant. Domine deus omnipotens exaudi orationem meam et clamor meus ad te perueniat quia tibi soli peccaui et malum coram te feci. Peccata mea domine innumerabilia sunt ualde propterea a te domine ueniam peto pro omnibus peccatis et neglegentiis meis, pro uana gloria pro concupiscentia carnali pro pollutione corporali pro detractione et murmuratione pro inuidia et superbia pro somnolentia et pigritia pro adulterio et fornicatione pro hoc quod ad opus dei tarde ueni quod et neglegenter preteriui atque pro omnibusque in iuuentute mea comisis peccatis que nec dicere nec premultitudine excogitare queo. Pro his omnibus ueniam a te domino deo et indulgentiam meritis omnium sactorum tuorum opto et deposco. Exaudi me domine sicut exaudisti sussanam et eam liberasti de manibus duorum falsidicorum. Exaudi me domine sicut exaudisti petrum in mare et paulum in uinculis. Parce domine anime mee. Pone domine angelorum tuorum custodiam circa me et benedictio tua iugiter precedat me ut uigilando siue dormiendo tua sancta custodia securus protegar ab insidiis omnium inimicorum uisibilium et inuisibilium. Exaudi me domine et misericorditer miserere mihi seruo tuo. Tu enim es deus meus uerus. Tu es pater meus sanctus. Tu es rex meus aeternus. Tu es medicus meus potentissimus. Tu es panis uiuus. Tu es sacerdos in aeternum. Tu es misericordia mea magna. Tu es redemptio mea salutifera. Tu es spes mea futura. Te domine deprecor te supplico te rogo ut in te uiuam, per te ambulem, in te requiescam, per te surgam et ad te deum meum feliciter perueniam domine ihesu christe deus omnipotens emitte spiritum tuum bonum et rectum qui animam meam et corpus meum in omni sanctitate et puritate custodiat et dona mihi peccatori domine deus ueram humilitatem patientiam tolerantiam sobrietatem fidem spem caritatem perfectam et filicem in tua sancta uoluntate consummationem ut ab omnibus peccatis emundatiis et spiritus tui gratia mente et animo illustratus ad misericordia beate et perpetue uisionis tue ualeam peruenire. Saluator mundi.
^{G} erraui, peccaui *C* ^{H} erraui: juravi *U* ^{I} nec . . . (end of damage): *om. CU*: *P (to* quia): nec te dereliqui deos alienos non adoraui; domine ueniam peto a te

★★★ (2 1t) quia[k] scio et credo et confiteor quod[J] pius es. Indulge, queso,[lK] mihi, Ihesu[mL] Christe; te laudo,[5] te[M] benedico, te magnifico teque[nN] glorifico,[O] trinitas *sancta*.[P] Tibi gratias ago in[Q] omni*bus* infirmitati*bus* meis quia non habeo in alio spe*m*[R] nisi in te, *deus* me*us*,[S] et[T] ad portam aecclesie tue,[U] Chri*ste*,[o] confugio, et ad pignera[V]

46[v] *sanctorum* tuorum prostratus[P] / indulgentia*m* peto. Precor et supplico te,[W] d*omine*,[X] ut illam[Y] mihi concedere digneris pro[Z] tua magna[A] misericordia[B] et pietate usque[C] in fine*m* meum et in[D] illa hora[q] tremenda[E] quando anima mea assumptura[r] erit[F] de corpore meo.[s6] Presta,[G] d*omine*,[t] ut rectum sensum[7] ★★★ (1–2 wd) fide*m* integra*m* ★★★ (1–2 wd)[u7] credulitate*mque* catholicam[v] mihi concedere[H] digneris,

---

[k] quia: *parts of two words are visible in the margin after this (adoru ★ mar ★(?))* et confiteor: *expuncted*   [l] queso: *added above*   [m] Ihesu: *in margin*   [n] teque: '-que' *added interlinearly*   [o] Christe: *added above*   [p] prostratus: *added below*   [q] hora: *add. above*   [r] assumptura erit: *gl.* uel egredietur   [s] meo presta: *see note 6 below*   [t] domine: *add. above*   [u] *see note 7 below*   [v] catholicam: *add. interl.*

[J] quod . . . es: quoniam tu pius pater es *C*: quia tu pius es pater *P*: quia tu pater es *U*   [K] queso: *om. CPU*   [L] Ihesu: *om. CPU*   [M] te benedico: *om. CPU*   [N] teque: te *PU*   [O] teque glorifico: *om. C*   [P] sancta: *om. C*   [Q] in . . . meis: omnibus diebus uitae meae *P*   [R] spem in alium *U*   [S] meus et: *om. C*   [T] et: *om. U*   [U] tue Christe: Christi *C*   [V] pignera: faciem *C*: suffragia *P*: pignora *U*   [W] tibi *CU*   [X] deus *U*   [Z] pro tua: perpetua *P*   [A] magna: *om. CU*   [B] misericordia: *U adds* misericordiam   [C] usque: *om. C*   [D] in: *om. C*   [E] tremenda: *om. C*   [F] egressa erit a *C*: migratura *U*: fuerit *P*   [G] *C reads* (Presta) mihi domine rectum sensum rectum mentum rectam fidem rectam credulitatem ut (mihi): *P reads* (Presta) mihi domine ut rectum sensum rectam fidem rectam credulitatem (mihi) *U reads* (Presta) mihi sensum rectum fidem rectam et credulitatem (omnipotens)   [H] concedere . . . Christe: *om. U*

---

[5] Cf. Dn. 4: 34.

[6] *meo presta* One line and a half have been erased and expuncted between these two words; *presta* is added interlinearly.

[7] This is one line in the MS. The text to *fidem* has been erased and expuncted; *integram* is added interlinearly, and the rest of the line has been erased.

f. 47[r]   Christe[I] omnipotens deus. Domine[J] deus omnipotens, exaudi me ut /
animam meam[w] liberare dign⟨eris⟩ de[x] inferno inferiori [liberes].[y]
Domine deus omnipotens libera me de igne inextinguibili. Domine deus
omnipotens, libera me de protoplasto satane. Domine deus omnipotens,
libera me de uerm⟨e immorta⟩li[z] eterna[a] et[b] ★★★ (5–6 wd). Domine
deus omnipotens, libera me de omni tribulatione. Domine deus

---

[w] meam: *followed by a word expuncted and erased: MS. damaged*   [x] de: *a word erased*
before this   [y] liberes: *extraneous*   [z] *MS. damaged*   [a] immortali eterna: *in*
margin   [b] et . . . (lost passage): *expuncted and erased*

[I] Christe . . . deus: *om.* C   [J] *These petitions are as follows in* C, P *and* U:

C reads:
Domine omnipotens exaudi me ut animam meam liberare digneris de inferno inferiori.
Deus tu me libera de igne inextinguibile;
Deus tu me libera de poena infernali;
Deus tu me libera de uermis immortalibus;
Deus tu me libera de protoplasto satanae;
Deus tu me libera de supplicio aeterno;
Deus tu me libera de damnatione et confusione aeterna;
Deus tu me libera de tormenta impiorum;
Deus tu me libera de angustia aeternali;
Deus tu libera animam meam de tenebris exterioribus (quia)

P reads:
Domine deus omnipotens exaudi me ut animam meam de inferno inferiori salues.
Domine deus omnipotens libera me de inferno inferiori;
Domine deus omnipotens libera me de igne inextinguibili;
Domine deus omnipotens libera me de protoplasto satane;
Domine deus omnipotens libera me de uerme immortali aeterna;
Domine deus omnipotens libera me de omni tribulatione;
Deus omnipotens libera me de manibus inimicorum meorum;
Deus omnipotens libera me de tormentis impiorum;
Deus omnipotens libera me de angustia aeternale;
Deus omnipotens libera me de omnibus malis;
Deus omnipotens liberare digneris animam meam de tenebris exterioribus (quia)

U reads:
Domine deus omnipotens exaudi me ut animam meam liberare digneris de inferno
   inferiori.
Deus omnipotens libera me de poena infernali;
Deus omnipotens libera me de igne inextinguibili;
Deus omnipotens libera me de protoplasto satana;
Deus omnipotens libera me de uermibus immortalibus;
Deus omnipotens libera me de mansione impiorum;
Deus omnipotens libera me de angustia aeterna;
Deus omnipotens libera me de omnibus malis;
Deus omnipotens liberare digneris animam meam de tenebris exterioribus (quia)

omni*poten*s, libera me de manibus inimicorum meor*um*.[c] Domine d*eu*s
47[v] omni*poten*s, libera me de tormentis impiorum. / D*omin*e d*eu*s
omni*poten*s, libera me de angustia aeternali. D*eu*s omni*poten*s, libera
me de dampnatione et confusione aet*ern*ali. D*eu*s omni*poten*s, libera
me de omnibus malis.[d] D*omin*e[e] d*eu*s omni*poten*s, liberare, queso,[f]
digneris anima*m* meam de tenebris exterioribus quia in te confido.[8]
Chri*ste*,[K] quia[gL] opera[M] manuu*m* tuaru*m* su*m* ego,[N9] ne[O] despicias
48[r] me.[P] Rogo s*anc*tam ac[Q] beatissimam matrem / d*omi*ni Ih*es*u Chri*sti*[R]
Mariam; rogo uiginti quattuor seniores qui[S] sine fine[T] deum laudant.[10]
Omn*es* s*anc*t*os* angelos atque[U] archangelos tuos deprecor, omn*es*que[hV]
patriarchas[i] et prophetas[W] tuos[jX] supplico; omn*es* apostolos[Y] et
martyres tuos,[Z] confessores[A] et[BC] uirgines similiter rogo;[D] omn*es*que[kE]
s*anc*t*os* tuos[l] et[F] electos tuos[mG] inuoco in auxilium[H] mihi[I] in illa hora
treme⟨n⟩da[nJ] quando[K] anima mea egr⟨es⟩sura[no] erit[L] de[M] corpore[p]
48[v] meo.[N] Te[O] ergo[qP] supplico / s*ancte* Michael[Q] archangele qui ⟨ad⟩[nR]
animas suscipiendas accepisti potestatem ut anima*m* mea*m* suscipere
digneris quia[rS] ⟨de⟩[T] corpore meo erit[U] egres⟨sa⟩, et libera eam de

---

[c] meorum: *add. above*   [d] malis: *one line and a half after this expuncted and
erased*   [e] domine: *in margin*   [f] queso: *add. above*   [g] quia: *expuncted*
[h] omnesque: *'-que' added above*   [i] patriarchas: *first 'a' added above*
[j] tuos: *partially erased*   [k] omnesque: *'-que' added above*
[l] tuos: *erased*   [m] tuos: *added above*   [n] *MS. damaged*   [o] egressura: *there
is a partly legible OE gloss,* þoga-   [p] corpore: *corrected*
[q] ergo: *followed by an erasure*   [r] quia . . . inimici: *erased (by washing?)*

[K] Christe: *om.* UC   [L] quia: quoniam C   [M] opus CU   [N] ego: *om.* C
[O] me despicias C   [P] me: U *adds* Christe   [Q] ac . . . Christi: *om.* C
[R] domini Ihesu Christi: nostram U: *after* domini P *adds* nostri
[S] qui . . . laudant: *om.* CU: C *cont. with* omnesque . . . supplico
[T] sine fine: cotidie P   [U] atque archangelos: *om.* CPU   [V] omnesque: P *om.* -que
[W] omnibus sanctis patriarchis ac prophetis U   [X] tuos: *om.* U
[Y] apostolos: C *adds* tuos   [Z] tuos: *om.* CU: CPU *add* et
[A] confessores: U *adds* tuos   [B] et: atque U   [C] et . . . et: humiliter depraecor C
[D] rogo similiter U   [E] omnesque: '-que' *om.* PU   [F] et: C *adds* omnes sanctos
[G] tuos: *om.* P: dei U   [H] auxilium mihi: exitu meo C: meum U
[I] mihi: CU *add* et   [J] tremenda hora U: tremendo P
[K] quando: qua U   [L] assumta exiet C: egressa erit P: egressura U   [M] a C
[N] meo: *om.* C   [O] te . . . supplico: *om.* U   [P] ergo: *om.* CP: P *adds* rogo et
rogo C: P *adds* et deprecor
[Q] Michael: *om.* U   [R] ad: *om.* P: animarum accipiendarum U: accipiendas P
[S] quia: *om.* CPU   [T] de: a C   [U] erit egressa et: *om.* C: egressura U

---

[8] Cf. Mt. 8: 12; Ps. 24: 2.
[9] Ps. 137: 8; Ib. 10: 3.
[10] Cf. Ap. 4: 10–11. 5: 8, 14 and 19: 4.

potestate inimici^V ut te duce^{sW} pertransire possit^X portas infernoru*m*^Y et uias tenebrarum, ut non^t se ei^Z [de]^u obponat leo uel^{vA} draco¹¹ qui consuetus *est* animas in infernu*m*^B rapere^C et ad tormenta aeterna^D

f. 49^r p*er*ducere.^E Te deprec⟨or⟩^{wF}/ *sanct*e Petre, princ⟨eps ap⟩ostoloru*m*^{wG} qui^H claues¹² ⟨re⟩gni^w caeloru*m*^I accipiendas^J accepisti potestatem^K ut portas^L paradysi mihi aperire digneris. D*omin*e Ih*es*u Chr*ist*e, fili^M *sanct*e^N Marie,^x preces^{O13}fundo^P tibi ut^Q de^R anima mea agas^S pietatem^T et misericordiam quia in te speraui,^U Chr*ist*e^V redemptor mundi.^W Peto ut ⟨quan⟩do^y accussatus fuero non sim^z expulsus a facie

f. 49^v tua quia non merear^X coronam uel ueniam nisi inuen⟨i⟩-^{yY}/ re a ★★★ (1–2 wd)^Z Chr*ist*e.¹⁴ Auxil⟨iat⟩ri⟨x⟩^y sis^A m⟨ihi⟩^y trinitas *sanct*a.^B Exau⟨di⟩^y me, d*omin*e; tu es d*eu*s m*eu*s uerus, tu es pater meus sanctus, tu es d*eu*s m*eu*s pius, tu es d*eu*s m*eu*s magnus, tu es magister m*eu*s oportunus, tu es medicus meus potentissim*us*, tu es dilectus m*eu*s pulcherrimu⟨s⟩,^y tu es panis meus uiuus, tu es sacerdos m*eu*s in aeternum, tu ⟨es⟩^y misericordia mea magna, ⟨tu e⟩s^a uictima mea

---

^s te duce: *added above, another hand* ^t ut non: *partially erased* ^u de: *expuncted*
^v uel: *followed by an erasure* ^w MS. *damaged* ^x MS. sancta Maria
^y MS. *damaged* ^z sum MS. ^a MS. *damaged*

---

^V inimici . . . uias: infernorum et de uia *C* ^W te duce: *om. PU* ^X possim *U*
^Y inferorum *U* ^Z se ei: *om. C: PU om.* ei ^A uel: et *C*
^B in infernum: miserorum *C*: inferorum *U* ^C rapere: recipere *U*
^D aeterna tormenta *CPU* ^E pertrahere *U* ^F te deprecor *C*
^G apostole *C* ^H qui: *U adds* tenes ^I caelorum: *U cont.* et accipiendarum animarum (accepisti) ^J accipiendas: *om. C* ^K potestatem: *om. C*
^L portam *U* ^M filius *C* ^N sancte: *om. U* ^O preces fundo: processum do *U* ^P tibi fundo *C*: effundo *P* ^Q ut agas de anima mea *U* ^R de: *om. C*
^S agas: habeat *C* ^T misericordiam et pietatem *C* ^U spero *C*
^V Christe: *P adds* miserere mei ^W *C reads* (mundi) quando ego occursurus fuero coram te ad iudicium ut (non): *P reads* (mundi) Peto ut quando accussatus (non sim): *U reads* (mundi) quando occursurus sum ne (sim expulsus a facie tua)
^X mereor *C* ^Y inuenire nisi te auxiliare Christe *C* ^Z inuenire . . . Christe: mihi conceder⟨e⟩ digneris Christe *P*: mihi concedere digneris *C*
^A sit *U* ^B sancta trinitas *PU* ^C domine . . . tota: *U reads*: (domine) qui es deus meus uiuus et uirtus mea iudex iustus tu medicus potentissimus tu es sacerdos in aeternum tu dux ad patriam tu lux mea uera tu dulcedo mea sancta tu sapientia mea clara tu simplicitas mea pura tu anima mea catholica tu concordia mea pacifica tu custodia mea tota tu perfectio mea tota tu salus mea sempiterna tu misericordia mea magna tu uita mea immaculata tu patientia robustissima tu redemptio mea facta tu resurrectio mea sancta tu uita perpetua (te)

---

¹¹ Cf. Ps. 88: 23.
¹² Mt. 16: 19.
¹³ Note the interesting scribal misreading in *U* of processum do for preces fundo.
¹⁴ *Christe.* Analogue *C* ends here.

66

50^r immaculata, tu es redemptio mea facta, tu es spes mea futura, tu es concordia mea bona, ⟨tu es cust⟩odia^a mea tota.^C Te dep⟨recor⟩,^a / te supplico, te rogo^D ut p*er* te ambulem *et*^E ad te p*er*ueniam,^F in te requiescam *et*^G ad te surgam. Exaudi me, d*omi*ne; mem*ento*^15 Dauid^H sicut Dauid patris n*ost*ri ut auertas iram tuam a^I me,^J famul⟨o⟩ tu⟨o⟩,^16 N.^K Archangelus^L Michael, archangelus^L Gabrihel, archangelus^L Raphael, om*nes* s*ancti*^M angeli, om*nes* s*ancti*^M archangeli,^N om*nes*^O s*ancti*^P patriarche, om*nes* s*ancti*^Q prophete,^O om*nes* s*ancti*^R ap*ostoli*, om*nes*^S s*ancti*^T martyres, om*nes* s*ancti*^U confessores, om*nes*^V s*ancte*^W uirgines, om*nes*^X s*ancti*^Y uirtutes, om*nes*^Z s*ancti* *et* electi d*ei* in

50^v adiutorium *et*^A auxilium m⟨ihi adsistant⟩^bB / p*er* d*omin*um n*ost*r*um* Ih*esu*m ⟨Christu⟩m.^b Matheus, Marcus, Lucus et^C Iohannes, sanctus^D Gregorius *et* om*nes* s*ancti*, cuncti, famule^E d*ei* int*er*cedant p*ro* me. D*omi*ne, de limo terre formasti me,^17 ossib*us*,^F uenis^G *et* neruis^H formasti^I me. D*omi*ne, p*ro* tua pietate custodi me;^J saluu*m* me fac, hic pax, hic d*eus*.^K D*omi*ne,^18 exaudi orationem meam^L *et* clamor m*eus* ad te ueniat quia t*ibi* soli peccaui *et* malu*m* cora*m* te feci.^M Quia peccata mea innumerabilia sunt^N ego^O ueniam^P peto ad te,^Q d*omi*ne, p*ro*^R

---

^b *MS. damaged*

---

^D te . . . rogo: te rogo, te deprecor *U*   ^E et *om.* *PU*   ^F ueniam *P*
^G et . . . surgam: *om.* *P*   ^H Dauid . . . nostri: mei fili Dauid sicut iurasti patribus nostris *P*: domine sicut jurasti patribus nostris *U*   ^I de *P*   ^J me: *om.* *PU*
^K N: *om.* *U*   ^L angelus *U*   ^M sancti: *om.* *PU*   ^N archangeli: *U adds* omnes dominationes, omnes principatus et potestates   ^O *P om. whole line*
^P sancti: *om.* *U*   ^Q omnes sancti: et *U*   ^R sancti: *om.* *PU*   ^S omnes sancti: et *U*   ^T sancti: *om.* *P*   ^U sancti: *om.* *PU*   ^V omnes sancte: et *U*
^W sancte: *om.* *P*   ^X omnes . . . dei: *om.* *U*   ^Y sancti: *om.* *P*
^Z omnes . . . dei: *om.* *P*   ^A et: *P adds* in   ^B assistant mihi *PU*
^C et: *om.* *PU*   ^D sanctus . . . me: *U reads* (iohannes) sancte Georgi famule ⟨Christi⟩ intercede pro me famulo tuo. Sancte Christophore intercede pro (me)
^E cuncti famule: famuli *P*   ^F ossibus: *U adds* et   ^G ueni *P*
^H et neruis: *om.* *U*   ^I formasti: compegisti *U*   ^J custodi me: *om.* *U*
^K pax hic, deus hic *PU*   ^L meam: *om.* *P*   ^M feci: *P adds* miserere mei deus
^N sunt: *U adds* valde   ^O ego: *om.* *U*: propterea *P*   ^P ueniam: *U adds* pro his
^Q ad te: *om.* *U*   ^R pro: *om.* *U*

---

^15 *memento . . . nostri.* There are textual problems here; see the apparatus. Cf. Ps. 131: 1.
^16 *famulo tuo.* The endings, which were probably masculine, have been erased.
^17 Gn. 2: 7.
^18 Ps. 101: 2.

peccatis^S meis^T neglegentiisque,^U pro uana gloria, pro concupiscentia /

f. 51^r carnali,^V pro pollutione corporis,^W pro detractione,^X pro murmuratione, pro inuidia, pro superbia, pro somnolentia, pro uisione,^Y pro cogitatione^Z iniqua,^A pro adulteriis ⟨pro⟩ fornicatione, pro hoc quod ego ad opus dei¹⁹ tarde ueniam^B reus^C apparui pro^D peccatis meis nec dicere nec nominare possum,^E iniquitates meas et malitias meas non abscondi. Omnipotens^F sempiterne deus, credo²⁰ quia tu pius es pater sed dignare indulgere quod male^G egi.^c Succurre mihi pietas^H inuisibilis, dulcis et amabilis antequam me fauces^I inferni absorbeant, /

f. 51^v antequam ueniat^J pars inimici super^K me.^L Mihi^d manum^M porrige²¹ et^N lumen ostende ut^O illic^P hora quando anima mea egressa^Q fuerit de corpore meo possum,^R piissime deus, misericors deus, clementissime pater,^S te laudare,^T tibi gratias agere^U qui me saluasti per diem,^V iube^W me saluare^X per noctem. Fac me,^Y domine, op^Z tuam gratiam ad^A te uenire,^B te amare, te laudare,^C tibi,^D seruire, te^E diligere per^F omnes dies. Deus, tibi commendo animam^G meam;²² miserere^H mei,^e deus,^I miserere deus glorie qui es uiuus et uerus, qui es solus et iustus,

---

^c MS. ęgi   ^d mihi: MS. in   ^e mei: MS. me

---

^S peccatis: U cont. et neglegentiis meis   ^T meis: P adds pro
^U neglegentiisque: P om. '-que'   ^V carnali: U adds pro delectatione
^W corporis: om. U   ^X pro detractione: om. U
^Y visionibus U   ^Z cogitationibus meis iniquis U   ^A iniqui P
^B uenio P   ^C reus . . . meis: peccata mea U   ^D pro: et P
^E possum: possim P: U adds reus sum   ^F omnipotens . . . pater: P reads
(omnipotens) sempiterne deus miserere michi peccatori. Credo quia tu pius pater es non
me derelinquas pie (pater): U reads (abscondi) quia scio et credo quod tu pius pater es.
Ne me derelinquas pater misericors (sed)   ^G malum U   ^H pius U
^I fauces inferni me absorbeant P: porta inferorum absorbeat me U   ^J ueniat . . .
inimici: pars inimici ueniat P   ^K super me: mei U   ^L me: PU add tu
^M manus U   ^N et: om. P   ^O ut: U adds nulla potestas inferni invadat me in
^P illa PU   ^Q assumptura erit U   ^R possim P: om. U   ^S pater: deus U
^T laudo U, and adds te magnifico   ^U ago PU   ^V diem, noctem inverted U
^W iubeas U   ^X servari U   ^Y me: P adds salua   ^Z op: om. PU
^A ad te: om. U   ^B invenire U   ^C laudare: U adds et timere
^D tibi: te P   ^E te: et U   ^F per . . . dies: omnibus diebus vitæ meæ U
^G vitam U   ^H U reads (miserere) mei domine gloriae qui es unus et uerus et solus
et iustus et (in quo): P adds mei   ^I deus: rex P

---

¹⁹ The preservation of this reference to the opus dei is perhaps another small piece of
corroborative evidence that G was written for use in a monastic institution.
²⁰ G has textual problems here; cf. the readings of the analogues.
²¹ Ecli. 7: 36.
²² Ps. 30: 6; Lc. 23: 46.

52^r in quo / omnia,^{J} per quem omnia facta sunt.^{23} Exaudi me, domine,
orantem te,^{K} sicut exaudisti Susannam$^{L\,24}$ et liberasti^f eam de manu
inimicorum duorum testium. Exaudi me, domine,^{M} orantem te,^{N} sicut
exaudisti Petrum in mare, Paulum in uinculis.^{25} Parce anime mee,
parce malis meis et cunctis^O criminibus meis, Christe.^{26} Deus meus,
pone me^P ante te, sicut^Q exaltat inimicus^R contra me arma.^{S} Tu^T
pius, domine, pius ante me. E⟨go⟩^{g} dormio,^{U} cor meum uigilat;^{V}
angeli tui, domine, illi^W mihi custodiant tam per diem quam per

52^v noctem. Deus omnipotens, / emitte^X spiritum tuum bonum et rectum
qui animam meam et corpus meum custodiat. Peccaui tibi,^{Y} domine,
peccaui coram^Z te in lege dei,^{A} in^B uerbis, in^C factis, in^D cogitationibus
multa sunt peccata mea; neglegens sum^E de opere dei^{27} et de ordine
meo. Misereator^F sit mihi, omnipotens deus; donet mihi, dominus,
ueram humilitatem ueramque^G penitentiam, sobrietatem et tollerantiam,^{H} bonam perseuerantiam. Inluminet me, spiritus sanctus;
indulgeat mihi, dominus, omnia peccata mea hic et in^I futuro seculo.^{J}
Amen.

Incipit confessio.^{28}/

---

^{f} liberasti: *corrected above* ^{g} MS. *damaged*

---

^{J} omnia: *PU add* et ^{K} te: *om. PU* ^{L} Susannam . . . testium: *U reads*
(exaudisti) tres pueros de camino ignis ardentis Sidrac Misac et Abdenago (exaudi)
^{M} domine: *om. P* ^{N} te: *om. PU* ^{O} cunctis: *om. P* ^{P} *U inverts* me, te
^{Q} si exsultat *U* ^{R} inimicus: *U adds* meus ^{S} arma: *om. U*
^{T} tu . . . me: *om. U* ^{U} dormiam et *U* ^{V} vigilet *U* ^{W} illi mihi: me *U*:
illi me *P* ^{X} mitte *P* ^{Y} tibi: *om. U* ^{Z} coram te: *om. U*
^{A} dei: *om. P* ^{B} in: *om. U* ^{C} in: *om. U* ^{D} in: et *U* ^{E} sum: fui *U*
^{F} misereator . . . perseuerantiam: *U reads* (meo) Misereatur mei omnipotens deus et
donet dominus deus uerus ueram humilitatem ueram poenitentiam ueram indulgentiam
sobrietatem tolerantiam bonam fidem bonam (perseuerantiam) ^{G} ueramque: *P*
om. '-que' ^{H} tollerantiam: *P adds* bonam fidem ^{I} in: *om. P*
^{J} seculo: *om. U*

---

^{23} Io. 1: 3.
^{24} See the history of Susanna, vv. 52–62.
^{25} Mt. 14: 30–33; Ac. 16: 25–26.
^{26} Cf. Ib. 17: 3.
^{27} *opere dei.* See above, p. 68, n. 19.
^{28} This was perhaps intended as a rubric; see below, pp. 70, n. 1 and 130, n. 2.

26

⟨'Deus inestimabilis misericordie':
A Prayer of Confession to God the Father⟩

f. 53[r] Deus[1] inestimabi⟨li⟩s[a] misericordie et[A] inmense pietatis,[B] conditor ac[C] reparator humani generis, qui confitentium tibi corda purificas et accusantes se ante conspectum diuine clementie tue ab omni uinculo iniquitatis absoluis, uirtutem tuam totis exora gemitibus ut secundum multitudinem miserationum tuarum de omnibus peccatis[D] meis, de quibus me accusat[E] mea conscientia, puram mihi coram te concedas agere[b] confessionem; ueramque ex his[F] omnibus et condignam mihi

f. 53[v] tribuas / penitentiam[c] quecumque peccaui in cogitationibus[G] prauis, in consensu malo et in consilio iniquo, in concupiscentia carnali[H] atque[I] delectatione inmunda, in uerbis otiosis, in factis malitiosis, in uisu, in auditu,[dJ] gustu,[K] odoratu et tactu. Tu enim, misericors deus, ad operandam mihi anime mee salutem membra singula humanis usibus apta dedisti; sed ego miserrima[eL] omnium[M] peccatrix,[fN] te eterne salutis auctorem contempsi et eterna mihi inimico incendia preparanti[g]

f. 54[r] ac[O] suadenti consensi.[P] Lapsa[Q] sum[R] in / peccatis corru⟨i⟩[h] in delict⟨is⟩,[h] occidi[S] in cunctis criminibus et sceleribus ac facinoribus in

---

[a] MS. damaged   [b] MS. ager   [c] MS. pententiam   [d] MS. audito
[e] miserrima: gl. '-mus'   [f] peccatrix: gl. '-tor'   [g] preparanti: '-ti' a gl. on earlier '-di'   [h] MS. damaged

---

[A] et: UV add deus   [B] pietatis: UV add deus   [C] et UV   [D] iniquitatibus V
[E] mea conscientia accusat U: accusat conscientia mea V   [F] omnibus his V
[G] cogitationibus: V adds pessimis, in meditationibus   [H] carnali: om. UV
[I] atque: et in V   [J] auditu: U adds in   [K] gustu: U adds in
[L] miserrimus UV   [M] omnium: UV add et   [N] peccator UV
[O] ac: om. U   [P] ac . . . consensi: promerui V   [Q] lapsus UV
[R] sum: V adds domine   [S] occidi . . . facinoribus: om. UV

---

[1] The analogues for this text are U (101.523–26) and V (ff. 175[v]–177[v]); the latter has an interlinear Old English gloss. In U, this is entitled the 'Confessio peccatorum pura Alcuini'; it is for feria II of the Officia per ferias. See also Ma (col. 679) and Wi (pp. 21, 56, 73). The extensive list of parts of the body with which the penitent claims to have sinned is characteristic of the effusiveness of early Celtic piety. Kuypers discusses the Roman and Celtic characteristics of early prayers, and concludes that 'the complete fusion of the two influences was effected in the great English school of York' (op. cit. p. xxix). There are several instances of words with feminine inflections, some having masculine glosses; attention has been drawn to these where they occur.

membris singulis nature modum excessi, et impiis ac^T prauis atq*ue*
p*er*uersis laboribus^U obn*oxium*^{i} me feci; id est,^{V} pedes mei ad
currend*um* in malu*m*, sequendo libidine*m* supra modu*m* ueloces
fuerunt, *et* in obedientia mandatorum tuorum inbecilles. Crura mea
ad me sustinendum^j in malum ⟨for⟩tia^{kW} fuerunt.^{l} Genua mea ad
fornicatione*m* potius qua*m* oratione*m*^{m} libenter^X flexi. In femorib*us*
54^v et^Y genitalib*us* meis supra modu*m* in omnib*us* me / inm⟨u⟩ndi-
tiis^{h}c⟨o⟩ntaminare^h n*on* metui, et reum me omni hora p*er*egi.^{Z} Uent*er*
m*eus* et uiscera mea^A omnia^B crapula^C sunt iugit*er* et ebrietate
distenta. In renib*us* et lumbis, inlusione diabolica ac flamma^D libidens^E
turpissimo ardeo desiderio. Latera enim^F mea luxuria*m* malitie n*on*
formidant p*er*petrare; dorsu*m* meu*m* ad iniqua roboraui^G op*er*a et
collu*m*^{H} in carnali erexi sup*er*bia. Humeros^I meos ad portanda
nequitie onera subdidi, et brachia^J inlecebrosis iugit*er* / amplexib*us*
55^r prebui. Manus mee plene sunt sanguine omnib*us*que sunt^K sordib*us*
pollute, prompte ad omne opus prauu*m*, pigre ad aliquid^L op*er*andum
⟨bonum⟩.^{n2} Os meu*m* nefario pollutum^M osculo *et* iniqua *est* con-
cupiscentia^o maculatu*m*, uerbisq*ue* luxuriosis ac fabulis otiosis
sup*er*habundant*er* me et^N m*en*dacio coinq*ui*naui. Gule semp*er*^{O} et
ebrietate^P dedita,^{Q} carnalibus^R numqu⟨am⟩^{p} desideria^S satiata,^{T} sed
et lingua mea omni *est* fallacio^U prof⟨anat⟩a.^{P} Guttur meu*m* insatiabil⟨i⟩^{p}
55^v semp*er* ardet ingluuie. Aures mee / dolosis s*unt* obtunse loquelis,
pr*om*pte ad omne malu*m*, surde ad omne bonum. In^V naribus nanq*ue*^{W}
sepius iniqu*is* delectata^X sum odorib*us* in quib*us* etiam putredine*m*
delictor*um* meor*um*^{Y} minime horrui.^{Z} Quid^q igit*ur*^{A} dica*m* de oculis

---

^{i} obnoxium: *corrected* ^{j} MS. sustenta dum ^{k} fortia: *1st syllable damaged, but*
may have read 'sen-' ^{l} fuerunt: *added interlinearly* ^{m} MS. adorationem
^{n} bonum: *add. ed.* ^{o} MS. concupiscentiam ^{p} MS. *damaged*
^{q} quid: '-*d*' *added above*

---

^{T} ac . . . peruersis: *om. UV* ^{U} me laboribus obnoxium feci *UV*
^{V} id est: *om. UV* ^{W} fortes *V* ^{X} libenter: *om. UV* ^{Y} et: *V adds* in
^{Z} perfeci *V* ^{A} mea: *om. UV* ^{B} omni *V* ^{C} crapula et ebrietate iugiter
sunt distenta *V* ^{D} libidinis flamma *V* ^{E} libidinis *U* ^{F} enim: *om. V*
^{G} curuaui *V* ^{H} collum: *U adds* meum ^{I} humera mea *U*
^{J} brachia: *V adds* mea ^{K} sordibus sunt *UV* ^{L} aliquod *V*
^{M} pollutum: *UV add* est ^{N} et: *om. V* ^{O} semper: *om. V* ^{P} ebrietati *U*
^{Q} deditus *UV* ^{R} numquam carnalibus *V* ^{S} desideriis satiatus *UV*
^{T} satiata: *V adds* sum ^{U} fallacia profanata *U* ^{V} in: *om. V*
^{W} nanque: meis *V* ^{X} delectatus *UV* ^{Y} meorum: *om. UV* ^{Z} exhorrui *V*
^{A} igitur: *V adds* domine

---

^{2} *bonum*. Note the same antithetical structure below, f. 55v.

qui omnib*us* meis^B criminib*us* ⟨me⟩^r fecer*unt* obnoxium omne*mque*
sensu*m* cordis mei euerterunt,^C quibus in omni consensi^D libidine?^s
Q*ui et* me quamuis raro in sanctuario tuo te,^E d*omine*,^F adorante*m*

f. 56^r intuitu p*er*uerter*unt* iniqu*o*, omne*mque* motum corpo- / ris mei ⟨ad⟩^t
inmunda pertraxer*unt* desideria. Capud^G meum^H omnib*us* sup*er*eminens
me*m*bris, raro umqua*m* ad te, d*ominum* creatore*m* meu*m*, incuruaui,
sed insuper^I etia*m* ceteris^u membris in omni malitia^J consentaneu*m*
feci. Cor meu*m* plenum dolo *et* malitia, nu*m*quam pura purgaui
penitentia; semperque^K diabolica pollui inlusione, numqua*m* uera
ablui confessione. Non eni*m* hec narrans tua*m*, d*omine*, in me
blasphemio^L creatura*m*, sed mea*m* ad^M te, d*eus* piissime,^N exposco

f. 56^v medicinam, qui etiam in omnib*us* mem⟨bris⟩^v / meis reu*m* intellego^O
sup*er* mensura*m*; quia ut astra celi atq*ue* arena^P maris³ ita^Q mea
innumerabilia agnosco delicta. Insup*er* etia⟨m⟩^v ira, tristitia, ocidia^R
atq*ue* desidia omnib*usque* octo principalib*us* uitiis obnoxiu*m*^w me^S *esse*
profiteor. Sed t*ibi*,^T d*omino*,⁴ occultoru*m*^x cognitori,^U q*ui* dixisti⁶ penitentia*m* potius^V te male⁵ peccatoru*m*^W qua*m* mortem,^X omnia cordis
mei reuelo^yY archana. Respice^Z6 in me,^A miserere mei, fontemque
⟨l⟩acrimaru*m*^v et remissionem ⟨om⟩niu*m*^v peccatoru*m* meoru*m*^B atqu*e* /

f. 57^r intima*m*^C mihi^z cordis confessione*m* ⟨e⟩t^a intentionem^D tribue posconti.
Renoua et^E inuoca in me, piissime pat*er*, q*ui*cqu*id* actione, q*ui*cquid^F

---

^r me: *add. ed.*   ^s *MS.* bilidine   ^t *MS. damaged*   ^u *MS.* ceteri
^v *MS. damaged*   ^w *MS.* obnox um   ^x *MS.* occutorum   ^y *MS.* reuolo
^z mihi: *MS.* in   ^a *MS. damaged*

---

^B meis criminibus: *om. U: V om.* meis   ^C auerterunt *UV*   ^D libidine
consensi *V*   ^E te: *om. U*   ^F domine te *V*   ^G capud: *U adds* vero
^H deum meum *U: om. V*   ^I insuper: *om. UV*   ^J malitia: *V adds* me
^K semperque . . . confessione: numquam uera ablui confessione sed diabolica semper *V*
^L blasphemo *UV*   ^M a *UV*   ^N piissime deus *UV*   ^O intellego: *V adds* esse
^P arenam *U*   ^Q ita: *U cont.* innumerabilia cognosco delicta: ita mea innumerabilia
esse cognosco delicta *V*   ^Q acedia *U, adds* jactantia: accidia *V, cont.* iactantia
desidia atque omnibus   ^S me: *V adds* scio et   ^T tu domine *UV*
^U cognitor *V*   ^V potius: *om. UV*   ^W peccatorum: *om. V*   ^X mortem: *V*
adds tibi   ^Y revelabo *U*   ^Z respice: *V adds* domine   ^A me: *UV add* et
^B meorum atque: *om. U:* meorum *om. V*   ^C intimam cordis confessionem mihi *V*
^D et intentionem: *om. UV*   ^E et: *om. U:* atque *V*   ^F quicquid: quod *U*

---

³ Cf. Ib. 6: 3 and Ir. 33: 22.
⁴ Cf. Dn. 13: 42.
⁵ *male.* Read *malle.*
⁶ Ez. 18: 21 and 33: 12.

uerbo, quicquid^G denique in cogitatione diabolica fraude uitiatum^H est; et unitati corporis^b ecclesie membrum tue redemptionis acnecte, et non habentem fiduciam nisi in tua misericordia, ad sacramentum tue reconciliationis admitte, per Ihesum Christum unigenitum filium tuum dominum^I et saluatorem nostrum qui tecum una^J cum sancto spiritu unus est deus,^K per immortalia regnans in secula seculorum. Amen./

---

^b *MS.* corpori

---

^G quicquid: quod *U, adds* ipsa: *V cont.* ipsa locutione diabolica   ^H uitiatum: uiolatum *V*   ^I dominum et: *om. V*   ^J una: et unus *V, ends* uiuit et regnat deus per inmortalia secula   ^K deus: dominus *U*

27

⟨Various Incipits and Rubrics⟩

f. 57ᵛ   Quicumque uult;[1] Pater; et Credo in deum; Benedicamus patrem et filium cum sancto spiritu, laudemus et superexaltemus eum in secula.

Benedictus[2] es, domine, in firmamento celi et laudabilis et gloriosus; et superexaltate eum in secula. Benedicat et custodiat nos, omnipotens dominus. Amen.

Te[3] trina deitas unaque poscimus ut culpas abluas noxia subtrahas; des pacem famulis nobis[a] quoque gloria per cuncta tibi secula.

Ego dixi:[4] Domine, miserere mei . . . /

---

[a] *MS*. nos

---

[1] The texts on this folio, consisting of rubrics, various Biblical verses and a liturgical response, also occur on f. 114ᵛ where they are not incomplete as they are here. This is one of the two items that appears twice in the manuscript as edited here; the other appears as nos. **6** and **11** above.

[2] Dn. 3: 56.

[3] This is from the *Liber responsalis* (*PL* 78.811) of Gregory I, for the vigil of the feast of All Saints. The clause 'Te trina deitas, unaque poscimus' was adopted by St. Thomas Aquinas as the first line of the seventh verse of his famous hymn 'Sacris sollemnis'.

[4] Ps. 40: 5. This verse is used for the Graduale of Holy Trinity Sunday (cf. *H*, p. 23); see below, p. 147, where its contextual significance is more apparent.

28

⟨The Psalter Collects⟩

f. 59ʳ Domine,[1] ne ★★★ (1–2 wd)[a] usque in finem. Kyriele⟨ison⟩.[b] Christe⟨leison. Kyri⟩eleison. Christe audi nos. Pater noster.

Domine,[2] ⟨c⟩onuertere et eripe animam meam; saluum me fac propter misericordiam tuam.

Respice,[3] et exaudi me, domine deus meus. Inlumina oculos meos ne umquam obdormiam in morte; ne quando dicat inimicus meus : preualui aduersus eum. Ab[4] ocultis meis munda me, domine, et ab alienis parce seruo tuo.

Collecta

Oremus.

Exauditor[5] omnium, deus, exaudi nostrorum fletum[c] supplicem uocem et tribue infirmitatibus nostris perpetuam[d] sospitatem ⟨ut⟩[e] dum

---

[a] MS. damaged   [b] kyrieleison (2nd) . . . nos: add. interl.
[c] MS. fleuium, it seems   [d] MS. perpetum   [e] MS. damaged

---

[1] In W, Dom Louis Brou presents the three different series of collects, the Africana, the Hispana and the Romana; all of those in G are from the Romana series. There is at least one collect for each psalm. The seven collects in G appear to have been chosen because they correspond to the seven 'penitential psalms', 6, 31, 37, 50, 101, 129 and 142. This is the first of two sets of devotions based upon these psalms in G; the other begins on f. 110ʳ. The Penitential Psalms were said after Prime and before the litany in the Benedictine Office. In the Office, the 'trina oratio' was a kind of threefold prayer in honour of the Trinity, consisting of the Penitential Psalms and various collects performed three times daily (Symons, op. cit., p. 12, n. 2). J. B. L. Tolhurst has noted that these psalms were to be said in three groups, each with a special intention, and followed by 'Pater noster' and a collect relative to the intention (The Monastic Breviary of Hyde Abbey, Winchester VI, HBS LXXX, London, 1942, p. 57).

The format in G is as follows: there is a rubric indicating that the 'Kyrie' and the 'Pater noster' must be said first; this followed by another rubric indicating which psalms are to be recited, at least one of which is from the psalm upon which the collect is based; and lastly, there is the collect itself. W is the analogue for all these collects.

Folio 59 is out of place in the manuscript. A whole line has been lost at the top of the folio.

[2] Ps. 6: 5.
[3] Ps. 12: 4–5.
[4] Ps. 18: 13.
[5] Collect Romana 6; the analogue is W (p. 175).

75

f. 59ᵛ dign⟨an⟩t⟨er⟩ᵉ gemitu*m* ⟨nostri labor⟩isᵉ s⟨uscipis / tua nos semper⟩ᵉ
miserico⟨rdia conso⟩leris.ᵉ P*er* omn*i*⟨a . . .

Psalmu⟩sᵉ Dauid⁶: Beati quor*um* ⟨remisse⟩ . . .ᵉ Chri*st*eleison.ᶠ
Kyriele⟨ison. Christe au⟩diᵍ nos. P*ate*r n*oste*r . . . *et* ne nos inducas
in . . .

Delicta⁷ iuuentutis mee *et* ignorantias meas ne memineris, deus.
S*ecundu*m misericordia*m* tua*m* memento mei, tu, p*ropte*r bonitate*m*
tua*m*, d*o*mine.

Propte*r*⁸ nomen ⟨tu⟩u*m* propitiaberis,ʰ d*o*mine, peccato meo, multu*m*
est enim.

Delictu*m*⁹ meu*m* cognitum tibi feci, *et* iniustitias meas non abscondi.

Coll*ec*ta

Orem*us*.

S*anct*e¹⁰ d*o*mine, qui remissis aute*m* delictis beatitudinemⁱ te c*on*fessis
adtribuis, exaudi uota p*r*e⟨s⟩entis famili⟨e⟩ᵍ et confractis ⟨aculeo⟩ᵍ

f. 58ʳ pecca⟨ti spiri⟩tali nos exult- / atione. P*er* ⟨omnia . . .⟩ ★★★ᵍ D*o*mine
★★★ (1–2 wd) eas tuas ★★★ (1 wd).ʲ Kyrieleison. P*ate*r n*oste*r . . . *et* ne
nos inducas in . . . D*o*mine,¹¹ ante te omne desideriu*m* meu*m*, et
gemitus meus a te non est ⟨a⟩bscondit*us*.ʲ

Exaudi¹² orationem mea*m*, d*o*mine, *et* deprecatione*m* mea*m*; auribus
p*er*cipe lacrimas meas.

Conplacent¹³ t*ibi*, d*o*mine, ut eripias me; d*o*mine, in auxiliu*m* meu*m*
respice.

Coll*ec*ta

Orem⟨us⟩.

Emitte,¹⁴ d*o*mine, salutare tuu*m* ⟨infir⟩mitatibusʲ n*os*tris uulnerum
⟨cicatri⟩cumqueʲ mortaliu*m* potent⟨issime me⟩di⟨c⟩atorʲ ut omne
gemitu*m* doloremq⟨ue⟩ᵏ n*ost*rum coram te deplorantes ualeam*us*

ᶠ *MS.* Christeleson ᵍ *MS. damaged* ʰ *MS.* propiaberis
ⁱ *MS.* beatitudine ʲ *MS. damaged* ᵏ *MS.* dolorumque

⁶ Ps. 31: 1.
⁷ Ps. 24: 7.
⁸ Ps. 24: 11.
⁹ Ps. 31: 5.
¹⁰ Collect Romana 31; the analogue is *W* (p. 183).
¹¹ Ps. 37: 10.
¹² Ps. 38: 13.
¹³ Cf. Ps. 39: 14.
¹⁴ Collect Romana 37; the analogue is *W* (p. 185).

58ᵛ euincere insultationes aduersantium uitiorum. Per . . . ★★★ (1 wd)-
erem estis. Kyriel⟨eison ★★★ʲ / ★★★ (2–3 wd). Pater⟩ noster . . . et ne
nos . . .¹ Domine,¹⁵ miserere mei; sa⟨na⟩ animam meam quoniam
peccaui tibi.

Miserere¹⁶ mei, deus, miserere mei; quoniam in te confidit anima mea,
et in umbra ⟨al⟩arum¹ tuarum sperabo donec transeat iniquitas.

Domine,¹⁷ auerte faciem tuam a peccatis meis, et omnes iniquitates
meas dele.

Domine,¹⁸ ne ⟨memi⟩neris¹ iniquitatum nostrarum ⟨antiqua⟩rum,¹ cito
anticipet nos ⟨misericordi⟩æ¹ tuæ quia pauperes ⟨facti sum⟩us¹
⟨n⟩imis.¹

Adiuua ⟨nos, deus⟩¹ salutaris noster: propter gloriam nominis tui,
domine, libera nos et propitius esto peccatis nostris ⟨pro⟩p⟨ter nomen
tuum⟩.¹

Collecta

Oremus.

60ʳ ⟨D⟩omine,¹⁹ miserationes tuas ★★★ (1–2 wd)¹ / ★★★ (1–2 wd) ⟨nomen⟩ᵐ
tuumᴬ tr⟨ini⟩tasᵐ deus qui human⟨i pect⟩orisᵐ antrum emundans
uitiis super ⟨cando⟩remᵐ efficis ⟨ni⟩uis,ᵐ ⟨innoua, quesumus, in
uisce⟩ribusᵐ nostris spiritum sanctum tuumᴮ quo laudem tuam amareᶜ
posimus ut rec⟨t⟩oᵐ principalique spiritu confirmatoᴰ mereamur
eternis sedibus in Hierusal⟨em ce⟩lesti componi. Per . . .

Item, ⟨psalmus⟩ᵐ Dauid: Domine,²⁰ exaudi orationem meam et clamor
meus ad te ⟨ueniat⟩ ★★★ (1 wd).ᵐ Kyrieleison. Christe⟨leison. Christe
au⟩diᵐ nos.

Deus,²¹ tu scis insipientiam meam et delicta mea non suntⁿ abscondi⟨ta.
60ᵛ In⟩ᵐ multitudine²² mi⟨seri⟩cor⟨die tue⟩ᵐ [et]ᵒ exaudi ⟨m⟩eᵐ / in
ueritate salu⟨tis tue⟩.ᵐ

---

¹ *MS. damaged*   ᵐ *MS. damaged*   ⁿ sunt: '-nt' *in ligature*   ᵒ et: *extraneous*

ᴬ tuum: *om. W*   ᴮ tuum: *om. W*   ᶜ annuntiare *W*   ᴰ confirmati *W*

---

¹⁵ Ps. 40: 5.
¹⁶ Ps. 56: 2.
¹⁷ Ps. 50: 11.
¹⁸ Ps. 78: 8–9.
¹⁹ Collect Romana 50; the analogue is *W* (p. 189). The first line of the analogue is not
close to the text of *G*; it reads, *Profluae miserationis ineffabile nomen* . . .
²⁰ Ps. 101: 2.
²¹ Ps. 68: 6.
²² Ps. 68: 14.

Exaudi[23] me, domine, quoniam benigna est misericordia tua; secundum multi‹tudi›nem[p] miserationum tuarum respice in me. Et ne a‹uert›as[p] faciem tuam a pu‹ero›[p] tuo; quoniam tribulor, ue‹loc›iter[p] exaudi me. ‹Intend›e[p] anime meæ, et libera ‹eam; propter›[p] inimicos meos eri‹pe me›,[p] domine.

Collecta

Oremus.
Exorabilis[24] domine, intende in o‹rationem su›pplicum[p] tuorum ut qui ‹in peccatis›[p] detenti tam quam ‹fenum aruimus›,[p] respectu[q] c‹e›l‹e›s‹tis misericordie›[p] subleue‹mur›.[p] Per . . . ★★★ (1–2 wd).[p] ‹Ore›mus.

f. 61[r]   Deus ★★★ (2 ll.)[p]
Kyrieleison. Christe audi nos. Kyrieleison. Christe audi nos. Pater noster . . . et ne nos in . . .
Domine deus,[25] de ★★★ (2 wd)[p] meam et laborem meum ‹et dimitte›[p] uniuersa delicta mea.[r]
Ne[26] perdas cum impiis animam meam, ‹deus›,[s] et cum uiris sanguinum uitam m‹eam›;[s] in quorum manibus iniquitates sunt, dextera eorum repleta est muneribus. Ego[27] autem in innocentiam meam ingressus sum; redime me, domine, et miserere me‹i›.[s]

Collecta

Oremus.
‹I›ntendant,[28] quesumus domine, pietatis ‹tue›[s] aures in or‹ationem›[s] suppli‹cum›[s] quia apud ‹te est propitiatio peccato›rum[s] ut non
f. 61[v]   obserues iniquitates ‹nostras›,[s] sed impertias nobis miser‹icor- / dias tuas. Per . . .› ★★★ (1–2 wd).[s]
Domine,[29] exaudi oratio‹nem›[s] meam auribus percip‹e›[s] obsec‹ratio›nem[s] meam.

---

[p] MS. damaged   [q] MS. respetu   [r] mea: MS. meam   [s] MS. damaged

[23] Ps. 68: 17–19; Ps. 101: 3.
[24] Collect Romana 101; the analogue is W (p. 206).
[25] Cf. Ps. 24: 18 which, however, begins, 'Uide humilitatem meam (et) . . .'
[26] Ps. 25: 9–11.
[27] Cf. Ps. 129: 8.
[28] Collect Romana 129; the analogue is W (p. 220).
[29] Ps. 142: 1.

Kyrieleison. Christeleison. Kyrieleison. Christe audi nos. Pat⟨er⟩ˢ
noster qui es in celis . . . et ne nos inducas . . .
Cl⟨amaui⟩ˢ ad te,[30] domine, dixi : tu es spes mea, portio mea in terra
uiuen⟨tium⟩.ˢ Intende in orationem meam ⟨quia humilia⟩tusᵗ sum
nimis. Liber⟨a m⟩eᵗ a persequentibus me quoniam confortati sun⟨t⟩ᵗ
super me. ⟨Educ⟩ᵗ de carcere animam meam ⟨ad⟩ᵗ confitendum nomini
⟨t⟩uo;ᵗ ⟨me⟩ᵗ expecta⟨n⟩tᵗ iusti donec re⟨tribuas mihi.

Co⟩llectaᵗ

Oremus.
D⟨eus³¹ qui matutinam sacre⟩ᵗ resur⟨rectionis tue auditam⟩ᵗ fe⟨cisti /
iocunditatem³² cum ex inferno rediens replesti⟩ᵗ terram gaudiis
⟨q⟩uam ⟨reli⟩q⟨ue⟩r⟨as in⟩ᵗ absconditis,ᴱ rogamus potentiæ tue
ineffabilem ⟨maie⟩s⟨tat⟩emᵗ ut sicut tunc cateru⟨am apos⟩tolicamᵗ
gaudere ⟨fecistiꟳ sacr⟩aᵗ in astasi,ᴳ ita h⟨anc ecclesiam⟩ᵗ tuam
misericordiam expansis manibus flagitantem splendore celestis iubaris
inlustrareᴴ digneris, qui cum patre et spiritu sancto uiuis et regnas,
deus per omnia ⟨secula⟩.ᵗ
Respice, domine ★★★ (5–7 wd) sui corporis ★★★ (3 ll.)ᵗ /

62ʳ (margin left of second paragraph)

ᵗ *MS. damaged*

ᴱ obscuris *W*   ꟳ sacra fecisti *W*   ᴳ extasi *W*   ᴴ inlustare *W*

---

³⁰ Ps. 141: 6–8.
³¹ Collect Romana 142; the analogue is *W* (p. 224).
³² There is a marginal note on the right side of this folio which reads, I⟨n⟩ *omnibus*
emendata continuo se sentiat tuam medicinam sa ★★★ *atum.*

29

⟨Prayers for Eastertide⟩
Collecta

f. 62ᵛ

O⟨remus⟩.ᵃ

D*eus*[1] qui nos re⟨surr⟩ectionisᵃ annuaᴬ dominice solle*m*pnitate
letificas, concede *pro*pitius ut *per* te*m*poralia ⟨f⟩estaᵃ que agimus
*per*uenire ad gaudia eterna mereamur, *per* . . .

Alia.[2]

Omnipotens sempiterne d*eus* qui paschale sacramentum in reconciliationis humane federe contulisti, da mentibus n*os*tris ut quod
*pro*fessione celebramus imitamur affectu.ᴮ

Alia.[3]

⟨Concede⟩,ᵇ q*uesumus*, om*nipoten*s d*eus* ut qui ⟨fe⟩staᵇ paschaliaᶜ
uenerandaᴰ egimus *per* hec conting⟨ere⟩ ★★★ᵇ (1 wd) ad uidi ★★★
(1 wd) ⟨gaudi⟩a mereamur, *per* . . .ᵇ

f. 63ʳ Presta, q*uesumus*, d*omi*ne ut ★★/★ (8–9 wd) *per* . . .[4]

Incipit ⟨oratio⟩nesᵇ cotidianisᶜ diebus[5]

D*eus* qui conspicis omni nos ⟨uir⟩tuteᵇ destitui, interius exteriusque
custodi ut ab omn⟨ibus⟩ᵇ aduersitatibus muniamur in corpore, et a
prauis cogitationibus m⟨unde⟩murᵇ in m⟨ente⟩.ᵇ

ᵃ *MS. damaged*   ᵇ *MS. damaged*   ᶜ *MS.* cotdianis   ᶜ *MS. damaged*

ᴬ dominice annua *M*   ᴮ imitemur effectu *M*   ᶜ paschalia festa *M*
ᴰ uenerando *MH*

---

[1] This is the collect for feria 4 of Easter Week; the analogue is *M* (I. 311). See also *De*
(no. 408)
[2] This is the collect for feria 6 of Easter Week; the analogue is *M* (I. 318). See also *De*
(no. 423).
[3] This text is the collect for Easter Saturday; the analogues are *M* (I. 320) and *H* (p. 1).
See also *De* (no. 429).
[4] This badly damaged text has not yet been identified, but may also be for Eastertide.
[5] This text is the collect for the second Sunday of Lent; the analogue is *M* (I. 131). See
also *De* (no. 202).

Alia.[6]

63^v Subueniad ⟨nobis⟩^{c} quesumus, domine misericordia tua ut ab inminentibus peccator⟨um⟩^{c} nostrorum periculis te^E ★★★(4 ll.) / offic ★★★(1 wd).^{c}

Alia.

★★★(1 wd)^c domine fidelibus tuis ★★★(1 wd)^c te ★★★(1 wd)^c celestis auxilii ut te toto corde perquirant et que ★★★(1 wd)^c digne postulant adsequatur, per . . .

Alia.[7]

Da no⟨bis⟩,^{c} domine, quesumus perseue⟨rantem in tua⟩^{c} uoluntate fa⟨mu⟩latum^c ut ⟨in die⟩bus^i nostris et ⟨mer⟩ito^c et numero populus tibi ⟨s⟩eruiens^c augeatur, per . . .

Collecta[8]

Dies nostros quesumus, domine, placatus^F ★★★(2 wd)^d pariter quid et ⟨pec⟩catis^d ⟨absolue⟩^{d} p⟨ro⟩pitius^e ⟨et^G a cunc⟩tis^H ★★★(3–4 wd)^d Da,^{I} quesumus, domine ★★★(3–5 wd)^d /

---

^{d} MS. damaged ^{e} propitius: 'i' (2nd) and 's' add. interl.

---

^{E} De cont. (te) mereamur protegente saluari per dominum.
^{F} placatus: De cont. intende pariterque nos ^{G} et: De cont. a peccatis
^{H} cunctis: De cont. eripe benignus aduersis, per ^{I} da: a new petition, 8–10 wd

---

[6] This is the 'oratio super populum' for feria 2 'ad sanctam Mariam'; the analogue is De (no. 235).
[7] This is the prayer 'super populum' for feria 4 of Passion Week; the analogue is M (I. 215). See also De (no. 295).
[8] This is one of the 'orationes cotidiane' in the analogue De (no. 891).

30

⟨Fragments⟩[1]

f. 64ʳ   Fu*n*de ★★★(1 wd)ᵈ ⟨om⟩niu*m*ᵃ conditor et redemptor ★★★(1 wd)ᵃ
animabus famulor⟨um⟩ᵃ famularumque tuaru*m*, omniu*m* episcoporum
tuoru*m*, canonicorum, monachorum siue regu*m* et gubernatorum
atque consanguinu*m* nostrorum et eo*rum* qui se in n*os*tris comme*n*-
dauerunt orationibus et q*ui* nobis suas largiti ᵇ sunt elemosinas seu
etia*m* ceterorum utriusq*ue* secus defunctoru*m* illorum et illaru*m*
omniu*m*que in Chr*is*to quiescentiu*m* remissione*m* cuncto*rum*, tribue pec
★★★(1 wd)ᶜ indulgentia*m* qua*m* sempe*r* ★★★(2–3 wd)ᶜ supplicationib*us*
f. 65ʳ   ★★★(2 wd)ᶜ consequant ★★/★(4 ll.)ᶜ igne quos sub extremis ★★★(2 wd)ᶜ
accendit fidei ★★★(1 wd)ᶜ psallite cuncti ★★★(2 wd)ᶜ sollemnis redit
annuat ★★★(2 wd)ᶜ dantis reuerendos here sint magni meriti patronalis
ortu.

★★★(1 wd)[1] modwento nu*m* pius hi*n*c sacer⟨dos⟩ᶜ ★★★(1 wd)ᶜ tutu*m*
f. 65ᵛ   nituit con ★★★(3–4 wd)ᶜ ndem re ★★/★(15–17 wd)ᶜ tus ★★★(1 wd)ᶜ
buc ★★★(1–2 lt)ᶜ do ★★★(3–4 wd)ᶜ Qui suos nosmet ★★★(2–3 wd)ᶜ
gubern*et* ★★★(3–4 wd)ᶜ ado ★★★(1–2 lt)ᶜ *et* ★★★(3–4 wd)ᶜ ca ★★★(1–2
lt)ᶜ sus ★★★(1 wd)ᶜ choreis ★★★(1–2 wd)ᶜ uoco. per sacerdote*m* suas
★★★(1–2 wd)ᶜ adsit trinitas nobis ★★★(1 wd)ᶜ illo ★★★(1–2 lt)ᶜ uisit ad
n*os*tra*m* ★★★(2–3 wd)ᶜ n. Gloria p⟨atri⟩ ★★★(6–7 wd).ᶜ/

ᵃ *MS. damaged*   ᵇ *MS.* largiasunt   ᶜ *MS. damaged*

---

[1] The prayers on the next two folios are fragmentary and unidentified, and are
presented here as a single item. The opening section indicates that it is a prayer for
the souls of the departed and for the monastery's deceased benefactors. The verso of
this folio is blank.

[2] A new prayer may have begun here. If *modwento* is a proper name or part of a name, it
has not yet been identified.

31

⟨'Domine deus meus omnipotens ego humiliter te adoro:
A Confessional Prayer⟩

75^r Domine[1] deus meus^A omnipoten⟨s, ego h⟩u⟨mi⟩liter^a te ado⟨ro⟩;^a tu es
rex reg⟨um⟩^a et dominus dominantium,[2] tu es arbiter omnis^b saeculi,
tu es redemptor animarum, tu es liberator credentium, tu es spes
laborantium, tu es paraclytus dolentium, tu es uia errantium, ⟨tu es⟩^b
75^v magist⟨er⟩^b gentium, tu es ⟨cre⟩ator^{bB} creaturarum,^C tu es / ⟨amator
omnis⟩^b boni, tu es pri⟨n⟩cep⟨s⟩^b omnium uirtutum, tu^D es ⟨g⟩audium^b
sanctorum tuorum, tu es uita perpetua^E in ueritate, tu es exultatio in
aeterna patria, tu es lux lucis, tu es fons sanctitatis, tu es gloria dei
patris in excelso,[3] tu es saluator mundi, tu es plenitudo spiritus sancti;
tu sedis ad dexteram dei patris,[4] ⟨i⟩n^F thron⟨o r⟩egnas^b in saecula. Ego
66^r te p⟨eto⟩[5] / ★★★^b nem pe⟨ccato⟩rum cord ★★★(1–2 lt).^b Deus meus
Ihesu Christe, tu^G qui neminem uis p⟨erir⟩e,^c sed omnes^H saluos fieri[6]
et ad agnitionem ueritatis uenire, tu, deus,^I ore tuo sancto et casto

---

^a MS. damaged   ^b MS. omni   ^b MS. damaged   ^c MS. damaged

---

^A meus: om. X   ^B creator: C adds omnium   ^C creaturarum: om. X
^D X reads (tu) es amator uirginum tu es fons sapientium tu es fides credentium tu es lux
lucis tu es fons sanctitatis tu es gloria dei patris in excelso (tu sedis)
^E perpetua: C adds tu es laetitia   ^F in: X adds alto   ^G tu: X adds es
^H omnes: X adds uis   ^I deus: es qui X

---

[1] The analogues used for this text are C (no. 10, pp. 95–99), X (pp. 185–87) and O
(f. 34^{r–v}); the beginning of analogue O is wanting, as indicated in the notes. There is
a witness for this text in ILH (II. 213–16) which has the rubric 'incipit confessio
sancti Patricii episcopi'; it is from a tenth-century continental MS. now at Angers.
That witness is much longer than any of the others and differs from them greatly at
several points. For this and other reasons it has not been used in the collation of the
apparatus.
    This confessional prayer is characterized by the same effusive Celtic piety
witnessed in no. **26** (see above, p. 70). As indicated by the folio numbers, this folio is
bound out of place as the manuscript now stands.
[2] 1 Tm. 6: 15 and Ap. 19: 16.
[3] Io. 4: 42.
[4] Col. 3: 1.
[5] C has peto remissionem omnium peccatorum; X has peto ut des mihi remissionem omnium
peccatorum meorum. G seems to have read remissionem peccatorum cordis, or something
close to this.
[6] 1 Tm. 2: 4.

dixisti[7] in quac⟨u⟩mque die conuersus fuerit peccator uita uiue*t et* non
morietur.[8] Ego nunc[J] reuertar ad[9] te,[K] d*eus* m*eus*; tibi[L] nunc uolo

f. 66[v]   confitere omnia peccata mea. Multiplicata sunt debita / mea sup*er* me
quia peccat⟨a⟩ mea numerum n*on* habent. Confitebor tibi,[M] ⟨domine⟩
d*eus* m*eus*, quia[N] peccaui in celum *et* in terram,[10] *et*[O] coram te *et* coram
angelis tuis s*an*ctis,[P] et coram faciem omniu*m* s*an*c*t*orum. Peccaui[Q]
p*er* neglegentiam mandatorum tuorum *et* facinoru*m*[R] meoru*m*;[S]
peccaui p*er* superbiam *et* p*er* inuidia*m*; peccaui per detr⟨a⟩ctionem[T]

f. 67[r]   et p⟨er⟩[U] / auariti⟩am *et*[V] per ★★★(1–2 wd)[d] iam; peccaui p*er* fornicatione*m et* per[W] gulam; peccaui p*er* falsum testimonium *et*[X] hodium
hominum; peccaui p*er* furtum *et* p*er* rapinam; peccaui p*er* blasphemiam
et p*er*[Y] desiderium carnis;[Z] peccaui per ebrietate*m et* p*er* otiosas
fabulas;[A] peccaui p*er* contentionem[B] *et* per[C] rixam;[D] peccaui p*er*

f. 67[v]   iuramentum *et*per[E]⟨i⟩racundiam;[d] peccaui per[Γ] letitia*m* / terream *et*
transitoriam; peccaui p*er* suauitatem[G] mentis mee; peccaui p*er* dolorem
et per[H] murmurat⟨io⟩nem;[d] peccaui in oculis[e] meis *et* in auribus meis;
peccaui in[I] naribus[J] meis[K] *et* in lingua mea[L] *et* in gutture; peccaui in
collo[M] *et* in pectore; peccaui[N] in corde *et* in cogitationibus; peccaui in
manibus *et* in[O] pedibus; peccaui[P] in ossibus[Q] *et* in carne; peccaui in

---

[d] *MS. damaged*   [e] oculis: '-*cu*-' *added interlinearly*

[J] nunc: *om.* C   [K] te: X *adds* domine   [L] tibi . . . habent: delictum meum
cognitum tibi facio et iniustitiam meam non abscondo X
[M] tibi humiliter confiteor X   [N] quia: quod ego C   [O] et: *om.* X
[P] sanctis: *om.* C   [Q] peccaui: tam X
[R] facinorum: factorum C: malefactorum X   [S] meorum: X *adds* ego corde ego ore
ego opere et omnibus uitiis coinquinatus sum   [T] detractationem CX
[U] per: *om.* X   [V] et . . . (damaged part of next line ending -*iam*): peccaui per
superbiam et per malitiam CX   [W] per: *om.* X   [X] et: X *adds* per
[Y] per: *om.* X   [Z] carnis desiderium X   [A] fabulas: X *adds* peccaui in dictis in
factis in cogitationibus   [B] contentionem CX   [C] per: *om.* X   [D] rixas X
[E] per: *om.* X   [F] per: X *cont.* terrenam et transitoriam letitiam
[G] mentis mee suauitatem X   [H] per: *om.* X   [I] in naribus meis et: *om.* X
[J] C *reads* (naribus) et in auribus peccaui in manibus et in pedibus peccaui in lingua et in
guttore peccaui in collo et in pectore peccaui in corde et in cogitationibus (peccaui in
ossibus)   [K] meis: *om.* C   [L] mea: *om.* X   [M] collo, pectore: X *inverts*
[N] peccaui . . . cogitationibus: *om.* X   [O] in *om.* X   [P] peccaui . . . carne: *om.* X
[Q] ossibus: O *begins here*

---

[7] Ez. 33: 12.
[8] Ez. 18: 21.
[9] *ad te.* A clause has been left out here through homoeoteleuton; CX read *ad te* et in
omni (X toto) corde meo (X *adds* clamabo) *ad te.*
[10] Cf. Lc. 15: 18, 21.

68^r medullis *et* in^R renis;^S peccaui / in anima ⟨m⟩ea^{fT} *et* ⟨in o⟩mni^{fU} corpore meo. Si^V nunc erit uindicta tua^W tanta quanta in me^X fuerint^Y peccata mea *et*^Z multiplicata^A fuerint^B iudicium tuum,¹¹ quomodo sustineo?^C Sed^D habeo te, sacerdotem^E summu*m*; ideo^F confitebor^G peccata^H mea tibi,^I d*eus* m*eus*. Tu^J es unus sine peccato;^{K12} obsecro te,^L *deus* m*eus*,^M *per* passione*m* tuam^N atque^O *per* lignum^P ligni salutife⟨r⟩e^g

68^v crucis¹³ tue atque *per* effusione*m*^{hQ} / sanguinis ⟨tui⟩^g quod ⟨tu⟩^g concedas remissionem o⟨mni⟩u*m*^g peccatorum meorum. Precor^{iR} te, domine d*eus* m*eus* Ih*es*u Chr*ist*e, quod mihi¹⁴ n⟨o⟩n^g reddas^S secundum merita mea,^{jT} sed secundum magnam misericordiam tuam. ⟨I⟩udica^g me,¹⁵ d*omi*ne,^U secundum iudicium indulgentie tue.^V Ego^W te adiuro, d*eus* m*eus* om*n*ipote*n*s,^X quod^Y tu collocas^{kZ} in me amo⟨r⟩em^g

---

^f *MS. damaged*   ^g *MS. damaged*   ^h *MS.* fusionem   ⁱ *MS.* percor
^j *MS.* meritis meis   ^k *MS.* colloca

---

^R in: *om. C*   ^S renibus *X*   ^T mea: *om. X*   ^U toto *X*
^V si . . . tanta: si iniquitates obseruem domine domine quis sustinebit *X*
^W tua: *CO add* super me   ^X me: *CO add* ipso: ipsa *X*   ^Y fuerunt *XO*
^Z et: *om. CO*: si *X*   ^A multiplicaueris *X*   ^B fuerint: *om. CXO*
^C sustineam *X*: susteneo *O*   ^D sed . . . summum: si nunc erit uindicta tua *X*
^E sacerdote *O*   ^F ideo: proinde *C*: *om. O*   ^G confiteor *X*
^H peccata mea: *om. X*   ^I tibi: *X adds* domine   ^J tu . . . peccato: qui solus sine peccato es *X*   ^K peccato: *X adds* et   ^L te: domine deus meus *CO*: Ihesu Christe deus misericordiarum *X*   ^M meus: *om. C*   ^N tuam: *om. CO*
^O et *X*   ^P lignum: signum uel lignum *C*: signum + lignum salutiferae: lignum . . . concedas *O*: effusionem sanguinis tui atque per signum ligni salutiferi crucis tue ut concedas mihi *X*   ^Q effusionem: *CO add* sancti   ^R peto *CO*: precor . . . mihi: *om. X*   ^S reddas: *om. X*   ^T meritum meum *X*: meritis meis *O*
^U domine: *om. X*   ^V tue: *C adds* ac misericordiae tuae   ^W ego: *X adds* homo
^X omnipotens deus meus *CX* (*X om.* meus)   ^Y quod . . . tuo: *X reads* (omnipotens) ut non reddas mihi peccatorum poenam meorum sed suscita timorem et amorem tuum perseuerantem in me ac ueram penitentiam peccatorum meorum et fletum praeteritorum propter nomen sanctum tuum (da)   ^Z in me collocas *CO* (colloca *O*)

---

¹¹ Cf. Ps. 129: 2; Ps. 147: 17; Ecli. 16: 22.
¹² Cf. Heb. 9: 28.
¹³ *lignum . . . crucis.* GC have textual problems here; XO have good readings. In C, *uel* is added interlinearly; the corrector of C has misinterpreted the cross sign (+) for 'l' with a stroke through it, the regular abbreviation for *uel*. The scribe of G has omitted the sign altogether, probably through confusion; see also below, p. 113, n. 6.
¹⁴ Cf. Ps. 50: 3.
¹⁵ Ps. 7: 9.

f. 69[r]   tuum *et* timor⟨em⟩.[g] / Suscita in me[l] penitentiam[m] peccatorum meorum[A] pro nomine tuo.[B] Da mihi memoriam mandatorum tuorum[C] *et*[D] adiuua me,[E] d*eus* m*eus*;[F] dele iniquitatem meam a[G] conspectu tuo.[16] *Et* ne auertas[17] faciem tua*m* ab oratione mea,[H] ne proicias me a facie tua.[18] Ne[I] derelinquas me, d*eus* m*eus*, ne disces⟨s⟩eris[n] a me,[19]

f. 69[v]   sed confirma / me in tua uoluntate.[J] Doce me facere uoluntatem tuam, quid[K] debeam agere, quid facere aut loquere, quid debeam[oL] tacere. Defende me, d*omine* d*eus* m*eus*,[M] contra[20] iacula diaboli *et* contra angelum tartari suggerentem[N] *et*[O] docentem[P] multa mala ne deseras

f. 70[r]   me, d*omine* d*eus* m*eus*, ne derelinquas unum *et* m⟨i⟩-[P] / serum ancillu⟨m[Q] tu⟩um;[P] sed adiuua me,[R] d*eus* meus, *et* perfice in me doctrinam tuam[21] quia tu es doctor meus *et* deus meus qui regnas in se*cu*la seculor*um*. Amen.

---

[l] me: *followed by a space*   [m] MS. penitentiae   [n] MS. damaged
[o] MS. debitam *with the 'i' erased*   [p] MS. damaged

[A] meorum: *CO add* et fletum   [B] tuo: *X adds* et   [C] tuorum: *X adds* ut faciam
[D] et: *om. X*   [E] me: *X adds* domine   [F] meus: *om. C; X adds* secundum multitudinem miserationum tuarum   [G] a conspectu tuo: usque semper *X*
[H] mea: *X adds* et   [I] ne discesseris et ne derelinquas me *X*   [J] uoluntate: *X adds* et doce . . . tacere: *CO add* doce me quid debeam agere quid facere aut quid loquere quid tacere (*O* . . . aut loquere quid debeam tacere)   [K] quid . . . tacere: et quae debeam loqui a⟨ut⟩ tacere *X*   [L] debitam *G*   [M] deus meus: *om. X*
[N] suggentem *CO: om. X*   [O] et . . . amen: *X reads* (suggerentem) de quo dixisti uenit princeps mundi huius et in me non habet quicquam. Quapropter extingue mea peccata et carnalia desideria in me. Redemptor animarum ne me derelinquas unum miserum indignumque famulum tuum N. sed ut per te ambulem et ad te perueniam et in te requiescam domine deus meus quia siue† te nil possumus qui uiuis et regnas cum deo patre deus in unitate spiritus sancti per omnia saecule saeculorum amen.
[P] docentem: *C adds* me   [Q] *CO* famulum tuum   [R] me: *C adds* domine

---

[16] Ps. 50: 3.
[17] Cf. Ps. 101: 3.
[18] Ps. 50: 13.
[19] Ps. 37: 22.
[20] *contra*. A clause has been left out here in *G* through homoeoteleuton; *CO* read '*contra* omnes inimicos meos uisibiles et inuisibiles (*O* uses the ablative) domine deus meus defende me *contra* (iacula)'. *X* has 'ab omnibus inimicis meis inuisibilibus et uisibilibus. Defende me, domine deus meus, contra iacula.'
[21] *tuam*. A clause has been left out here in *G* through homoeoteleuton; *CO* read *tuam*. Doce me uoluntatem *tuam*.

32

⟨Domine qui me fecisti : A Prayer to God the Father for Guidance⟩

Domine[1] qui me[a] fecisti[b] *et* uitam meam[c] dedisti[d] quando de fonte crucis inde portaui[e] in fronte p*er* hoc non timeo[f] diabolum nec eius temtationem nisi te, d*omin*um saluatorem omnium, ★★★(2 wd)[g]/ deprecor ⟨te⟩[g] p*er* unigenitu*m* filiu*m* tuu*m* ut ap*er*ias cor meu*m*[h] [illius][i] tui ad intelligendum uerba scie⟨n⟩tie,[g] et da mihi[j] p*er* tua*m* misericordiam g*ra*t*i*am de sp*irit*u s*an*c*t*o, sp*irit*u*m* sapientie et intellectus, sp*irit*u*m* consilii et fortitudinis, sp*irit*u*m* scientie et pietatis; et reple me, N.,[k] sp*irit*u timoris tui quia de limo terre[2] me, N.,[k] formasti,[l] p*ro*prio sanguine tuo me, N.,[k] redemisti. Pater, ne despicias me[m] famula*m*[n] ⟨tuam⟩[g] querente*m* te[3] sed sal ★★★[g]/

70[v] (left margin)

---

[a] me: *gl.* te   [b] fecisti: *gl.* fecit   [c] meam: *gl.* tuam   [d] dedisti: *gl.* dedit
[e] portaui: *gl.* -tasti   [f] timeo: *gl.* -mes   [g] *MS. damaged*   [h] meum: *gl.* tuum
[i] illius: *extraneous, perhaps an earlier gloss now incorporated into the text*
[j] mihi: *gl.* eum uel ei   [k] N: *gl.* eum uel eam   [l] formasti: *gl.* fecisti
[m] me: *gl.* eum uel eam   [n] famulam: *gl.* uel -um -eam

---

[1] There are no known analogues for this incomplete prayer for guidance. Its original personal forms have been glossed to make it suitable for more general use.
[2] Gn. 2: 7.
[3] Cf. Ps. 26: 9.

33

⟨Various Fragments and Two Collects⟩

f. 71ʳ ★★★(9–11 wd).ᵃ

Om*nipoten*s d*eu*s ★★★(1–2 wd)ᵃ inimicos uirtute ★★★(1 wd)ᵃ tue
co*m*prime ★★★(2 wd)ᵃ populus tuus et fidei in ★★★(1 wd)ᵃ letetur et
te*m*poru*m* tranquillitate semper exultet. Per . . .

D*eu*s qui misericordie tue p*re*tendis auxiliu*m* et p*ro*spera tribuis *et*

f. 71ᵛ aduersa depellis uniuersa obstacula que seruis tuis aduersam / ★★★
(6–7 wd)ᵃ osti ★★★(6–7 wd)ᵃ te ★★★(2–3 wd)ᵃ eterne. P*er* . . .

Famulum¹ tuum ⟨quesumus domine⟩ tua se*mper* protectione custodi
ut libera tibi in mente deseruiat et te protegente a malis omnibus sit
securus. P*er* . . .

D*eu*s² a quo s*anct*a desideria recta consilia et iusta sunt opera, da
seruis tuis illa*m* qua*m* mundus dare . . .ᴬ/

ᵃ *MS. damaged*

ᴬ dare: *PM conclude* non potest pacem ut et corda nostra mandatis tuis dedita et
hostium sublata formidine tempore sint tua protectione tranquilla. Per . . .

---

¹ This is a collect from a votive mass; the analogue is *De* (no. 1296).
² The analogues for this collect are *P* (I. 78) and *M* (II. 1147); see also *De* (no. 1343).

34

⟨A Formula for Curing Ailments in the Foot⟩

72ʳ Wið fot⟨coþe singe man⟩ᵃ¹ þas fers ærest : S*ancta* Marina, Dominus
⟨reg⟩nauitᵃ¹ decoremᵇ induit² *and* Cantate domino *and* In omnem
terram;³ be s*anc*te Eadwarde *and* be s*anc*te Grimbalde, posuisti⁴
domine et per capud eius; *and* be s*anc*ta Bridæ, Offerentur regi
firgines; *and* be s*anc*teᶜ Ceadda, Am⟨a⟩uitᵃ eum d*omin*um; *and* biddan
drihten ⟨and þa⟩sᵃ halgan þ*æt* him gesc⟨ilde⟩ᵃ wið þam ⟨coþe⟩.ᵃ /

ᵃ *MS. damaged*   ᵇ decorem: *MS. seems to read* decesam   ᶜ *MS.* sancta

---

¹ These emendations are based on Wanley (*op. cit.* Art. X, p. 231); his rubric is,
'Carmen siue Exorcismus contra pedum dolorem; Saxonice'.
² Ps. 92: 1, which however reads, 'indutus est'.
³ Ps. 95: 1; Ps. 18: 5.
⁴ The three incipits given here must be to hymns or prayers that were well known at the
time, but which can no longer be identified. If Wanley was consistent in cataloguing
the contents of *G*, as is my contention, then this recipe came after that on f. 118
below before the fire.

35

⟨Collect for the Feast of the Birth of St. Brigid⟩

f. 72ᵛ   ⟨Deus¹ ce⟩lorumᵃ ⟨atque terrarum⟩ᵃ conditor et guberna⟨tor⟩,ᵃ
om*nipoten*s ⟨deus p⟩recantiᵃ populo tuo succurre pietate *et* presta ut
qui honore *sancte* Brigide presentem diei hui⟨us⟩ gerimus sollempni-
tatem *per* ipsius suffragia perenni misericordia tua potiamur. P*er* . . .

ᵃ *MS. damaged*

---

¹ The analogue is *H* (p. 68).

36

⟨A Fragment of an unidentified Collect⟩

Deus qui sanctorum tuorum meritis ecclesiam toto orbe diffusam decorasti presta, quesumus, ut intercessione . . ./

37

f. 73ʳ   ★★★(3–4 ll)ᵃ pis ★★★(4–5 wd)ᵃ hega pius¹ ★★★(4–5 wd)ᵃ ede ★★★(2–3 wd).ᵃ

ᵃ *MS. damaged*

---

¹ *-hega pius.* This fragment of a prayer may have been to Ælfheah, as is the next (no. **38**) on the same folio.

38

⟨Collect for the Feast of the Birth of St. Ælfheah⟩

D*eus*[1] elector*um* cor⟨on⟩a[a] pontificum[A] ⟨qui⟩[B] c⟨onfes⟩sore*m*[a] tuu*m*
Ælphegu*m* summi sacerdot⟨ii dign⟩itate[a] et martirii palma decorasti,
⟨conce⟩de[a] pro*p*itius ⟨it⟩a[a] nos aput te sup⟨plication⟩ib*us*[a][C] adiuuari
⟨ut e⟩i[a] in eterna beatudine possimus adunari. P*er* . . ./

---

[a] *MS. damaged*

[A] pontificum: *H adds* et gloriosa uictoria certantium   [B] qui: *H adds* beatum
[C] intercessionibus *H*

---

[1] The analogue is *H* (p. 86).

93

39

⟨Fragments⟩

f. 73ᵛ ★★★(3 ll) eleg ★★★(4–5 wd)ᵃ hostes pugna ★★★(3–4 wd)ᵃ bile uirtute tua ★★★(2–3 wd)ᵃ oire et sicut beatum Marcu⟨m⟩¹ ★★★(1 wd)ᵃ ce exercitu ualid ★★★(1 wd)ᵃ sol ★★★(1 wd)ᵃ super*are* fecisti. It ★★★(1–2 lt)ᵃ ipso pides ★★★(3–4 lt)ᵃ e et a ★★★(2–3 lt)ᵃ mundemur debitis ★★★(3–4 lt)ᵃ ra inimicos no*str*os uisi biles atq*ue* in⟨uisi⟩biles dexter*am*

f. 74ʳ tue in ★★★(3–4 lt)ᵇ sta eis ex / ★★★(5 ll)ᵇ salua me famu⟨lum⟩ᶜ tu⟨um⟩;ᵈ ⟨do⟩ceᵇ me facere uoluntatem² tuam omnibus dieb*us* uite mee,ᵉ saluator mundi, qui uiuis et regnas, d*eus* in *secula secu*lorum. Am*en*./³

ᵃ *MS. damaged*   ᵇ *MS. damaged*   ᶜ famulum: *gl.* '-am'
ᵈ *MS.* tue *gl.* tuum   ᵉ mee: *gl.* '-eu*m*' *and* '-eam' *and followed by an erasure*

---

¹ A search for prayers for the feast of St. Mark has not been able to discover an analogue for this text.
² Ps. 142: 10.
³ *f. 74ʳ. The verso of this folio is blank.*

40

⟨Litany I⟩

76r ★★★
★★★
★★★
★★★
★★★
De p★★★[a]
Domine, exaudi orationem.
Kyrieleison.
Christeleison.
Christe audi nos.
Pater de celis, deus,
miserere nobis.
Filius redemptor.

S ★★★
S ★★★
S ★★★[a]
⟨miser⟩ere nobis.
S⟨ancta M⟩aria,
⟨dei⟩ genetrix. Ora.
Sancta uirgo uirginum.
Sancte Michahel.
Sancte [Michahel].[b]
Sancte Gabrihel.
Sancte Raphahe⟨l⟩.[a]
Omnes sancti ang⟨eli⟩[a]
et archange⟨li⟩.[a][1]

76v ★★★
★★★
★★★[a]
Omnes sancti patri-
arche et prophete.[2]
Sancte Iohannes ba⟨ptista⟩.[a]
Sancte Petre. Ora
Sancte Paule. Ora.
Sancte Andrea. Ora.
Sancte Iohannes. Ora.
S⟨ancte Ia⟩cobe.[a] Ora.
⟨Sancte⟩[a] Philippe. Ora.
⟨Sancte Ba⟩rtholomee.[a] Ora.

★★★
★★★[a]
Sancte Simon. ⟨Ora⟩.[a]
Sancte Iuda. Ora.
Sancte Mathia. Ora.
Sancte Marce. Ora.
Sancte Luce. Ora.
Sancte Marcialis. Ora.
Sancte Barnaba. Ora.[c]
Omnes sancti apostoli et
euangeliste. Orate.
Omnes sancti discipuli
domini. Orate.
Omnes sancti inno⟨centes⟩.[a]/

---

[a] *MS. damaged*   [b] Michahel: *deleted*   [c] sancte Barnaba ora: *added above*

---

[1] The response is wanting here.
[2] The response is wanting here.

f. 77ʳ ★★★ᶠ Or*a*.
★★★ᶠ Or*a*.
★★★ᶠ Or*a*.
★★★ᶠ Or*a*.
★★★ᶠ Or*a*.
★★★ᶠ Or*a*.
S*ancte* ‹Ci›priane.ᶠ Or*a*.
S*ancte* Laurenti. Or*a*.
S*ancte* Vincenti. Or*a*.
S*ancte* Pancrate. Or*a*.
S*ancte* Geruasi. Or*a*.
S*ancte* Protasi. Or*a*.
S*ancte* Cristophore. Or*a*.
S*ancte* Oswalde. Or*a*.
‹Sancte› Eadweard‹e. Or*a*›.ᶠ

★★★ᶠ Or*a*.
S ★★★ᶠ Or*a*.
S*ancte* ★★★ᶠ Or*a*.
S*ancte* Eadmund‹e›. Or*a*.
S*ancte* Eustachi‹e› [Or*a*].ᵈ
cum sociis tuis. Or*a*.
S*ancte* Gereo‹n› c*um* soc*iis*.ᵉ Or*a*.
Omnes s*ancti* martyres.
Or*ate*.
S*ancte* Benedicte. Or*a*.
S*ancte* Martine. Or*a*.
S*ancte* Hilari. Or*a*.
S*ancte* Silue‹ster›.ᶠ Or*a*.
S*ancte* Gregor‹ii›.ᶠ Or*a*.
/

f. 77ᵛ ★★★
S*ancte* ★★★ Or*a*.
S*ancte* ★★★ᶠ Or*a*.
S*ancte* Swið‹un›.ᶠ Or*a*.
S*ancte* Cuðberhte. Or*a*.
S*ancte* Cuðman. Or*a*.
S‹ancte›ᶠ Guþlace. Or*a*.ᵍ
S*ancte* Ercenwalde. Or*a*.
S*ancte* Remegi. Or*a*.
S*ancte* Germane. Or*a*.
S*ancte* Maure. Or*a*.
S*ancte* Placide. Or*a*.
S*ancte* Colu*m*bane. Or*a*.
S*ancte* Antoni. Or*a*.
S‹ancte›ᶠ Machari. Or*a*.

★★★
★★★ᶠ
S*ancte* Her ★★★
S*ancte* Brendane. ★★★
S*ancte* Mach‹ute›.ᶠ ★★★
S*ancte* Bern‹stane›.ᶠ ★★★
S*ancte* Ælfh‹egi›.ᶠ Or*a*.
S*ancte* Grimbald. Or*a*.
S*ancte* Hædda. Or*a*.
S*ancte* Dunstani arch*iepiscop*i. Or*a*.
S*ancte* Oswoldi arch*iepiscop*i. Or*a*.
S*ancte* Æþelwold. Or*a*.
S*ancte* Byrnwold. Or*a*.
Omnes s*ancti* confessores.
‹Orate›.ᶠ/

f. 78ʳ ★★★
★★★
★★★ Or*a*.
★★★ Or*a*.
★★★ʰ Or*a*.

★★★
★★★
O ★★★ᶠ
propitius esto.
‹Par›ceʰ nob*is*, d*omi*ne.

ᵈ ora: *superfluous*   ᵉ *MS*. gereocums   ᶠ *MS. damaged*
ᵍ sancte Guþlace ora: *added interlinearly*   ʰ *MS. damaged*

★★★^h Ora.
Sancta Ag⟨atha⟩.^h Ora.
Sancta Agnes. Ora.
Sancta Cecilia. Ora.
Sancta Lucia. Ora.
Sancta Brigida. Ora.
Sancta Baldhild. Ora.
Sancta Eugenia. Ora.
Sancta Eulalia. Ora.
Sancta ★★★ dryþ.^h Ora.

Ab omni malo, libera.
Ab insidiis diaboli, libera.
A peste superbie, libera.
A carnalibus desideriis,
libera.
A peste et fame et clade,
libera.
A subita et ★★★(1 wd)^h
morte.
★★★^h Ora.ⁱ/

78^v P ★★★(1 l.) P ★★★(1 l.) Per ★★★(1 l.)^h
Per glo⟨riosam⟩^h ascensionem tuam;
Per gratiam ⟨sancti spiritus paracliti⟩;^h
Peccatores ★★★(4–5 wd)^h
Vt pacem et co ★★★(3–4 wd),^h te rogamu⟨s au⟩di^h nos.
Vt locum istu⟨m⟩^h et omnes habitantes in eo^j uisitare
et consolari digneris, te . . .
Vt sanctam ecclesiam tuam catholicam regere et
defensare digneris, te . . .
⟨Vt⟩ donum^k apostolicum et omnes gradus ⟨ecclesi⟩e^h
custodire et conseruare digneris, te . . ./

79^r ★★★(2 ll)^l ⟨e⟩piscopum et abbatiss⟨am⟩,
omnem congregationem ★★★(1 wd)^l mis ★★★^l
(3–4 lt)^l in sancta religione conseruare digneris,
te . . . ★★★(4 wd)^l inum pretioso sanguine ★★★^l
(1 wd)^l redemptum conseruare dign⟨eris⟩, te . . .
Vt nos hodie sine peccato custodias, te . . .
Vt inimicos sancte dei ecclesie conprimere digneris,
te rogamus audi nos.
Vt nos in tuo sancto seruitio confortare digneris,
te rogamus audi nos.
Vt angelum tuum sanctum ad tutelam /

79^v Vt ★★★(4–5 wd)^l tate ★★★(2 wd)^l te roga⟨mus⟩ . . .
Vt remissionem omnium peccatorum nostrorum nobis ⟨dones,
te rogamus⟩ . . .^l

ⁱ *added later*   ^j MS. ea   ^k donum: *corrected from* domum
^l MS. *damaged*

97

Vt omnibus benefa⟨ctoribus⟩ ★★★(2 wd)¹ sempiterna
★★★(3–4 wd).¹
Vt omnibus f⟨amuli⟩s¹ defunctis requiem eternam
donare digneris, te . . .
Vt nos exaudire digneris, te . . .
Fili dei, te rogamus audi nos.
Agnus dei qui tollis peccata mundi, miserere nobis.
★★★(1 wd)¹ ⟨au⟩di¹ nos. Kyrieleison. Christeleison.
Kyrieleison. ★★★(1 wd)¹ deus ★★★(1 wd)¹ speraui. /

f. 86ʳ   hic et in per⟨petua⟩.³

---

³ *f. 86ʳ*. This folio is out of place in *G*.

41

⟨Collect from the 'Missa pro prelatis et subditis'⟩[1]

Om*nipoten*⟨s sempi⟩terne[a] d*eus*, qui facis mirabilia magna solus, pretende sup*er* me, m⟨i⟩sera⟨m⟩[a] famula*m* tua*m*, et sup*er*[A] cunctam congregatione*m* mihi indigna*m* co*m*missam sp*iritu*m gratie salutaris et ut[B] in ueritate tibi conplaceamus[C] p*er*petuu*m* nobis[D] ror⟨em⟩[a] tue benedictionis effunde. P*er* . . .

[a] *MS. damaged*

[A] super . . . commissam: famulos tuos et super cunctas congregationes illis commissas *M*
[B] ut et *M*   [C] complaceant *M*   [D] eis *M*

[1] The analogue is *M* (II. 1143–44); see also *De* (no. 1308).

42

⟨Collect from the 'Missa pro congregatione'⟩[1]

Familiam huius sacri cenobii q*uesumu*s, d*omi*ne, intercedente beata[A] d*e*i genitrice Maria se*mperqu*e uirgine et beato Michahele archangelo nec- /

f. 86ᵛ non et[2] b⟨eato Petro apostolorum⟩[a] principe ⟨atque sancto⟩[a] Benedicto confessore tuo cu*m* om⟨ni⟩bus[a] s*anc*tis perp⟨et⟩ue[aB] guberna moderamine ut adsit nobis et in securitate cautela et inter aspera fortitu⟨do⟩.[aC]

---

[a] *MS. damaged*

[A] beato . . . tuo: sancta Maria et beato petro apostolo tuo et beato edwardo patrono nostro *M*　　[B] perpetuo *M*　　[C] fortitudo: *M cont.* et iram tue indignacionis quam iuste meremur propiciatus auerte. Per.

---

[1] The analogue is *M* (II. 1145).
[2] These emendations are based upon a text from BL MS. Cotton Titus D. xxvi cited by E. Bishop (*op. cit.* p. 388).

43

⟨Collect for the second Sunday in Lent⟩[1]

Actiones nostras, quesumus, domine, et[A] aspiran⟨do⟩ preueni et adiuuando prosequere ut cuncta nostra operatio et a te semper incipiat et per te cepta finiatur.

[A] et: *om.* M

---

[1] The analogue is *M* (I. 126–27); see also *De* (no. 198).

44

⟨Collect for the Feast of the Commemoration of the Holy Spirit⟩[1]

D*eus* cui omne cor patet[a] et omnis uoluntas loquitur et[A] nullu*m* latet
secretu*m*, purifica p*er* infusionem *sancti* sp*iritu*s cogitationes cordis
n*ost*ri ut te[B] / ⟨perfecte di⟩ligere[b] et digne laudare mer⟨eamu⟩r.[b]
P*er* . . .

f. 80[r]

---

[a] patet: *corr.*   [b] *MS. damaged*

[A] et: *M adds* quem   [B] perfecte te *MS*

---

[1] The analogue for this text is *M* (II. 500–01); it is also found in *S* (p. 24).

45

⟨A Petition for Spiritual Protection⟩[1]

Defende, quesumus, domine, intercedente beato Benedicto ab omni aduersitate congregationem istam et tibi toto corde prostratam ab hostium tuere propitius clementer insidiis.

---

[1] The analogue is *P* (II. 1).

46

⟨Collect from the 'Missa pro uiuis atque defunctis'⟩[1]

Item alia.

Om*nipoten*s semp⟨itern⟩e[a] d*eu*s, qui uiuorum domin⟨aris⟩ simul et mortuorum omniu*m*que misereris quos tuos fide et opere futuros esse prenoscis, te suppliciter[A] exoro[B2] ut p*ro* quibus effundere preces decreui[C] quosque uel / presens adhuc[D] seculu*m* ⟨in⟩[a] car⟨ne⟩[a] retin⟨et⟩[a] uel fu⟨turum iam exu⟩t⟨o⟩s[a] ⟨cor⟩pore[a] sus⟨cepit pi⟩etatis[a] tue cle⟨m⟩entia[a] ⟨omnium delictorum suorum ueni⟩am[a] et gaudium[E] cons⟨equi mereatur eterna. Per.⟩[a]

f. 80^v

---

[a] *MS. damaged*

[A] supplices *M*   [B] exoramus *M*   [B] decreuimus *M*   [D] seculum adhuc *M*
[E] gaudia *M*

---

[1] The analogue is *M* (II. 1179).
[2] Note that in *G* the verbs have been converted to the personal singular.

47

⟨Collect from the 'Missa pro familiaribus'⟩[1]

D*eu*s, qui car⟨itatis⟩ᵃ dona p*er* gratia*m* s*an*cti sp*iritu*s tuoru⟨m⟩ᵃ cor⟨di⟩busᵃ fideliu*m* infudisti,ᴬ da f⟨amu⟩lisᵃ et famulabus tuisᴮ ★★★ (4–5 lt)ᵃ bus pro quibus tuam deprecam⟨ur⟩ᵃᶜ clementiam salute*m* mentis et corporis ut te tota uirtute diligant et que tibi placita sunt tota dilectione perfi⟨ci⟩ant.ᵇ P*er* . . .

ᵃ *MS. damaged*   ᵇ perficiant: '*-nt*' *in ligature*

ᴬ infundis *MQ*   ᴮ tuis: *Q adds* N. cunctisque benefactoribus meis (pro): *there is no corresponding word in M for the one partially lost after this*   ᶜ deprecor *Q*

---

[1] The analogues are *M* (II. 1156) and *Q* (p. 446); see also *De* (no. 1304). This collect also appears in *S* (the *Regularis Concordia* MS.) as part of the 'trina oratio', with this rubric: 'He shall now go to the second prayer in which he shall recite the next two Penitential psalms for the King, Queen and the benefactors with this Collect . . .' (trans. Symons, pp. 12, 14; see also p. 137.13 nt.).

⟨Fragments⟩

f. 81ʳ Da famulat ★★★(2–3 lt)ᵃ / Pre ★★★(1 l.)ᵃ coru*m* n*ostru*m ★★★(4–5 wd)ᵃ
amus ★★★(1–2 wd)ᵃ core plac⟨e⟩m*us*.ᵃ

ᵃ *MS. damaged*

48

⟨Collect from the 'Missa in agenda mortuorum plurimorum'⟩[1]

⟨Inuen⟩iant,[a] q*uesumu*s, d⟨omi⟩n⟨e ani⟩me[a] famulor*um* famularu*m*que tu⟨o⟩rum[a] lucis eterne consortiu*m* qui[2] in hac luce positi tuu*m* consecuti sunt sacram*entum*.

---

[a] *MS. damaged*

---

[1] The analogue for this text is *S* (p. 13), where it is preceded by this rubric: 'Passing thence to the third prayer he shall say the last two Penitential psalms, for the faithful departed with this Collect . . . (trans. Symons, pp. 12–13, and see 13.1 nt.); see also *De* (no. 1436).

[2] There is a note in the right margin at this point, although there is no indication that it was to be inserted into the text. Though damaged, it seems to read, *fratrum christianorum nostr⟨orum⟩ omn⟨ium⟩ in Christ⟨o⟩*. It was added by another hand.

49

⟨Collect from the 'Missa pro quacumque tribulatione'⟩[1]

Ineffabile*m* misericordia*m* tua*m*, d*o*mi*n*e,[A] nobis clementer ostende[a] ut simul nos et a peccatis exuas et a poenis quas pr*o* his meremur[B] eripias.

---

[a] ostende: '-*nde*' *added above*

[A] nobis domine *M*   [B] meremur: *M adds* clementer

---

[1] The analogue is *M* (II. 1149); see also *De* (no. 1346).

50

⟨Collect from the 'Missa generalis'⟩[1]

81ᵛ Sancte dei genetricis,ᴬ Marie, et beatorum / ⟨omnium celestium uirtutum sanctorum quoque patriarchar⟩u⟨m, apostolorum, martirum, confes⟩so⟨rum, uirginum atque omnium sancto⟨rum⟩,ᵃ quesumus, omni⟨potens deus, m⟩eritisᵃ ac precibus placa⟨tus⟩ᵃ tribue nob⟨is miser⟩icordiamᵃ tu⟨am⟩,ᵃ et da popul⟨o tuo⟩ᵃ inuiolabilem fidei firmitatem et pacem; repelle a nobis hostem et famem et pestem.ᴮ Da nobis in tua uirtute constantiam et fortitudinem; inmitte hostibus nostris formidinem,ᶜ retribue omnibus nobis bona facientibus uite

87ʳ eterne beatitudi- /² ⟨nem. Da inimicis nostris et perseq⟩uenti⟨bus nos recognitionem et ind⟩ul⟨gentiam. Concede infirm⟩isᵃ nostris³ et omnibus ⟨in Christo⟩ᵃ quiescentibus ⟨remis⟩sion⟨em omnium pecca⟩torum,ᵃ et re⟨quiem⟩ᵃ sempiternum. Per.

ᵃ MS. damaged

ᴬ genetricis: M adds perpetue uirginis   ᴮ pestem: M adds et omnem inmundiciam
ᶜ formidinem: M adds et inualitudinem

---

¹ The analogue is M (II. 1180).
² f. 87ʳ. This folio is out of place as G is presently bound.
³ nostris. A phrase has been left out here through homoeoteleuton; M reads, 'nostris ueram corporis et anime sanitatem defunctis nostris (et omnibus)'.

51

⟨A Prayer for Spiritual Progress⟩[1]

Om*nipoten*s sempiterne d*eu*s, respice propitius ad preces ecclesie tue; da nobis fide*m* rectam, caritate*m* perfecta*m*, humilitate*m* uera*m*. Concede, d*omi*ne, ut sit in nobis simplex affectus, patientia fortis, obedientia perseuerans, pax perpetua, mens pura, rectu*m* et mundu*m* /

f. 87ᵛ cor⟨dem⟩ ★★★(3 ll.)ᵃ inrepreh ★★★(3–4 wd)ᵃ currentos ★★★(3–4 wd)ᵃ ⟨me⟩reamur in ★★★(1–2 wd)ᵃ regnum ★★★(1 wd).ᵃ

ᵃ *MS. damaged*

---

[1] There is no known analogue for this incomplete prayer.

52

⟨A Prayer 'pro inimicis'⟩

Deus pacis caritatisque amator ⟨et⟩[a] custos, da omnibus inimicis nostris pacem caritatemque ueram cunctorumque eis remissionem tribue peccatorum nosque ab eorum potenter insidiis eripe.

---

[a] *MS. damaged*

---

[1] The analogue is *Q* (p. 449).

53

⟨Collect for the Blessing of the Ashes Ceremony and
for the Mass for the Penitent⟩[1]

D*eu*s qui non[A] morte*m* sed penitentia*m*[2] desideras peccatoru*m*
populu⟨m⟩[aB] . . .[3] /

---

[a] *MS. damaged*

[A] non: *M adds* uis   [B] populum: fragilitatem *MZ*

---

[1] The analogues are *M* (II. 553) and *Z* (p. 16); see also *De* (no. 1007).
[2] Cf. Ez. 18: 21.
[3] *MZ* continue: 'condicionis humane benignissime respice et hos cineres quos causa
proferende (*Z* preferende) humilitatis atque promerende uenie capitibus nostris
imponi decernimus benedicere pro tua pietate digneris ut qui nos in cinerem (*Z* (nos)
cineres esse uoluisti) et ob prauitatis nostre meritum in puluerem reuersuros
cognoscimus (*Z* creasti) peccatorum omnium (*Z om.*) ueniam et premia (*Z adds* nobis)
penitentibus repromissa (*Z* repromissa petentibus) misericorditer consequi mereamur
(*Z* concedas). Per . . .'

54

⟨The Celtic Capitella⟩[1]

82[r] Pro ⟨fratribus et sororibus nostri⟩s:[a]

Pro⟨pter fratres⟩[a] meos ⟨et proximos⟩[a]meos loquebar[2] pacem de te
★★★(2 wd).[a]

Pro fratribus et sororibus[A] no*str*is absentibus:

Saluos[3] fac seruos tuos et ancillas[B] tuas, d*eus* m*eus*, ⟨spe⟩rantes[b] in te.

Pro p⟨e⟩nitentibus:[c]

Conuertere,[4] d*omin*e, usque q*uo*, et deprecabilis esto super ⟨ser⟩uos[c]
tuos.

Pro elemosinas facientib*us*[C] nob*is*:

Disp*er*sit,[5] dedit pauperibus, et iustitia[d] eius[e6] manet in s*eculum*
s*ecu*li.

Pro iter agentib*us*:

O d*omin*e,[7] saluu*m* me fac; O d*omin*e, bene pr*os*perare.

Pro fidelibus[D] nauigantibus:

---

[a] *MS. damaged*   [b] *MS.* sperantem   [c] *MS. damaged*   [d] iustitia: *expuncted*
[e] eius: *MS.* et

[A] et sororibus: *om. D*   [B] ancillas tuas: *om. D.*   [C] nobis facientibus *D, and*
adds in hoc mundo   [D] fidelibus: *om. D*

---

[1] The analogue for these texts is *D* (ff. 79[v]–81[v]), which has been printed twice by the
Surtees Society: firstly by J. Stevenson as vol. 10 for 1840, and secondly by U.
Lindelöf and A. H. Thompson as vol. 140 for 1927. Though these 'capitella' survive
in a number of manuscripts, *D* alone has been used as an analogue, firstly because its
text is very close to that of *G*, and secondly because it is close to *G* in time and place of
origin. Its text, while of continental origin, was transcribed in southern England
(probably in Wessex) in the tenth century. It is not known how it came to the North,
but the interlinear gloss (in Old English) in red ink is of Northumbrian character, and
it is thought to be earlier than the year 1000. The 'Capitella' have been edited
critically from many manuscripts of both insular and continental provenance by
J. B. L. Tolhurst (*The Monastic Breviary of Hyde Abbey, Winchester* VI, HBS LXXX,
London, 1942, pp. 18–30). This edition includes a discussion of the origin of the
'Capitella' and of the difference between the three different series.
[2] Ps. 121: 8.
[3] Cf. Ps. 16: 7.
[4] Ps. 89: 13.
[5] Ps. 111: 9.
[6] *eius. G* reads *et*, which is incorrect, and which is perhaps a misreading of the
abbreviation for *eius*.
[7] Ps. 117: 25.

f. 82^v   Exaudi ⟨nos, deus salutaris noster, spes omnium finium terre et in mare longe⟩. ★★★(2 ll.)^c corda illorum[8] ★★★(3 wd) ro^c capit ★★★(3–4 wd)^c deus Israhel ex omnibus ★★★(2 wd)^c

Pro^E aduersantibus et calumniantibus nobis:

Domine Ihesu Christe, ne^e statuas illis hoc^F peccatum quia^G nesciunt^{fH} quid faciunt.[9]

Pro fructibus terre:[10]

Et[11] enim dominus dabit benignitatem et terra nostra dabit fructum suum.

Pro infirmis Christianis:^{gI}

f. 83^r   Et[12] cla- / ⟨mauerunt ad dominum cum tri⟩bulantur^h ⟨et de necessitate⟩^h eorum libe⟨rauit eos.

Pro fidelibus def⟩unctis:^h

Requiem eternam ⟨dona eis⟩,^{hJ} et lux perpetua luceat eis.^K Requiescant in pace. Amen.

Oremus^L pro peccatis et neglegentiis nostris:

Domine,^M ne memineris[13] iniquitatum nostrarum antiquarum, cito nosⁱ anticipiet misericordia^j tua quia pauperes facti sumus.

⟨Pro nobismet ipsis⟩:^k

Adiuua nos, deus salutaris^l noster, et^N propter honorem nominis tui, domine, libera nos, et propitius esto peccatis nostris propter nomen /

f. 83^v   ⟨tuum⟩.^m ★★★(2 ll.)^m et da ★★★(4 wd)^m

Proba no⟨s, domine⟩,^m et tempta nos;[14]

---

^e MS. nestuas   ^f nesciunt: '-nt' in ligature   ^g christianis: added above
^h MS. damaged   ⁱ nos: added above   ^j MS. misericordie tue
^k add. ed.   ^l MS. saluataris   ^m MS. damaged

---

^E pro: D adds omnibus   ^F hoc: D adds in   ^G quia: om. D
^H nesciunt: D adds enim   ^I christianis: et captiuis D   ^J eis: D adds domine
^K eis: D adds animæ illorum illarumque   ^L oremus: om. D   ^M domine: om. D
^N et: om. D

---

[8] Perhaps there is a reference here to Eccli. 17: 7: 'Posuit oculum suum super corda illorum ostendere illis magnalia operum suorum.'
[9] Lc. 23: 34.
[10] This petition is not in D.
[11] Ps. 84: 13.
[12] Ps. 106: 13, 19.
[13] Ps. 78: 8–9.
[14] Ps. 25: 2.

Non uen⟨iat⟩[m] no⟨bis⟩[m] pe⟨s⟩[m] superbie;[15]
Mitte eis, domine, auxilium de sancto;[16]
Exsurge, domine, adiuua nos;[17]
Domine, exaudi orationem meam.[18]/

84[r] ★★★(3 ll.)[n]
⟨Memor esto⟩[n] congregationis tue ⟨quam creasti[19] ab initio⟩.[n]
★★★(4 wd)[n] sana ani ★★★(1–2 wd)[n] tus et ★★★(1 wd)[n] aliquantulum.

Orem*us*[O] *pro* omni gradu ecclesie:[P]
Sacerdotes tui, d*omi*ne, induantur iusti⟨tiam⟩.[20]

Pro pastore n*os*tro:
Beatus[21] qui intellegit sup*er* egenu*m* et pauperem, in die malo liberauit
eum d*omi*nu*s*.[Q]

Pro rege n*os*tro:

84[v] D*omi*ne,[22] saluum fac regem, et exaudi ⟨nos⟩[n] / ★★★(1 ll.)[n] et uiuifi ★★★
(3–4 wd)[n] ei em ★★★(4–5 wd)[n] non trad⟨at⟩ ★★★(1 wd)[n] in manus
inimi⟨corum⟩.[23]

Pro cuncto[R] ⟨populo Christiano⟩:[n]
Saluu*m* fac populu*m* tuu*m*,[24] d*omi*ne, et be⟨nedic⟩[o] hereditati tue, et
rege eos et extolle illos usque in eternum.

Pro nobismet[p] ipsis:
Fiat misericordia[S] tua, d*omi*ne, sup*er* nos[25] que*m* ad modu*m*
sperauimus[T] in te.

---

[n] *MS. damaged*   [o] *MS. damaged*   [p] *MS.* nosmet ipsos

---

[O] oremus: *om. D*   [P] æcclesiastico *D*   [Q] deus *D*   [R] omni *D*
[S] domine misericordia tua *D*   [T] speramus *D*

[15] Ps. 35: 12.
[16] Ps. 19: 3.
[17] Ps. 43: 26.
[18] Ps. 101: 2.
[19] Cf. Ps. 101: 26.
[20] Ps. 131: 9.
[21] Ps. 40: 2.
[22] Ps. 19: 10, which, however, continues 'in die qua inuocauerimus te'.
[23] Cp. Ps. 40: 3, 'Dominus conseruet eum et uiuificet eum et beatum faciat eum in terra et non tradat eum in animam inimicorum eius'.
[24] Ps. 27: 9.
[25] Ps. 32: 22.

Pro pace et unitate[U] ecclesie:[q]
Fiat[26] pax in uirtute tua, et habundantia in turribus tuis. /

f. 85[r] ★★★ (6 2/3 ll.)[o]
Saluos fac seruos tuos et ancillas tuas.[27]
Saluum fac populum tuum,[28] domine, ★★★(1 ll.)[o]
Proba nos, domine; et, non ueniat mihi[29] ★★★(2–3 wd)[o] Exsurge, domine, adiuua nos; et, libera nos . . .[30]

---

[q] *MS.* ecclesia

[U] unitate: sanitate *D*

---

[26] Ps. 121: 7.
[27] Cf. Ps. 16: 7; see above, n. 3.
[28] Ps. 27: 9; see above, n. 24.
[29] Cf. Ps. 25: 2, Ps. 35: 12; see above nn. 14 and 15.
[30] Ps. 43: 26; see above n. 17; Ps. 78: 9 and Is. 2: 27.

55

⟨Collect for the First Sunday after the Octave of Christmas⟩[1]

Om*nipoten*s sempiterne d*eu*s, dirige actus n*os*tros in beneplacito tuo /
5ᵛ ut in nomine ⟨di⟩le⟨cti fi⟩lii[a] tui mereamur bonis operibus habundare.
Per . . .

---

[a] *MS. damaged*

---

[1] The analogue is *M* (I. 57); see also *De* (nos. 85 and 1093).

56

⟨Collect for the Seventh Sunday after Pentecost⟩[1]

D*eu*s uirtutu*m* cuius *est* totu*m* quod[A] optimu*m* insere pectoribus n*os*tris amore*m* tui nominis[2] augmentu⟨m⟩ ut que sunt bona nutrias ac p⟨i⟩etatis studio que sunt[b] nutrita custodias. Per . . .

---

[a] *MS. damaged*   [b] sunt: 'n' and 't' in ligature

[A] quod: *HPM add* est

---

[1] The analogues are *H* (p. 30), *P* (I. 74) and *M* (I. 411); see also *De* (no. 1147).

[2] *nominis*. A clause has been omitted through homoeoteleuton; *HPM* read, 'nomi*nis* et presta in nobis religio*nis* augmentum . . .'

57
⟨Prayer of Confession⟩[1]

Domine Ihesu Christe, filii dei uiui, miserere mei peccatrici[a] atque culpabili, et omnium populorum Christianorum uiuentibus et defunctis[b] indulge nobis, domine, et miserere nostri / ★★★ (3 ll.) tioni[c] ★★★ (2–3 lt)[c] anqu ★★★ (4–5 lt).[c] Per . . .

39[r] (margin)

---

[a] *MS.* peccatrice, culpabile   [b] *MS.* defunctibus   [c] *MS. damaged*

---

[1] No analogue has yet been found for this short prayer of confession; note the feminine form *peccatrici*.

58

⟨Collect for the 'Missa pro uiuis atque defunctis'⟩[1]

Omnium sanctorum intercessionibus quesumus, domine, gratia tua nos semper[A] proteg⟨at⟩[a] et Christianis[2] omnibus uiuentibus atque defunctis misericordiam tuam ubique pretende ut uiuentes ab omnibus inpugnationibus defensi[B] tua opitulatione saluentur, et defuncti remissionem mereantur suorum omnium[C] accipere peccatorum. Per . . ./

---

[a] *MS. damaged*

[A] semper: *om.* M   [B] defensi . . . saluentur: sint tua opitulatione defensi M
[C] omnium: *om.* M

---

[1] The analogue is M (II. 1182).
[2] *et Christianis*. Several phrases have been omitted here through homeotopy; M reads, '*et* cunctis coniunctis nobis oracione uel confessione consanguinitate aut familiaritate et pro quibus promisimus uel obnoxii sumus orare *et* christianis . . .'

59

⟨Collect for the Feast of St. Benedict⟩[1]

9ᵛ D ★★★(2 ll.)ᵃ *sancti* Bened⟨icti⟩ ★★★(1–2 wd)ᵃ duca in conuersatione perseuerare posces labentis uite descessum ad eterna*m* peruenire requiem. P*er* . . .

ᵃ *MS. damaged*

---

[1] No analogue has yet been found for this text which is probably a Collect for the feast of St. Benedict.

60

⟨Prayer for King Æthelred⟩[1]

Da, quesumus, omnipotens deus, animam famuli tui Æþelredi regis requiem sempiternam omnibusque qui hoc monasterium suis elemosinis ditauerunt[a] ad laudem et ad gloriam tui sancti nominis. Per . . . /

---

[a] ditauerunt: 'n' and 't' in ligature

---

[1] No analogue has yet been found for this text, a prayer for the repose of the soul of King Æthelred (ob. 23 April 1016). Bishop cited this text as evidence for the date of the MS.; see Introduction, p. xv.

61

⟨Litany II⟩[1]

0[r] ★★★
★★★
S ★★★[a]
Sancte Michahel. Ora.
Sancte Gabrihel. Ora.
Sancte Raphahel. Ora.
Omnes sancti angeli et
archangeli. Orate.
Omnes sancti beatorum
spirituum ordines
angelorum. Orate.
Omnes sancti patri-
arche et prophete. Orate.
Sancte Iohannes baptista.[c] Ora.

★★★ (2–3 lt)[a] Kyri-
eleison. ⟨Christe a⟩udi nos.[a] Ora.
Sancte Pe⟨t⟩re.[a] Ora.
Sancte Paule. Ora.
Sancte Andrea. Ora.
Sancte Iohannes. Ora.
Sancte Iacobe. Ora.
Sancte Philippe. Ora.
Sancte Bartholomei.[b] Ora.
Sancte Iacobe. Ora.
Sancte Mathee. Ora.
Sancte Thoma. Ora.
Sancte Simon. Ora.
Sancte Iuda. Ora. /

0[v] Sancte ★★★[a] Ora.
Sancte ★★★[a] Ora.
Sancte L⟨uce⟩.[a] Ora.
Sancte ★★★[a] Ora.
Omnes sancti apostoli. Orate.
Omnes sancti discipuli. Orate.
Omnes sancti innocenti. Orate.
Sancte Stephane. Ora.
Sancte Line. Ora.
Sancte Tite. Ora.
Sancte Clete. Ora.
Sancte Clemens. Ora.

★★★[a]
★★★[a] O⟨ra⟩.
★★★[a] Ora.
Sancte Laurent⟨i⟩. Ora.
Sancte Ypolite. Ora.
Sancte Dionisie. Ora.
Sancte ★★★[d] Ora.
San⟨c⟩te[a] Adriane. Ora.
Sancte Quirice. Ora.
Sancte Iuuenalis. Ora.
Sancte Salui. Ora.
Sancte Albane. Ora.

---

[a] *MS. damaged*   [b] Bartholomei: *corrected above from earlier '-e'*
[c] *MS.* baptiste   [d] *The name in the second column erased*

---

[1] This litany has been published previously by E. S. Dewick and W. H. Frere, *The Leofric Collectar II*, HBS LVI, London, 1921, pp. 619–626. Edmund Bishop was struck by its inordinate length, and further remarked, 'I think our second Galba litany much more interesting than Leofric's, as being wholly of a non-liturgical and quite personal character' (*op. cit.* p. 389).

Sancte Corneli. Ora.
Sancte Cypriane. Ora.

Sancte Eadmunde. Ora.
Sancte Ealchmunde.^e Ora. /

f. 91^r

★★★^a Ora.
★★★^a Ora.
Sancte ★★★^a Ora.
Sancte ★★★^a Ora.
Sancte Victor. Ora.
Sancte ★★★ olde.^a Ora.
Sancte Saturnine. Ora.
Sancte Geruasi. Ora.
Sancte Protasi. Ora.
Sancte Nazari. Ora.
Sancte Georgii. Ora.
Sancte Sabastiane. Ora.
Sancte Fabiane. Ora.
Sancte Quintine. Ora.

S⟨ancte⟩ ★★★^a Ora.
S⟨ancte⟩ ★★★^a Ora.
S⟨ancte M⟩arcelle.^a Ora.
Sancte Ioannes. Ora.
Sancte Paule. Ora.
Sancte Urbane. Ora.
Sancte Chrisogene.^g Ora.
Sancte Cosma. Ora.
Sancte Damiane. Ora.
Sancte Prote. Ora.
Sancte Iacinte. Ora.
Sancte Alexander. Ora.
Sancte Vincent. Ora.
Sancte Tiburtii. Ora./

f. 91^v

Sancte ★★★^a
Sancte Vitali⟨s⟩.^a Ora.
Sancte Cyriace. Ora.
Sancte Timothei. Ora.
Sancte Nicomedis. Ora.
Sancte Landberht. Ora.
Sancte Luciane. Ora.
Sancte Gereon cum sociis. Orate.
Sancte Celse. Ora.
Sancte Abdon. Ora.
Sancte Sennes. Ora.
Sancte Simphoriane.^h Ora.
Sancte Iuliane. Ora.
Sancte Bonefaci. Ora.

★★★ erici.^a Ora.
S⟨ancte⟩ ★★★^a Ora.
S⟨ancte⟩ ★★ leode ★^a Ora.
Sancte Crist⟨ophore⟩.^a Ora.
Sancte Oswalde. Ora.
Sancte Æþelb⟨er⟩hte.^a Ora.
Sancte Cenelme. Ora.
Sancte Anthiri. Ora.
Sancte Proiecte. Ora.
Sancte Auguli. Ora.
Sancte Torpete. Ora.
Sancte Sigismunde.ⁱ Ora.
Sancte Caste. Ora.
Sancte Milite. Ora./

f. 92^r

★★★^a Ora.
S⟨ancte⟩ ★★★^a Ora.
S⟨ancte⟩ ★★★^a Ora.
S⟨ancte⟩^a Marcelline. Ora.

S⟨ancte⟩^a Felix. Ora.
S⟨ancte⟩^a Simplex. Ora.
S⟨ancte⟩^a Faustine. Ora.
Sancte Beatrice. Ora.

---

^e Ealchmunde: '-e' added later
^h Simphoriane: '-ne' added above
^g Chrisogone: 'h' added later
ⁱ Sigismunde: corrected from 'Siges-'

Sancte Petre. Or*a*.
S⟨ancte⟩[a] ★★ce. Or*a*.
S⟨ancte⟩ ★★★[a] Or*a*.
Sancte Processe. Or*a*.
Sancte Martiniane. Or*a*.
Sancte Apollonaris. Or*a*.
Sancte Pantaleon.[k] Or*a*.
Sancte Basilidis. Or*a*.
Sancte Cirini. Or*a*.
Sancte Naboris.Or*a*.

Sancte Marce. Or*a*.
Sancte Marcelliane.[j] Or*a*.
Sancte Prime. Or*a*.
Sancte Feliciane. Or*a*.
Sancte Magne. Or*a*.
Sancte Audacte. Or*a*.
Sancte Caprase. Or*a*.
Sancte Ermete. Or*a*.
Sancte Prisce. Or*a*.
Sancte Gorgoni. Or*a*.

92[v]
Sancte ★★firine.[a] Or*a*.
Sancte Iuste. Or*a*.
Sancte Iust⟨ini⟩ane.[a] Or*a*.
Sancte Ci ★★a.[a] Or*a*.
Sancte Iustine. Or*a*.
Sancte Racnnulfe. Or*a*.
Sancte Theodore. Or*a*.
Sancte Menne. Or*a*.
Sancte Flauiane. Or*a*.
Sancte Chrissanti.[l] Or*a*.
Sancte Mansuete. Or*a*.
Sancte Seueri. Or*a*.
Sancte Longine. Or*a*.
Sancte Erasme.[m] Or*a*.

Sancte ★★★[a]
Sancte ★★ emma ★★★[a]
Sancte ★★★[a]
Sancte ★★genes★★[a] Or*a*.
Sancte ★★★ ane.[a] Or*a*.
Sancte ★★★.[a] Or*a*.
Sancte Iuliane. Or*a*.
Sancte Hilarini. Or*a*.
Sancte Mammetis. Or*a*.
Sancte Urane. Or*a*.
Sancte Dari. Or*a*.
Sancte Blasi. Or*a*.
Sancte Contestor. Or*a*.
Sancte Potite. Or*a*./

93[r]
⟨O⟩mnes *sancti* m⟨ar⟩tyres.[a]
Orate p*ro* . . . [Or*a*].[n]
Sancte ⟨Hilari⟩.[a] Or*a*.
Sancte ⟨Mar⟩tine.[a] Or*a*.
Sancte Ambrosi. Or*a*.
Sancte ⟨Au⟩gustini.[a] Or*a*.
Sancte ⟨Hie⟩r⟨o⟩nime.[a] Or*a*.
Sancte Gregorii. Or*a*.
Sancte Siluester. Or*a*.
Sancte Leo. Or*a*.

⟨Sancte Au⟩domare.[a] Or*a*.
Sancte ★★★[a] Or*a*.
Sancte ★★ce★★[a] Or*a*.
Sancte ★★ne★★[a] Or*a*.
Sancte Remigi. Or*a*.
Sancte Sulpici. Or*a*.
Sancte Marcelle. Or*a*.
Sancte Amande. Or*a*.
Sancte Elegi. Or*a*.
Sancte Richari. Or*a*.

---

[j] Marcelliane: '-e' *added above*   [k] Pantaleon: *an erasure after the* '-t-'
[l] Chrissanti: '-h-' *added above*   [m] Erasme: '-e' *added above*
[n] *added later, another hand; note the presently superfluous* ora *indicating that a name has been erased here, and probably in the preceding line also*

S*ancte* Eusebii. Or*a*.
S*ancte* Germane. Or*a*.
S*ancte* Medarde. Or*a*.
S*ancte* Vedaste. Or*a*.
S*ancte* Basili. Or*a*.
S*ancte* Cesari. Or*a*.
S*ancte* Philiberhte. Or*a*.
S*ancte* Antoni. Or*a*./

f. 93v S*ancte* Paule. ‹Ora›.[a]
S*ancte* Benedic‹te. Ora›.[a]
S*ancte* Maure. Or*a*.
S*ancte* Placide. Or*a*.
S*ancte* Hilarion. Or*a*.
S*ancte* Machari. Or*a*.
S*ancte* Guðlace. Or*a*.
S*ancte* Æþelmod. Or*a*.
S*ancte* Entferð. Or*a*.
S*ancte* Hemma. Or*a*.
S*ancte* Pachomi. Or*a*.
S*ancte* Frontoni. Or*a*.
S*ancte* Colu*m*bane. Or*a*.
S*ancte* Wulfmare. Or*a*.
S*ancte* Maurilione.[o] Or*a*.
S*ancte* Lata ⋆⋆⋆[a] Or*a*.[o]
S*ancte* ⋆⋆⋆[a] Or*a*.[a]/
S*ancte* ⋆⋆⋆ ‹Ora›.[a]
S*ancte* ⋆⋆⋆ ‹Ora›.[a]
S*ancte* Edoce.[2] ‹Ora›.[a]
S*ancte* Swiþune. Or*a*.
S*ancte* Winnoce. Or*a*.
S*ancte* Walerice. Or*a*.
S*ancte* Wandrag‹esi›le.[a] Or*a*.
S*ancte* Ywi. Or*a*.
S*ancte* Petroce. Or*a*.
S*ancte* Felix. Or*a*.
S*ancte* Deusdedit. Or*a*.
S*ancte* Benigne. Or*a*.
S*ancte* Furtunate. Or*a*.
S*ancte* Æþelwine. Or*a*.
S*ancte* Ecgwine.[o] Or*a*.

f. 94r S*ancte* ⋆⋆⋆ ‹Ora›.[a]
S*ancte* Lar ⋆⋆‹Ora›.[a]
S*ancte* ⋆⋆⋆ Or*a*.[a]
S*ancte* Branwalatore. Or*a*.
S*ancte* Canadir. Or*a*.
S*ancte* Rantfrit. Or*a*.
S*ancte* Siloc. Or*a*.
S*ancte* Triohoc. Or*a*.
S*ancte* Tula. Or*a*.
S*ancte* Twioric. Or*a*.
S*ancte* Mellite. Or*a*.
S*ancte* Pauline. Or*a*.
S*ancte* Byrnwolde.[q] Or*a*.
S*ancte* Byrhthelm. Or*a*.
⋆⋆⋆ Or*a*.
⋆⋆⋆ Or*a*.[a]
S*ancte* ⋆⋆⋆ Or*a*.[a]
S*ancte* Wilo‹br›ord. Or*a*.
S*ancte* Geroc. Or*a*.
S*ancte* Cherane. Or*a*.
S*ancte* Euticiani. Or*a*.
S*ancte* Maurille. Or*a*.
S*ancte* Basili. Or*a*.
S*ancte* Honorate. Or*a*.
S*ancte* Uiator. Or*a*.
S*ancte* Isidore.[p] Or*a*.
S*ancte* Samson. Or*a*.
S*ancte* Romane. Or*a*./

[o] *added in the lower margin, same hand*
[p] Isidore: *corrected interl. from earlier* 'Isa-'
[q] Byrnwolde: '-e' *added by another hand*

[2] Dewick and Frere read *Iudoce*.

94^v *Sancte* Fuss ★★★ ⟨Ora⟩.^a
    Sancte Bab ★★★ ⟨Ora⟩.^a
    Sancte Comes ★★★^a Or*a*.
    Sancte Gr⟨i⟩mba⟨lde⟩.^a Or*a*.
    Sancte Hædda. Or*a*.
    Sancte Ceadda. Or*a*.
    Sancte Iohannes æt Berenlic. Or*a*.
    *Sancte*³   Or*a*.
    *Sancte*³   Or*a*.
    Sancte Brendane. Or*a*.
    Sancte Machute. Or*a*.
    *Sancte*³   Or*a*.
    *Sancte*³   Or*a*.
    Sancte Pancrede. Or*a*.

    ★★★^a
    Sancte Aldelme. Or*a*.
    Sancte Botulfe. Or*a*.
    Sancte Indrahte. Or*a*.
    Sancte Patricii. Or*a*.
    Sancte Dor ★★★.^a Or*a*.
    Sancte Policarpe. Or*a*.
    Sancte Arseni. Or*a*.
    Sancte Perone. Or*a*.
    Sancte Donate. Or*a*.
    Sancte Babilli. Or*a*.
    Sancte Simeone. Or*a*.
    Sancte Leotfrede. Or*a*.
    Sancte Paterne. Or*a*./

95^r *Sancte* Theodore. ⟨Ora⟩.^a
    Sancte ★★ nwolde. ⟨Ora⟩.^a
    Sancte ⟨Wi⟩lfridi^a arch*iepisco*p*i*. ⟨Ora⟩.
    ★★★^a Or*a*.
    ★★★^a Or*a*.
    ★★★ tine.^a Or*a*.
    ★★★^a Or*a*.
    Sancte Piate. Or*a*.
    Sancte Abunde. Or*a*.
    Sancte Focate. Or*a*.
    Sancte Landwolde. Or*a*.
    Sancte Gangulfe. Or*a*.
    Sancte Byrnstane. Or*a*.
    Sancte Ælfeagi. Or*a*.
    Sancte Dunstani arch*iepiscop*e. Or*a*.
    ^r*Sancte* Oswolde^s arch*iepiscop*e. Or*a*.
    Sancte ⟨Æ⟩þelwolde. Or*a*.^r/

    Omn*es* s*ancti* con-
    ⟨f⟩essores.^a Orate
    pro nobis.
    Omn*es* s*ancti* monachi
    et heremite.
    Orate pro . . .
    Sancta Felicitas. Or*a*.
    Sancta Perpetua. Or*a*.
    Sancta Agnes. Or*a*.
    Sancta Agatha. Or*a*.
    Sancta Lucia. Or*a*.
    Sancta Petronella. Or*a*.
    Sancta Tecla. Or*a*.
    Sancta Eulalia. Or*a*.
    Sancta Hildeburh. Or*a*.

95^v *Sancta* Anasta⟨sia. Ora⟩.^a
    Sancta Eufem⟨ia. Ora⟩.^a
    Sancta Marin⟨a⟩.^a O⟨ra⟩.^a

    ★★★ onat ★★★^a
    ★★★ crist ★★★^a
    Sancta Iuliana. ⟨Ora⟩.^a

---

^r *added in lower margin*   ^s Oswolde: '-e' *added interl.*

---

³ These places may have been left blank so that the names of other saints—ones venerated locally—could be easily added later.

Sancta Brigida. Ora.
Sancta Baldhild. Ora.
Sancta Genofeua. Ora.
Sancta Geretrudis. Ora.
Sancta Radegundis. Ora.
Sancta Aldegundis. Ora.
Sancta Eugenia. Ora.
Sancta Scolastica. Ora.
Sancta Maria Magdalena. Ora.
Sancta Columba. Ora.
Sancta Prisca. Ora.
Sancta Osgyð. Ora.
Sancta Margareta. Ora.
Sancta Mar ✶✶✶ᵃ Ora.

Sancta Iulitta. ⟨Ora⟩.ᵃ
Sancta Sauina. ⟨Ora⟩.ᵃ
Sancta Praxedis. ⟨Ora⟩.ᵃ
Sancta Iustina. ⟨Ora⟩.ᵃ
Sancta Affra. Ora.
Sancta Barbara. Ora.
Sancta Æþelþryð. Ora.
Sancta Æþelbyrh. Ora.
Sancta Sexburh. Ora.
Sancta Endgyð. Ora.
Sancta Maria. Ora.
Sancta Martha. Ora.
Sancta Ælfgyf. ⟨Ora⟩.
Sancta Endburh. ⟨Ora⟩.ᵃ/

f. 96ʳ   ✶✶✶ᵃ Ora.
✶✶✶ᵃ Ora.
⟨S⟩anctaᵗ Uincentiana. Ora.
Sanctaᵗ Landrede. Ora.
Sanctaᵗ Anastasia. Ora.
Sanctaᵗ Berhte. Ora.
Sanctaᵗ Milgyð. Ora.
Sanctaᵗ Perdita. Ora.
Sanctaᵗ Cristina. Ora.
Sanctaᵗ Regula. Ora.
Sanctaᵗ Theodota. Ora.
Sanctaᵗ Corona. Ora.
Sanctaᵗ Reparata. Ora.
Sanctaᵗ Gaudentia. Ora./

Sancta ✶✶ oria.ᵃ Ora.
Sancta ✶✶✶ᵃ Ora.
Sancta ✶✶✶ᵃ Ora.
Sancta ✶✶ riwa.ᵃ Ora.
Sancta Gemma. Ora.
Sancta Regens ✶✶ᵃ Ora.
Sancta Opportuna. Ora.
Sancta P ✶✶ terna.ᵃ Ora.⁴

f. 96ᵛ   Omnes sancti. Orate pro nobis.
Propitius esto, parce nobis, domine.
Propitius esto, libera nos, domine.
Ab omni malo. Libera . . .
Ab insidiis diaboli. Libera . . .
A peste superbie. Libera . . .

Ab ira tua . . .
A persecutione
inimici . . .

ᵗ MS. sancte

---

⁴ Column b has been left blank; cf. above, n. 3.

A carnalibus desideriis.
Libera . . .
A peste et fame
et clade. Libera . . .
A subita eterna morte.
Libera . . .
A periculo mortis. Libera . . .

97ʳ ★★★ et protectio. Libera . . .
★★★ operatio. Libera . . .
Ab omni heres⟨e⟩.ᵃ Libera . . .
⟨A⟩bᵃ omni inmunditia
cordis et corporis.
Libera . . .
Per aduentum tuum. Libera . . .
Per natiuitatem tuam . . .
Per circumcisionem tuam . . .
Per baptismum tuum. Libera . . .
Per apparitionem tuam. Libera . . .
Per ieiunium tuum. Libera . . .
Per temptationem tuam. Libera . . .

97ᵛ Per uictoriam tuam. Libera . . .

A morte perpetua . . .
Ab ira uentura . . .
Ab omnibus eternis
suppliciis. Libera . . .
Ab omnibus laque⟨is⟩ᵃ
inimici diab⟨o⟩li.ᵃ
Libera . . ./

Per crucem et
passionem tuam. Libera . . .
Per mortem et
sepulchrum tuum. Libera . . .
Per sanctamᵘ
resurrectionem
tuam. Libera . . .
Per gloriosam
ascensionem tuam. Libera . . .
Per gratiam sancti
spiritus paracliti. Libera . . .
Per misericordiam
tuam. Libera . . .
Per omnipoten-/ tiam tuam.
Libera . . .

Per eternitatem tuam. Libera peccatores, te rogamus.
Audi nos, Fili dei, te rogamus. Audi nos. /

ᵘ MS. sancta

129

62

⟨A Confession for Two Priests⟩[1]

f. 98ʳ ⟨I⟩ncipitᵃ confessioᵇ inter presbiteros:[2]
Ego confiteor tibi pater celi et terre coram hoc altare tuo s*ancto* et
istius loci reliquiis[3] et cora*m* sacerdote tuo omnia peccata mea, et
quicquid d*e*i pietas mihi ad memoriam reducet de cogitationibus malis
et de sermonibus otiosis siue inmundis operibusᶜ quecumque ego feci
contra precepta d*e*i.

℟ Dimitat d*ominu*s omnia peccata tua.

f. 98ᵛ Ego confiteor omnia odia cordis / et corporis ★★★(2–3 wd)ᵈ ones pe
★★★(2–3 wd)ᵈ conuitia tuo ★★★(2–3 wd)ᵈ mendaci ★★★(2–3 wd)ᵈ
tiones, adolationes, tristitias, uigilias inutiles, carnales concupiscentias
*et*ᵉ pessimas propter corporis mei suauitates.

℟ Dimittat d*ominu*s omnia peccata tua.

Ego confiteor quia d*e*i precepta postposui et transgressa su*m*[4] p*er*
superbia*m* et elationem et pigritia*m* et uoluptates inmundas; p*er*petraui
f. 88ʳ omnem fornicationem,/[5] oblocutiones, luxurias, ebrietates, comessa-
tiones, homicidia manifeste et oculte in anima et corpore.

℟ Dimittat d*ominu*s om*n*ia peccata tua.

ᵃ *MS. damaged*   ᵇ *MS.* confessionem   ᶜ operibus: *two letters erased before
this; it is followed by a blank space*   ᵈ *MS. damaged; the text on the recto side is visible*
ᵉ et: *added interl.*

---

[1] This new form of the *Confiteor* as a dialogue between two priests (or a priest and a
deacon) reached full development by the first third of the eleventh century; see J. A.
Jungmann, *The Mass of the Roman Rite : Its Origins and Development*, trans. F. A.
Brunner (New York, 1951), I, pp. 299 sqq. The text here seems to be based upon a
confessional prayer in the Carolingian *De psalmorum usu liber* (*U*) (*PL* 101.499–501)
which, however, is not in dialogue form. Correspondences between *G* and *U* have
been noted where they occur.
[2] The rubric was added later. F. 52ᵛ ends with the rubric *Incipit confessio*; it is possible
that this folio followed it directly at one time.
[3] Cp. *U* 101.501A.
[4] *transgressa sum*. The significance of this and other feminine forms is discussed in the
Introduction, p. xiv.
[5] f. 88ʳ. This folio is bound out of place in *G*.

Ego confiteor quia[f] patrem et matre*m*, fra*tres* et sorores, patruos *et*[g]
consabrinos siue om*nes* propinquos et parentes meos secundu*m* dei
preceptu*m* et dei uoluntate*m* honoris obsequiu*m* non exhibu⟨i⟩[h] nec
necessitatibus eoru*m* prout potui adfui, et omnes chr*ist*ianos sicut de*us*
    88[v]   precepit non dilexi,[6] et muliere*m* et filios et filias, sorores, / et ne potes
ue ★★★(3–4 lt)[h] omnes familias domus mee non corre ★★★(3–4 lt)[h],
sed luxuriosas et adulterias et fornicarias enutriui et non prohibui;
dominicu*m* die*m* ac sollemnitates sa*nct*orum non digne nec dux[i] *uel*
acceptabile duxi nec custodiui, et nescientibus non adnuntiaui, sed
ebriose et luxuriose in ipsis me pollui et alios ad hoc inuitaui et
incitaui. Decimas[7] omnium bonoru*m* meoru*m* non reddidi, sed
latrocinia[8] et furta abscondi et comedi.[9]

    99[r]   Ego[10] confiteor / quod infirmos et in carcere repositos non uisitaui,
nudos non cooperui, hospites propter de*um* non suscepi nec pedes
laui,[11] esurientes et sitientes non refeci, dolentes et flentes non
consolatus su*m*; inter se discordantes siue parentes meos siue
chr*ist*ianos rixantes plus ad iracundiam qua*m* ad pace*m* incitaui, quod
maxime credere debui non credidi.

Dimittat d*omin*us omnia peccata tu⟨a⟩.[j]

    99[v]   Ego[12] confiteor quia multu*m* peccaui in uisu, auditu, gustu, adoratu /
et tactu et multa mala cogitat⟨a⟩[j] et locuta fui et perpetraui et mala
uoluntate consensi; mala dedi consilia contra dei precepta et dei
uoluntate*m*.

Dimittat d*omin*us omnia peccata tua.

---

[f] quia: *an erasure after this*   [g] et: *an erasure after this*   [h] *MS. damaged*
[i] dux: '*u*' *added interl.*   [j] *MS. damaged*

---

[6] Ex. 20: 12.
[7] Mt. 25: 14–30; cp. *U* 101.500B.
[8] Cp. *U* 101.499D.
[9] The refrain is wanting after this verse.
[10] Cf. Mt. 25: 31–46; cp. *U* 101.499D–500A.
[11] Cf. Lc. 7: 44.
[12] Cp. *U* 101.500A–B.

131

Ego confiteor quia in sancta dei ecclesia multa mala cogitaui et locuta fui et perpetraui; inordinate[k] et superbe intra ecclesiam dei steti, oscitans[l] sedi, aspexi, respexi, lacui, consensi, intraui, tetigi et similiter exiui; in omnibus locis ubicumque uoluptas corporis /

f. 100[r] m★★★(3–4 lt)[m] exit et mecum perseuerauit et osculo nefando polluta fui; ⟨et⟩ per sanctum[n] altare et in ecclesia consecrata et in cruce benedicta et per sanctas reliquias[13] et per dei nomen et sanctorum nomina et corpora iuraui et periuraui.[14]

Ego confiteor quia fui[o] omnipotenti deo et omnibus sanctis et[p] omnibus bonis inobediens et contentiosa et inuidiosa et iracunda et auara et cupida et rapax et[p] incredula; consecratum dei misterium et

f. 100[v] reliquias et sanctos libros et sancta uasa indigna et pol-/ luta tetigi et p★★★(3–4 lt)[m] et oratione⟨m⟩[q] meam[15] neglegenti in conspectu t⟨uo⟩[q] effudi proste ★★★(4–5 lt)[q] cogitationes inanes et cor lapideum.[16]

Ego confiteor quia corpus domini et sanguinem eius polluta corde et corpore sine confessione et penitentia scienter indignus accepi et eum non custodiui nec iudicium domini super me perhorrui.[17]

Ego confiteor quia ieiunia et psalmodias et orationes et secutiones post

f. 101[r] cruces debens nudis uestigiis incedere / sic ★★★(8–10 lt)[q] hoc agere cum omni humilitate cordis et corporis sicut ★★★(3–5 lt)[q] edictum fuit et regibus et imperatoribus non custodiui nec adimpleui;[18] episcopos et presbiteros, abbates, monachos, canonicos et omnes clericos ecclesie dei sicut debui non amaui; non dilexi nec honoris obsequeis prebui sicut deus precepit, sed memetipsum per carnalia desideria et

f. 101[v] per malam[r] uoluntatem et per mala opera contaminat ★★★(2–3 lt)[s] / de honestate ★★★(3–4 lt)[s] perdidi et ★★★(2–3 lt)[s] tariæ diabolo consensi

---

[k] inordinate: 'in-' added interl.   [l] oscitans: 's' (1st) added interl.
[m] MS. damaged   [n] sanctum: an erasure before 'm'   [o] fui: added interl.
[p] et: added interl.   [q] MS. damaged   [r] MS. malum
[s] MS. damaged

---

[13] Cp. U 101.499C.
[14] The refrain is wanting after this verse.
[15] Cp. U 101.499C.
[16] The refrain is wanting after this verse.
[17] The refrain is wanting after this verse.
[18] Cp. U 101.500A.

et in peccata memet ipsum sensum subdidi de his autem omnibus
atque aliis innumerabilibus que contra Christi dei uoluntatem. Sic ego
hodie tibi, deus celi et terre,[19] omnia confiteor coram[t] sancto altare tuo
in pura et uera confessione et uoluntate ad emendandum et hec omnia
peccata deinceps dimittendum ut tu, omnipotens deus, qui dixisti[20]

02[r] nolo mortem peccatoris sed ut conuertatur et uiuat,/ miserearis anime
mee, et parcas et remittas et deleas[21] omnia peccata atque facinora,
crimina et scelera, et omnia delicta mea preterita, presentia et futura
★★★(3–4 lt)[s] sentia ★★★(3–4 lt)[s] ducas me absque macula per tuam
magnam misericordiam in uitam eternam ad omnium consortia sanctorum
et ad gaudia angelorum in celo habitantium. Per . . . Supplico te, dei
sacerdos, ut de his omnibus sis mihi testis in die iudicii ne gaudeat de

02[v] me inimicus meus et digne pro me deum / clementiam deprecas
★★★(5–6 lt)[u] et mihi ueniam et indulge⟨nti⟩am[u] et remissionem
omnium pecc⟨a⟩torum[u] predictorum hic et in eterna secula. Amen.

Tunc[22] cum ipso prosternat se ipse sacerdos ante altare et si fieri
poterit ambo pariter cum dicant[v] 'Pater noster'; deinde dicat capitula et
penitens respondeat ei 'Et ne nos inducas in temptationem', 'Conuerte
nos, deus salutaris noster',[23] 'Conuertere, domine, aliquantulum',[24]
'Adiutorium nostrum',[25] 'Fiat misericordia tua, domine',[26] 'Ostende
nobis, domine'.[27]/

---

[t] coram: *added interl.*   [u] *MS. damaged*
[v] dicant: *there is ligation between 'n' and 't'*

---

[19] Cp. *U* 101.501A.
[20] Ez. 33: 11; Mt. 18: 3.
[21] Cp. *U* 101:501B.
[22] *tunc . . . ei.* This rubric is in red.
[23] Ps. 84: 5.
[24] Ps. 89: 13.
[25] Ps. 123: 8.
[26] Ps. 32: 22.
[27] Ps. 84: 8.

63

⟨A Hymn by Ratpert of St. Gall⟩[1]

f. 103ra Versus[A] in letania mai⟨ore⟩:[a]

A⟨rdua spes⟩ mundi ⟨solidator et inc⟩lite celi
    Chri*ste* ⟨exau⟩di nos propitius ⟨famul⟩os.
Virgo dei ⟨ge⟩netrix rutilans in honore perrenn⟨is⟩
    ora pro famulis sancta Maria tuis.
5 Angele summe dei Michael miserescito no*st*ri;
    adiuuet et Gabrihel atq*ue* pius ⟨Ra⟩phahel.
Aspice nos ⟨o⟩mnes clemens baptis⟨ta⟩ Iohannes
    Petreq*ue* ⟨cum⟩ Paulo nos rege d⟨octriloquo;
f. 103rb cetus ap⟩ostoli⟨cus si⟩t nobis fautor ⟨et / omnis
10   ac patriarcha⟩rum propheticusqu⟨e⟩ chorus.
Poscere nu⟨nc⟩ Stephanum stude⟨a⟩mus carmin⟨e⟩ summum
    ut cum m⟨ar⟩tiribus nos iuuet trepidus
Inclite Laurenti, qui fla⟨m⟩mas exsuperast⟨i⟩
    cum Gentiano ★★★(3–4 lt) miserare pio ★★★(3–4 lt).
15 Splendide Silu⟨ester⟩, Gregor⟨i⟩ ac san⟨ct⟩e magister,
    no⟨s⟩ quoq*ue* cum soci⟨is f⟩er⟨te iuuan⟩do poli⟨s⟩.

---

[a] *MS. damaged*   1–3, 6–13] *MS. damaged*   1] ardua: *the first 'a' two spaces high*
8] cum . . . et (9): *added in lower margin although belonging here*   14–28] *MS. damaged*

[A] uersus: *I adds* Ratperti   12] trepidus: *I reads* ipse pius (*rightly*)
14] *I reads* uictor ab etherio nos miserare choro

---

[1] This well-known processional hymn by Ratpert of St. Gall (*ob. c.* 884) was sung on
Sundays and feastdays. The analogue is *I* (pp. 321–2). The poem is also printed in
Monumenta Germaniae Historica, Poetae Latini Aevi Carolini IV, pp. 321–2; see also
P. Stotz, *Ardua spes mundi* (Bern, 1972), pp. 36–72. The text in *G* has interlinear
musical notation, and is written in double columns.

03va His ★★/★(10–12 wd) gite nos ★★★(2–3 wd) q*ue* Dionisi.
⟨B⟩onifacius a ★★★(2 wd) osiusq*ue* cum pre ★★★(2–3 lt)
nos uestra laeti⟨ti⟩a pia.
Uirgi⟨neo⟩s flores Agnes ⟨Aga⟩thesque fe⟨ren⟩tes,
20 auxilio ues⟨tris⟩ addite nos so⟨ciis⟩.
Innocuos pue⟨ros⟩ resonemus for ★★★(3–4 lt) ymnos,
qui ⟨mo⟩do nos pue⟨r⟩os ⟨d⟩ant resonare ⟨melos.
Omnes O sancti, nostre succurrite uite
03vb perque crucem sanctam sal⟩-/ ua nos, Chr*iste* redemptor,
25 ⟨ira deque tua⟩ clemen⟨s nos erip⟩e, Chr*iste*.
Nos peccatores audi, ⟨te⟩ Chr*iste* rogamus;
U⟨t pa⟩c*em* nob*is* dones, te Chr*iste* rogam*us*;
crimen u⟨t⟩ omne tuis soluas, te Chr*iste* ro*gamus*;
aure ut temperiem dones, te Chr*iste* ro*gamus*;
30 ut pluuia*m* nobis dones, te Chr*iste* . . .;
ut fruges terre dones, te Chr*iste* . . .;
ecclesiamq*ue* tua*m* firmes, te Chr*iste* . . .;
fili cels⟨i⟩throni, nos audi ★★★(3 ll.)/

23] resonare: *there is a hole in the MS. after this* 26–9, 34] *MS. damaged*

21] for . . . ymnos: laude peractos *I* 30] *not in I* 31] Christe: *I adds* ut
populum cunctum salves te Christe rogamus

17–19] This severely damaged section of *G* seems to have had four verses here
originally. The following six completely different verses occur in *I* at this point:
O Benedicte, pater monachorum, Galleque frater,
Cum reliquis sanctis nos refovete polis.
Maxime de Suevis superis coniuncte catervis,
Sancte Otmare, tuum letifica populum.
Inclyte Magne, tuam clemens nunc inspice plebem;
Auxilio tutos undique redde tuos.
34] *I* concludes: tete rogamus; / Agne dei patris, nobis miserere pusillis; Christe,
exaudi nos, (and then in Greek) O KYRRIE YMON ELEYSON (but Latin letters).

135

64

⟨A Prayer of Confession in Old English begging
Forgiveness and Protection⟩[1]

f. 104[r] In[2] naman ⟨þære hal⟩g⟨an⟩[a] þrynesse þ⟨æt i⟩s[a] fæder ⟨and sunu and
se⟩[a] halga[A] gast god ælmihtig þam ic e⟨om and⟩etta[a] ⟨ecne⟩[a]
ælmihtigne god a wesendne *and* a wuniendne[B] to widan feore þam ic
bibiode minre sawle gehealdness⟨e⟩[a] *and* mines lichoman min word
and weorc *and* mine geþohtas, mine heortan *and* minne hyge, min
leomu *and* mine lioðu, min fell *and* flæsc, min blod *and* ban, min mod
and gemynd *and* min gewit eall *and* æghwæt þæs þe me lichomlices
oþþe gastlices sy mid rihte ⟨mæ⟩ge[a] cyrran⟨ne⟩,[a] *and* þurh drihtnes
f. 104[v] þone[C] halgan / lichoman ⟨and þurh drihtnes þa⟩[a] halgan rode, *and*
þurh s*ancta* Ma⟨rie⟩[D] mægþhad, *and* þurh Cristes ac⟨enned⟩nesse,[a]
and þurh his þ*æt* halige fulwiht, *and* þurh his halige festen, *and* þurh
his þrowunga, *and* þurh his æriste, *and* þurh his upastigenesse on
heofonas, *and* þurh þone halgan gast *and* þone hean dom þe nu
toweard is eallan mancynne, *and* þurh his þ*æt* halige godspell *and* eal
þa wundor þe þ*ær* on syn þurh þa ic me bebiode minu*m* drihtne ðam
ælmihtigum gode; *and* eac ic hine[e] bidde þurh ealle þas ðe ic nu
f. 105[r] arimde[b] þæt he me forgife ealle mine / synna milde ★★★(4–5 lt)[c] *and*
eac wuldor mid his halgu⟨m⟩[c] æfter þysse worlde, *and* eac þurh ealle
þas on godes noman ic me bebiode ðam nigu*m* stefnum engla *and* þam
halgu*m* s*ancte* Michahele mid ealra þara haligra sawlum þ⟨e⟩[dE] ealle ic

---

[a] MS. damaged   [b] ðe ic nu arimde: *added interl.*   [c] MS. damaged
[d] MS. damaged   [e] MS. hinne

[A] halge *Wanley*   [B] wuniende *Wanley*   [C] þone: ⟨þa⟩ *Banks*
[D] M⟨aria⟩n *Banks*   [E] þe: *om. Banks*

---

[1] The prayers printed here as nos. **64, 65** and **68** are all texts in Old English for which
there are no analogues. Two editions of them have appeared previously, both in the
same year: R. A. Banks, 'Some Anglo-Saxon Prayers from British Museum MS.
Cotton Galba A. xiv', *N&Q* 210 (1965) 207–13, and W. Braekman, 'Some Minor Old
English Texts', *Archiv* 202 (1965) 271–76. The article by Banks is a more detailed
study which identifies several of the Latin sources for the Old English texts, and
draws attention to the liturgical structure of no. **65** which is a series of prayers 'ad
horas'. Where appropriate, Banks' reconstructions have been cited in the notes.
[2] This is Wanley's Article IV, 'Invocatio S. Trinitati et 9 Ordinum Angelorum pro
protectione. Saxonice.' (*op. cit.* p. 231).

hi healsige on godes noman þurh ealle þas þæt hy me geþingian wið
ælmihtigne god ge her in þisse worulde ge a^e to widan fiore; *and* eac in
eallu*m* þyssu*m* þe ic nu arimde on godes noman hi^f me forbioden
eallu*m* fiondu*m* gesewenlicu*m* *and* ungesewenlicu*m* þæt hy me sceððan
ne / motan ne in ⟨þysse worulde n⟩e^d æfter in ecn⟨esse⟩.[3]

05^v

---

^e a: *added interl.*   ^f hi: *added interl.*

---

[3] This line is emended from Wanley (*op. cit.* p. 231).

65

⟨A Series of Prayers 'ad horas'⟩

⟨Introductory⟩[1]

Min drihten[a] hælend Crist, ic do þe þancas ⟨ea⟩lre[b] þara goda *and* þara unarimedlicra fremsumnessa þe þu me synfullum sealdest *and* lændest; sy æfre þinre micelnesse nama symble gebletsod mid gode *and* þe sy æfre ar *and* wuldor a on ecnesse ealles mines dæles *and* ealles þæs ðu me æfre on þisse worulde butan ælcan gewyrhtan geuþ⟨e⟩.[b]

f. 106[r]   Min drihten, þu gefyldest me mid þine / gyfe in dagum fyrlenum, gefyl me nu, min drihten, mid þinre micelan mildheortnesse forþon ⟨þe⟩ þu e⟨art⟩[b] gebletsod to gode ★★★(1 wd)[b] a but⟨an⟩[b] ende þu leofast mid fæder *and* rixast þurh ealra worulda world.

⟨Prime⟩[2]

Min drih*ten* hælen⟨d⟩[c] Crist, godes sunu, on þinum noman ic mine handa up ahæbbe; drih*ten* hælend Crist, þu ðe[d] me þisse uht*an*tide gesundne[e] þurh ðas nihtlican dimnesse becuman lete, geheald me nu todæg, drihten, þurh ealre tida fæc *and* b⟨ea⟩rhtmas[c] *and* mid þinre gyfe læd me ⟨unge⟩deredne.[f]/[g]

⟨Terce⟩[3]

f. 106[v]   Min drihten hæle⟨nd⟩[c] Crist, þu þe on þa ðriddan ⟨tide d⟩æges[c] rode ⟨þin⟩e[c] gelæded[h] wære for ealles middaneardes hælo, ic þe bidde eadmodlice þæet þu mine synna adilgie *and* ic minra forðgewitenra synna æt þe forgifennessa gemete *and* þæet þu me sy wið þan toweardum synnum arful hyrde.

---

[a] min drihten: *2 spaces high*   [b] *MS. damaged*   [c] *MS. damaged*
[d] ðe: *added interl.*   [e] gesundne: '*n*' *(2nd) added interl.*
[f] ungederedne: '*n*' *(2nd) added interl.*   [g] *Part of a word is visible in the lower margin*: awunia   [h] gelæded: '*ge*' *added interl.*

---

[1] This is Wanley's Art. V (*op. cit.* p. 231) 'Oratio ad Christum Jesum, cum gratiarum actionibus. Saxonice'. Banks notes that the opening formula is a translation of Lat. *Gratias tibi agimus . . .* (*op. cit.* p. 210). He is not certain if a new prayer begins at f. 106[r]; if it does, neither he nor I have been able to find a source for it. In line 8 he suggests the emendation *ælmihtigum* where the text is damaged. The first three lines on f. 106[v] were visible only by ultra-violet light.

[2] See Banks, *op. cit.* pp. 210–211.

[3] *Ibid.* p. 211.

⟨Sext⟩⁴
Min drih*ten* hælend Crist, þu þe on þa^i sixtan tide dæges rode treow
gestige for middaneardes onlesednesse^j *and* þes middaneard wæs eall
on þystre gehwyrfed, syle me s⟨y⟩mble^k þæt leoht minre / sawle *and*
mi⟨nes lic⟩homan^k þæt ic geearnian mo⟨te⟩^k *and* cuman to eacan life.

⟨None⟩⁵
Min drihten hælend Crist, þu þe on rode galgan ahangen wære *and*
þone scaþan þu onfenge þe on þe gelyfde on þa fægernesse
neorxnawonges gefean, *and* hine mid þe feran lete; þu wære rice
cyning þeah þu on rode hangadest. Ic þe eadmodlice mine synna
andette *and* ic bidde þe for þinre micelan mildheortnesse þæt ic mote
æfter minre forðfore neorxnawonges gatu agan.^l/

⟨Vespers⟩⁶
Þancas ic do ⟨min drihten⟩^k ælm⟨ihtig⟩^k god þæt þu me ges⟨undne⟩^k
þurh þisses dæges ryne to þisse æfentide becuman lete.

⟨Oratio horae duodecime⟩⁷
Min drihten waldend *and* gescyldend, þu þe leoht fra*m* þystru*m*
ascyredest, ic þe bidde gehyr mine bene.

⟨Prime⟩⁸
Drihten god almih⟨tig⟩,^mn þu þe to fruman þisses dæges me becuman
lete, gehæl^o me, min drih*ten*, mid þinu*m* mægene þæt ic on þissum
dæge on nane synne ne gehwyrfe, ac symble min word *and* min weorc
sy on þinre soðfæstnesse gehwyrfed þu þe l⟨eo⟩fast^n *and* rixast a to
worulde./

---

^i þa: *added interl.*   ^j onlesednesse: '*ed*' *added interl.*   ^k *MS. damaged*
^l There is a space between *gatu* and *agan*   ^m almihtig: *added in margin*
^n *MS. damaged*   ^o gehæl: '*3e*' *added interl.*

⁴ *Ibid.*
⁵ *Ibid.* p. 212.
⁶ *Ibid.*
⁷ *Ibid.*
⁸ *Ibid.* p. 213. The scribe who compiled these prayers seems to have been familiar with
a liturgy based upon six Offices. Banks concludes that 'there is a strong suggestion
that the compiler was intimately acquainted with a collectar, different from the
surviving Old English collectars, but firmly based on the work of Alcuin (p. 213)'.
The *Rule of St. Benedict* gives eight Offices whereas the *Old English Benedictine Office*
gives the liturgy for only six: Prime, Terce, Sext, None, Vespers and Compline.

66

⟨A Prayer of Confession⟩[1]

f. 108ʳ Meis culpis, domine, ueniam peto tibi quia plurima sunt[a] peccato
meo[2] et innumerabiles delicta mea aula transgressa sum regu⟨lariter⟩[b]
die cotidie noctuque. ⟨I⟩ncesso[b] contra mandatum dei quem[3] custodire
debeo, quia plenum[4] sum de ebrietate, de uanagloria, de mendacio, de
periurio, de furto, de fornicatione, de pullutione, de luxuria, de
superbia, de accidia, de inuidia iniquas[5] et perfidus,[c] malitiosus,
f. 108ᵛ odiosus, contu⟨ndo⟩[b] contra mandatum / omni quem[6] custodire debeo
die cotidie. Sed rogo, pater celestis, tuam pietatem et tuam misericordiam ut numquam dimittas me de ista luce discedere antequam mihi
peccatrice[7] talem penitentiam concedas qui[8] me de inferno liberet et ad
tuam sancta⟨m⟩[c] misericordiam perducat. Amen.

---

[a] sunt: *there is ligature between the 'n' and 't'*   [b] *MS. damaged*
[c] perfidus . . . odiosus: *gl. feminine*   [c] *MS. damaged*

---

[1] There is no analogue for this text. It is highly ungrammatical at times, as are a
number of other texts in *G* (see Introduction, p. xxi). The textual oddities have been
retained, but improved readings are given below in the notes. The mixture of
masculine and feminine forms is noteworthy; see Introduction, p. xiv.

[2] For *peccato meo, innumerabiles* read *peccata mea, innumerabilia.*

[3] For *quem* read *quod.*

[4] For *plenum* read *plenus* or *plena.*

[5] For *iniquas* read *iniquus.*

[6] For *omni quem* read *omne quod.*

[7] For *peccatrice* read *-i.*

[8] For *qui* read *que.*

67
⟨A Prayer for Guidance⟩

Domine[1] Ihesu Christe,[A] mane cum surrexero intende in[B] me[C] et guberna[D] actos[E] meos et uerba mea et cogitationes meas ut toto[F] die[G] tra⟨n⟩seam[aH] in tua[bI] uoluntate. Dona[J] mihi, domine, timorem tuum, cordis conp⟨unc⟩- / tionem,[a] mentis humilitatem, conscientie[K] purita⟨tem⟩[aL] ut terram despiciam, celum[c] aspiciam, peccata odiam, iustitiam diligam. Aufer[M] a corde[N] meo sollicitudinem[d] secularem,[O] gule appetitum,[eP] concupiscentiam fornicationis, amorem pecunie, pestem iracundie, tristitiam seculi, mentis[Q] accidiam, uanam letitiam, tyrannidam,[R] superbiam. Planta in me[S] uirtutes bonas, abstinentiam carnis et castitatem mentis, humilitatem ueram, caritatem perfect⟨am⟩;[f] custodi, domine,[T] os meum ne lo- / quatur[U] uana ne ★★★(1 wd)[f] cu ★★★ ne ⟨detraham⟩[f] absen⟨tibus⟩[f] ne[V] maledict ★★★ (6–8 lt)[f] tibus, sed ⟨e contr⟩ari⟨o⟩,[f] benedic⟨am⟩[f] domine, semper laus tua[W] sit[X] in ore meo; custo⟨di⟩,[f] Christe,[gY] oculos meos ne uideant[Z] ad[A] con-

09r

09v

---

[a] *MS. damaged*   [b] *MS.* tue   [c] *MS.* celorum
[d] *MS.* sollenitudinem seculare   [e] *MS.* appetitu   [f] *MS. damaged*
[g] *MS.* christi

[A] domine ihesu christe: *om. R*   [B] in: ad *RP*   [C] me: *RP add* domine
[D] guberna: *RP add* omnes   [E] actus *RP*   [F] tota *R*: totum *P*
[G] diem *P*   [H] in tua uoluntate transeam *R*   [I] tua *P*   [J] da *P*
[K] conscientiam puram *R*   [L] puritatem *P*   [M] aufer . . . secularem: abscide a me domine *P*   [N] corde meo: me *R*   [O] secularem: terrenam *R*
[P] appetem *P*   [Q] mentis: *om.* R   [R] tyrannidem superbiae *P*: terrenam *R*
[S] *R reads* (me) uirtutem abstinentium continentiam carnis castitatem humilitatem caritatem non fictam (custodi): *P reads* (me) domine uirtutem mentis uoluntariam paupertem ueram patientiam laetitiam spiritale animi stabilitatem cordis contritionem humilitatem non fictam fraternam caritatem (custodi)   [T] domine: *om. RP*
[U] loquar *RP*   [V] ne . . . domine: ne maledicam maledictionem presentibus sed e contrario benedicam domino et *R*: ne respondeam maledictum pro maledicto sed e contrario benedicam domino in omni tempore *P*   [W] eius *P*   [X] sit: *om. P*
[Y] christe: *om. RP*   [Z] uideant: *P adds* mulierem
[A] ad . . . proximi: gloriam saeculi concupiscendas eas et ne desiderem rem proximi *R* quod . . . proximi: eam ne desiderent rem proximi nec delicias huius seculi *P*

---

[1] The analogues for this prayer are *R* (f. 22a) and *P* (II. 7–8), neither of which is an exceedingly close analogue, but which together provide sufficient evidence for an almost complete reconstruction of *G*; see also *Ma* (col. 657) and *Wi* (pp. 10, 38).

cupiscenda*m* quod malu*m* es*t*, nec dilicias se*c*uli nec re*m* pr*o*ximi, ut^B cu*m* sp*iri*tu Dauid dica*m*, 'Oculi mei se*mper* ad d*e*um^C quo*niam*^D ipse^E euellet de laqueo pedes meos',² et iteru*m*, 'Ad te leuaui oculos meos q‹ui ha›bitas in celis'.^{F3} Custodi ‹aures›^f meas ne audiant^G ★★★(3–4

f. 110^r wd)^h / nec uer‹bum› otiosu*m*, sed aperiantur^H cotidie ad audiendum uerbu*m* dei,^I q*ui* audit et regnat in se*c*ula se*c*ulorum. Amen.

---

^h *MS. damaged*

---

^B ut . . . dicam: ut dicam spiritu Dauid *R*: sed dicam cum spiritu Dauid *P*
^C dominum *RP*   ^D quoniam: *om. R*: quia *P*   ^E ipse . . . meos: *om. RP*
^F celo *RP*   ^G audiant . . . nec: audiam detractationem nec mendacium nec *R*: audiant linguam detrahentem nec audiant mendacium nec *P*   ^H aperte sint *P*
^I dei: *R reads* custodi pedos meos ne circumeant domus otiosas sed sint in oratione dei; custodi manus meas ne porrigantur sepe ad capienda munera sed potius eleuentur in precibus domini mundae et purae quo possim dicere cum propheta eleuatio manum mearum sacrificium uespertinum: *P reads* custodi pedes meos nec circumeant domos otiosi sed stent in oratione dei; custodi manus meas ne porrigantur sede (†) ad accipienda munera sed potius eleuentur in precibus domini munde et pure, sine irae et sermone, eleuatio manuum mearum sacrificium uespertinum, qui cum patre.

---

² Ps. 24: 15.
³ Ps. 122: 1.

68

⟨Prayers from the Veneration of the Cross Ceremony⟩[1]

Ps*almus*[2]: D*o*mine, ne in furore tuo;

Ps*almus*: Beati quorum;

Ps*almus*: D*o*mine, ne in furore tuo.[3]

D*o*mine Ih*es*u Chri*st*e, adoro te in cruce ascendente*m*;[A] deprecor te[B] ut ipsa crux liberet me de[C] diabolo[D] percutiente.

D*o*mine Ih*es*u Chri*st*e, adoro te in cruce uulneratu*m*;[E] depreco⟨r t⟩e[a] ut ipsa[F] uulnera remediu*m*[G] sint ⟨anim⟩e[a] mee.

10[v] D*o*mine ⟨Ih*es*u Christe⟩[a] / adoro te in sepulc⟨h⟩ro positu*m*; deprecor te ut ipsa[H] mors sit[I] uita mea.[J]

D*o*mine Ih*es*u Chri*st*e, adoro te descendente*m*[b] ad inferos liberante*m* captiuos; deprecor te ut[K] non ibi[L] me dimittas introire.

---

[a] *MS. damaged*   [b] *MS.* ascendentem

[A] ascendentem: *C adds* et spinam coronam portantem: *P adds* spinam coronam in capite portantem deprecantem   [B] te: *om. C*   [C] ab *PV*   [D] angelo *CPV*
[E] uulneratum: *C adds* felle et aceto potatum   [F] ipsa: tua *C*   [G] sint remedium *V*
[H] ipsa: tua *C*   [I] fiat mihi uita *C*   [J] mea: *V adds* aeterna   [K] ut: *C cont.*
me non demittas introire ubi adam tibi dixit ecce manus que me plasmauerunt et dixerunt alii quis est iste rex gloriae. Dominus uirtutum scio quia ultra non hic discenderis   [L] ibi . . . dimittas: permittas me illuc *V*

---

[1] The 'Adoro te' petitions are from the service for the veneration of the Cross on Good Friday; the format here is identical to that in *S* (Symon's edition of the *Regularis Concordia*), pp. 43–44. Lilli Gjerløw has divided the manuscripts of the petitions into two groups, those with the phrase 'ab angelo percutiente' in the first invocation (her 'common' form), and those with the phrase 'de diabolo percutiente' (her 'Concordia' form); *G* falls into the 'Concordia' group, as might be expected. In her edition she collates a large number of Insular and Continental witnesses (*Adoratio Crucis*, Oslo, 1961, pp. 17–18). Although there are many witnesses for the Latin version of these prayers, there is only one other known version in Old English—analogue *P*. The longest and apparently oldest version, with fifteen invocations, is found in *C*. The Old English translation of 'Deus omnipotens Ihesu Christe qui tuas manus' (p. 200) is unique. The analogues are *S* (pp. 43–44), *C* (pp. 114–17), *P* (II. 18–21) and *V* (f. 172[r]); see also *Wi* (pp. 44–45).
[2] A line has been left blank for a rubric, probably *in prima quidem oratione*, which is found in *S*.
[3] The first three penitential Psalms: 6, 31 and 37.

Domine Ihesu Christe, adoro te[M] resurgentem[N] ab inferis ascendentem
ad celos;[O] deprecor te[P] miserere mei.

Domine Ihesu Christe, adoro te uenturu⟨m⟩[c][Q] iudicaturum; deprecor[R]
te ut in tuo aduentu non intres[d][S] in iudicio[T] cum me peccante[U] sed

f. 111[r]   deprecor te[V] ut ante[W] dimittas[X] / qu⟨am⟩[c][Y] iudices,[Z] qui uiuis.[4]

Drihten[5] hælend Crist, ic gebidde[A] þe on rode astigendne;[B] ic bidde
þe þæt seo sylfe rod me alyse fram deofles slege.

Drihten hælend[e] Crist, ic gebidde[C] þe on rode gewundodne; ic bidde
þe þæt ða[D] sylfan wunda syn to lacnunge and læcedome[E] minre sawle.

Drihten hælend Crist, ic gebidde þe on byrgenne[F] geledne;[f] ic bidde
þe þæt se sylfa deað weorðe me to life.

Drihten hælend Crist, ic gebidde þe adune to helwarum astigendne[G]

f. 111[v]   and þa[H] gehæftan / þanan alysendne;[I] ic bidde þe þæt ðu me ne
geþafie þæ⟨r⟩inne cumc.[g]

Drihten hælend Crist, ic gebidde þe arisendne[h][J] fram helwarum
upstigendne[i][K] to heofonu⟨m⟩;[g] ic bid⟨de⟩[g] þe þæt ðu gemiltsige me.

Drihten hælend Crist, ic gebidde þe toweardne deman; ic bidde þe þæt
ðu on þines domes tocyme wið me synfulne dom ne[L] healde, ac ær þu
deme mine synna me forgif, þu ðe leofast and rixast[M] mid god fæder
in annysse haliges gastes a in worlda worul⟨d⟩.[g][6]

---

[c] *MS. damaged*   [d] intres: *MS. seems to read* uid-ris, *with* uid- *added interl.*
[e] hælend: '*h*' *added interl.*   [f] *MS.* gebedne   [g] *MS. damaged*

[M] te . . . mei: te a mortuis resurgentem et ad caelos ascendentem *V*: deprecor te ut me a
peccatis liberes et caelum ascendere facias *C*   [N] resurgentem . . . inferis: *om. C*
[O] celos: *C adds* sedentem ad dexteram patris   [P] te: *om. C*
[Q] uenturum: *PV add* et   [R] te deprecor *C*   [S] intres *FCPV*
[T] iudicium *CV*   [U] peccatore *V*   [V] te: *om. C*   [W] ante . . . iudices: antea
mihi omnia peccata dimittas quam iudices *V*   [X] dimitte *C*
[Y] quam . . . uiuis: *om. C*   [Z] iudices: *V adds* saluator mundi   [A] bidde *P*
[B] astigende *P*   [C] bidde *P*   [D] ða: seo *P*   [E] læcedomas *P*
[F] byrigenne geledne *P*   [G] astigende *P*   [H] þa: *om. P*   [I] alysende *P*
[J] arisende *P*   [K] stigende *P*   [L] no gehealde *P*   [M] rixast: *P adds* god

---

[4] There is a corresponding Old English gloss for all of the prayers in no. 67 in *V*.
[5] This OE text is Wanley's Art. VI: 'Ejaculationes ad I. Christum in crucem
ascendentem, crucifixum, in sepulchro positum, descendentem ad inferos, ab inferis
ascendentem, mundum judicaturum, Latine et Saxonice' (*op. cit.* p. 231).
[6] Analogue *C* ends here.

12ʳ In se*cun*da duos medioximos / sequente oratione:ⁱ

Ps*almus* : Miserere mei, d*eu*s (primus);[7]
Ps*almus* : D*omi*ne, exaudi.[8]
D*omi*ne[9] Ih*es*u Chr*ist*e, gl⟨or⟩iosissimeᵏ conditor mundi, qui c*um* sis
splendor glorie coeternus patr⟨i⟩ᵏᑫ sanctoque spiritui, ideo dignatus
es carne*m*ᴿ ex immaculata uirgine sumere et gloriosas palmas tuasˢ in
crucis patibuloˡ p*er*misisti configere*m* ut claustra dissipares inferni et
humanum genus liberares de morte, respice et miserere mihi misero
12ᵛ op⟨p⟩ressoⁿ facinoru*m* pondere / mul⟨t⟩aru⟨m⟩queᵏ nequitiaru*m*
labe polluta;ᵒᵁ non me dignerisⱽ derelinquere, piissime pater, sed
indulge quod impie gessi. Exaudi meᵂ p*ro*stratu*m* coramᴾ adoranda
gloriosissimaˣ cruce tua,ʸ ut merear tibi mundusᑫ adsistere et placere
in conspecturᶻ tuo, qui uiuis.ᴬ
Drihten hælend Crist, se wuldorfullesta middaneardes scippend, þeah
þu sy wuldres beorhtnes efenece þinu*m* fæder *and*ᴮ þam halegu*m*ᶜ
13ʳ gaste, ðu þeahhwe- / þereˢ þe gee⟨a⟩dmeddest,ᵗ þ*æt* ðu flæsc under-
fenge of unwe*m*mu*m* mægdene *and* þine wuldorfullan handbreda on
rode galgan afæstnigeanᵘ lete, þ*æt* þu þurh þ*æt*ᴰ helle locu tostengdest
and mennisc cyn fra*m* deaþe alysdest, biseoh *and* gemiltsa me earmum
mid gylta byrþena ofþrihtumᴱ *and* mid smittan manegra manaᵛᶠ
besmitenu*m*.ᴳ Ne sy þe eaþe þ*æt* þu me forlæte, þu mildheortesta

---

ʰ *MS.* asendne   ⁱ upstigendne: '*up-*' *added interl.*   ʲ *MS.* orante
ᵏ *MS. damaged*   ˡ *MS.* pabulo   ᵐ configere: '*-g-*' *added interl.*
ⁿ oppresso: '*s (2nd)*' *added interl.; '-o' glossed 'a'*   ᵒ polluta: *corrected from earlier '-um'*
ᴾ coram: *altered to* corad   ᑫ mundus: *glossed* '*-a*'   ʳ *MS.* conspectui
ˢ *MS.* þeahhreþere   ᵗ *MS. damaged*   ᵘ *MS.* afæstnigen   ⱽ *MS.* manna

ᑫ patris *P*   ᴿ carnem sumere ex immaculata uirgine *V*   ˢ tuas: *P adds*
hodierna die   ᵀ promisisti *P*   ᵁ polluto *SPV*   ⱽ derelinquere digneris *V*
ᵂ me: *P adds* peccatorem: *V adds* domine   ˣ gloriosissime: *V om.*
ʸ tuam *V and adds* et tribue mihi gratiam tuam   ᶻ in conspectu: conspectui *V*
ᴬ uiuis: cum patre *PV*   ᴮ and: æc *P*   ᶜ halgan *P*   ᴰ þæt: þa *P*
ᴱ ofðryhtne *P*   ᶠ mana *P*   ᴳ besmitendne *P*

---

⁷ Ps. 50: 3 (not 55 or 56; note the rubric 'primus').
⁸ Ps. 101: 2.
⁹ This prayer and its Old English translation are Wanley's Art. VII: 'Oratio pro
Remissione Peccatorum, Latine et Saxonice' (*op. cit.* p. 231). See *Wi* (pp. 13–14) for
an additional analogue.

fæder, ac forgif ⟨me⟩,ʷᴴ þæt ic unrihtlice adreah. Gehyr meᴵ

f. 113ᵛ astrehtne *and* gebiddendneˣᴶ ætforan þinre / wuldorfullan ro⟨de, þæt⟩ᵗ ic geea⟨r⟩nige,ᵗ þæt ic ætfora⟨n þe⟩ stande *and* li⟨c⟩wyrðeᵗ sy on þinre gesihþe, ðe mid þinum efenecean ⟨fæ⟩derᵗ leofast *and* ricsast in annysse halig⟨e⟩sᵗ gastes geond ealra woruldaᴷ world.ʸ

In *tertia* ultimos duos cum oratione:ᶻ

Ps*almus*: De pr*o*fundis;¹⁰
Ps*almus*: Domine, exaudi (*secundus*).¹¹

D*eus*ᴸ omn*i*potens Ih*e*su Chr*ist*e, qui tuasᴹ man*us* mundasᴺ pr*o*pter nos in cruce posuistiᴼ et deᴾ tuo s*ancto* sanguine pretiosoQ nos redemisti, mitte in me sensu*m*ᴿ et intellegentia*m* quomodo habeam

f. 114ʳ uerama peni- / tentiamᵇ ⟨et ha⟩bea⟨m⟩ᶜ bonam p*er*se⟨ueran⟩tiamᶜ omnib*us* diebus uite mee.ˢ

God ǣlmihtig hǣlend cyning, ⟨ðu þe þin⟩eᶜ clǣnan handa for us on rode gesettest *and* of þinum halgum *and* deorwyrðum blode us alysdest, asete on me andgyt *and* gemyn⟨te⟩ᶜ hu ic soðe hreowsunge *and* dǣdbote habban mǣge, and gode þurhwununge gehealdanne on eallu*m* mines lifes dagu*m*, hit a swa geweorðe.¹²

ʷ me: *add. ed.*   ˣ *MS.* gebiddende   ʸ world: '-*l*-' *added interl.*
ᶻ oratione: '-*one*' *added in line below*   a *MS.* uera   ᵇ *MS.* penitentia, bona
ᶜ *MS. damaged*

ᴴ me *P*   ᴵ *P adds* sinfulne   ᴶ gebiddedne *P*   ᴷ weoruldo *P*
ᴸ quesumus *P*   ᴹ tuas: *V adds* sanctas   ᴺ *om. V*   ᴼ extendisti *V*
ᴾ *om. V*   Q *om. V*   ᴿ sensus *P*   ˢ *S adds* amen

¹⁰ Ps. 129: 1.
¹¹ Ps. 142:1.
¹² This is Wanley's Art. VIII : 'Oratio brevis pro Poenitentia et Perseverantia, Latine et Saxonice' (*op. cit.* p. 231).

69

⟨Prayers and Incipits⟩[1]

14ᵛ Quicumque uult; Pater noster; Credo; Benedicamus patrem et filium cum sancto spiritu, laudemus et superexaltemus ⟨eum in secula⟩.[a] Benedictus es, domine, in firm⟨amen⟩to[a] celi et laudabilis et gloriosus et superexaltatus in secula. Benedicat et custodiat nos[b] omnipotens dominus. Amen. Te trina deitas unaque poscimus ut culpas abluas noxia subtrahas; des pacem famulis nobis[c] quoque gloria per cuncta tibi secula.[2]

Ego dixi: Domine, miserere mei; sana anima mea quia peccaui tibi.[3]

15ʳ Mihi autem adherere deo bonum est, / ponere in domino deo spem meam.[4]

Recordare mei, domine, et tuere me ab his qui persecuntur me.[5]

Saluum fac seruum tuum, deus meus, sperantem in te.[6]

Saluam fac ancillam animam, deus meus, sperantem in te.

Saluos fac seruos tuos et ancillas tuas, deus meus, sperantes in te.

Dominus conseruet nos, et uiuificet nos et beatum[7] faciet nos et emundet in terra animam eius et non tradat eum in manus inimici eius.[8]

Protexisti me, deus, a conuentu malignantium; a multitudine operantium iniquitatem.[9] /

---

[a] *MS. damaged*   [b] nos: *om. MS*   [c] *MS.* nos

---

[1] These prayers and incipits (to *miserere mei*) appear earlier in *G* as no. **27**. The two texts are almost identical. In this instance, however, the incipits and the introductory prayer are followed by biblical florilegia. This item includes three prayers for Holy Trinity Sunday—an antiphon and two collects. It seems as if someone had originally brought these texts together to form a short devotional text for Trinity Sunday for his or her personal use, which, however, was firmly rooted in the liturgy with which that person was so intimately familiar.

[2] See the corresponding note to no. **27**, n. 3, and cf. Dn. 3:56.

[3] See the corresponding note to no. **27**, n. 4.

[4] Ps. 72: 28.

[5] Ir. 15: 15.

[6] Ps. 85: 2.

[7] *beatum*. The scribe is converting the Vulgate text to the plural, but has slipped up here.

[8] Ps. 40: 3.

[9] Ps. 63: 3.

f. 115ᵛ Fiat pax in uirtute tua, ⟨et⟩ᵈ ab⟨un⟩dantiaᵈ in turrib*us* tuis.¹⁰
Exortu*m est* in tenebris lumen rectis corde, misericors et miserator et
iust*us* d*omi*n*us*.¹¹
Pax mult⟨a⟩ᵈ et diligentibus lege*m* tua*m*, d*omi*ne, et n*on* es*t* in illis
scandalum.¹²
In d*e*o faciem*us* uirtute*m*, et ipse ad nihilu*m* deducet.¹³
Et*e* pax d*e*i qui exsuperat omne⟨m⟩ᵈ sensu*m* custodiat corda n*os*tra et
intellegentias n*os*tras.¹⁴
Beatus qui intellegit sup*er* egenu*m* et pauperem;ᶠ in die mala liberatbit
eu*m* d*omi*n*us*.¹⁵

f. 116ʳ In tribulatione in- / ⟨uocaui⟩ᵈ d*omi*num, et ad d*eum* m*eum* clamaui.¹⁶
D*omi*n*us* m*ihi* adiutor *est*, n*on* timebo q*ui*d f⟨acia⟩tᵍ ⟨mi⟩h⟨i⟩ᵍ
h⟨o⟩mo.¹⁷
Adiuua nos, ⟨deus⟩ᵍ salutaris n*os*ter, propter honore*m* nominis tui;
d*omi*ne, libera nos et propitius esto peccatis n*os*tris propter nom*en*
tuu*m*.¹⁸
Adiutorium n*os*tru*m* in nomine d*omi*ni, qui fecit celu*m* et terra*m*.¹⁹

In euangelium²⁰

Te d*eum* patre*m* ingenitu*m*, te filiu*m* unigenitu*m*, te sp*iritu*m* s*anctu*m*
paraclitu*m*, s*anctam*ʰ et indiuiduam trinitate*m* toto corde et ore^A
confitemur,^B laudamus atque benedicim*us* tibi^C gloria in secula. /

f. 116ᵛ ⟨Bened⟩ictusⁱ d*omi*n*us* d*eus* Isr*ahel*,²¹ qui facis mirabilia magna solus

---

ᵈ *MS. damaged* | *e* et: *preceded by an erasure* | ᶠ *MS.* pauperum
ᵍ *MS. damaged* | ʰ *MS.* sanctum | ⁱ *MS. damaged*

---

^A et ore: *om.* E | ^B confitebimur A | ^C tibi . . . secula: *om.* E

---

¹⁰ Ps. 121: 7.
¹¹ Ps. 111: 4.
¹² Ps. 118: 165.
¹³ Cf. Ps. 58: 9.
¹⁴ Ph. 4: 7.
¹⁵ Ps. 40: 2.
¹⁶ Ps. 17: 7.
¹⁷ Ps. 117: 6.
¹⁸ Ps. 78: 9.
¹⁹ Ps. 123: 8.
²⁰ This is the Gospel antiphon for Holy Trinity Sunday; the analogues are E (II. 140)
and A (col. 187). The rubric is abbreviated curiously as *INEŪ GL. Ā.*
²¹ Cf. Ps. 135: 4.

et benedictum nomen[22] magestatis eius in eternum et in seculum seculi. Benedicat nos sancta maiestas et in⟨di⟩uidu⟨us⟩[i] pater et filius et spiritus sanctus, qui est uerus deus in secula seculorum.[23] Regi seculorum inmortali, inuisibili, soli deo honor et gloria in secula seculorum. Amen.

Domine, exaudi orationem meam, et clamor meus ad te perueniet.[24]

Collecta[25]

Omnipotens sempiterne deus, qui dedisti[E] famulis tuis in confessione
7[r] uere fidei eterne trinitatis gloriam / agnoscere et in poten⟨tia[F] maies⟩tatis[j] adorare unitatem, quesumus ut eiusde⟨m⟩[jG] fidei firmitate ab omnibus semper muniamur aduersis, per.

Collecta[26]

Da ⟨p⟩opulo[j] tuo, domine, quesumus inuiolabile[H] dei firmitate ut qui unigenitum tuum in tua tecum gloria sempiternum in ueritate nostri corporis natum de matre uirgine confitentur et a presentibus liberentur aduersis et mansuris gaudiis inserantur, per.

Collecta[27]

Omnipotens sempiterne deus, trina maiestas et una deitas, qui in /
7[v] ⟨trinitate⟩[j] permanes et ⟨in unitate⟩[j] semper consistis, presta, quesumus ⟨ut qui⟩[k] peccatorum nos⟨trorum⟩[k] pondere ★★★(1–2 wd)[k] mimus ★★★(1 wd)[k] indulge⟨ntie ueniam con⟩sequi[k] meream⟨ur⟩,[k] per.[28] /

---

[j] *MS. damaged* 　　[k] *MS. damaged*

[E] dedisti: *AP add* nobis 　　[F] potentia maiestas *PH*: potentiam maiestas *A*
[G] eundem *P* 　　[H] inuiolabilem fidei firmitatem *De*

---

[22] Ps. 71: 19.
[23] 1 Tm. 1: 17.
[24] Ps. 101: 2.
[25] This is the collect for Holy Trinity Sunday; the analogues are *H* (p. 22), *A* (col. 188) and *P* (I. 68). See also *Wi* (p. 102).
[26] This is an 'oratio de natale domini'; the analogue is *De* (no. 61).
[27] This is the collect for matins on Holy Trinity Sunday; the analogue is *A* (col. 187).
[28] *per*. The rest of the folio is blank.

70

⟨Two Medical Recipes for Restoring the Body to Health through Prayer⟩[1]

f. 118ʳ To[2] gehealden⟨ne lichoman hælo mid⟩ᵃ drihtnes gyfe þis is æþele
lǽcedom: ⟨Geni⟩mᵃ mirran *and* ge⟨gni⟩dᵃ on win swylc sy⟨e te⟩laᵃ
micel steap f⟨ul⟩ᵃ *and* þige on niht ⟨ne⟩s⟨tig⟩;ᵃᴬ þon*ne* restan wi⟨ll⟩eᵃ
þ*æt* gehealdeð ⟨wun⟩dorliceᵃ lichoman hælo *and* hit ea⟨c⟩ᵃ ðeah wið
feondes yflumᴮ costungum.

Þonne is eft se æðelesta lǽcedom wiðᶜ þamᴰ ylcan: Genim myrran
and hwit recels,ᴱ sauinan *and* saluian *and* wurman *and* þæs rycelses
and myrran sy mæst *and* þa oþer⟨e⟩ᵃ syn awegene þ*æt*ᶠ þaraᴳ efenfela;
and æt⟨somne⟩ᵃ on mortere *and*ᴴ gegnide to duste; sette under weofod
þonne Cristes tid sy, *and* gesinge man þreo mæssan ofer þa þry dagas
oðᴵ midne winter *and* æt s*ancte*ᴶ Stephan⟨es ti⟩deᵃ *and* s*ancte* Ioh*annes*
euangelista *and* on þa þry ⟨dagas þ⟩igeᵃ on wine on niht nihstig *and*

f. 118ᵛ þ*æt* ⟨þær to lafe sie⟩ᵃ þæs dustes hafa *and* heald.ᴷ Hit / ⟨mæg wiþ
eallum fær³ untrymn⟩essumᵃ ge wið fefre *and*ᴸ wið lenct⟨en⟩ adle ge⁴
★★★(1 wd)ᵃ ge wið attre ⟨ge⟩ᵃ wið yfelre lyft⟨e⟩.ᵃ Gewritu eac
secg⟨aþ⟩ᵃ seᴹ þone lǽce⟨d⟩omᵃ begæðᴺ þ*æt* he hine mæge geh⟨eald⟩anᵃ
xii monað wiþ ealre u⟨ntrymn⟩ess⟨a⟩ᵃ frecenissum.ᴼ

ᵃ *MS. damaged*

ᴬ nestig: *L adds* ond eft   ᴮ costungum yflum *L*   ᶜ wið: to *L*
ᴰ þam: þon *L*   ᴱ recels: *L adds* ond   ᶠ þæt: *om. L*   ᴳ þara: *L adds* sien
ᴴ and: *om. L*   ᴵ oð: on *L*   ᴶ sancte: *om. L*   ᴷ geheald *L*
ᴸ and: ge *L*   ᴹ se: *L adds* þe   ᴺ bega *L*   ᴼ frecenesse *L*

---

[1] The analogue is *L* (vol. II, no. 264, pp. 294–97).
[2] *to . . . win*. This is the incipit for Wanley's Article IX, 'Pro Sanitate conservanda
Medicamenta bina, Sax.' (*op. cit.* p. 231.)
[3] *fær*. Cockayne suggests this should be *færlicum*.
[4] *ge*. This and the word lost after it are not in the analogue.

71

⟨A Prayer 'ad introitum' for Use in a Monastery⟩[1]

D*omine* Ih*es*u Chri*st*e, qui introitum portaru*m*[A] ⟨Hi⟩erusale*m*ª saluans[B]
s*anct*ificasti du*m* splendore gemmarum duodecim totidem[C] nomina
presignasti, *et* qui per organum pr*o*pheticum promisisti,[D] lauda
Hierusalem d*o*min*u*m, lauda de*u*m tuum Sion qu*o*nia*m*[E] confortauit
seras postarum[F] tuarum, benedixit filios[G] tuos in te, te q*uesumu*s ut
po⟨n⟩as[aH] in omnes fines templi istius pace*m* ut uelociter currens
inter⟨ius[a] . . .[2]/

ª *MS. damaged*

[A] portarum: *om. P*   [B] saluans: saluas *PꞀ*   [C] totidem: *P adds* apostolorum
[D] prompsisti *Ꞁ*   [E] quam *P*   [F] portarum *PꞀ*   [G] filiis tuis *P*
[H] pones *PꞀ*

---

[1] The analogues are *Ꞁ* (p. 280) and *P* (I. 165). Before the binding of *G* was lost this prayer
may have been positioned with the series of 'benedictiones in monasterio' found below
(no. **81**); see also *De* (no. 441) and *R* (f. 14ᵛ).

[2] *interius.* The rest of this prayer is missing in *G*; *Ꞁ* continues: 'sermo tuus adipe frumenti
satiet eos spiritus sanctus defendat illos ut numquam eis nocere praeualeat inimicus sed
omnes habitantes uel conuenientes in ea uoce corde et ore pariter decantant dicentes
magnus dominus noster Iesus Christus et magna uirtus eius et sapientiae eius non est
numerus qui cum deo patre.' *P* differs slightly, but not significantly.

151

72

f. 119ʳ Deus¹ qui sup⟨plicium tuorum uota per cari⟩tatisᵃ officia suscipere
dignerisᴬ famulis tuis tuasque famulas, in tua proficere dilectione et in
tua letari protectione ut tibi secura mente deseruiatᴮ et in tua pace
semper assiste⟨re⟩ᵃ mereantur, per.

ᵃ *MS. damaged*

ᴬ (dig.) da famulis tuis ill. et ill. (in) *De*   ᴮ deseruiant *De*

---

¹ This is the prayer 'ad complendum' from the 'missa pro familiaribus'; the analogue is *De*
(no. 1307).

73

Via[1] sanctorum omnium, domine[A] Ihesu Christe, qui ad te uenientibus æterne[B] claritatis gaudia contulisti, aditum[C] templi istius spiritus[D] sancti luce perfunde, qui locum istum[E] sanctorum[F] apostolorum Petri et Pauli atque Andreæ[a] patrocinio[G] consecrasti, præsta omnipotens,[H] ut omnes isti[I] in te ⟨cre⟩dentes[b] obtineant ueniam pro delicti⟨s⟩[b] ab omnibus liberentur angusti⟨is im⟩petrent[c] quicquid petierint / ⟨pro necessitatibu⟩s[b] suis placere sem⟨p⟩er[b] ⟨pre⟩ualeant[bJ] coram oculis ⟨t⟩uis[b] et obtentu[K] sanctae et gloriose dei genetr⟨icis⟩[b] Marie, nec non et beatorum apos⟨to⟩lorum,[b] martyrum, confessorum ★★★(2 wd)[b] omniumque ★★★(1–2 wd)[b] aulam paradysi mereantur introire cum ⟨s⟩ancto[b] patre.[d2]

19ᵛ

---

[a] MS. andrea   [b] MS. damaged   [c] MS. impeterent   [d] patre: *there is ligature between the 't' and 'r'*

[A] domine: *om.* P   [B] æterne: *om.* JP   [C] introitum JP   [D] spiritus sancti: *om.* J   [E] istum: J *adds* in honore beatae dei genetricis semperque uirginis mariae et (sanctorum): P *adds* in honore sanctae mariae   [F] beatorum apostolorum tuorum J   [G] patrocinio: *om.* J   [H] omnipotens: quesumus J   [I] istic J   [J] ualeant P   [K] obtentu . . . patre: P *reads* ⟨tuis⟩ quatinus per te et sanctam Mariam genetricem tuam muniti mereantur aulam paradysi introire saluator mundi qui uiuis: J *reads* ⟨tuis⟩ quatinus per te omnium sanctorum intercessionibus muniti aulam paradysi mereantur introire saluator mundi qui cum patre

---

[1] This is a prayer to be said outside the church; the analogues are J (p. 279) and P (I. 165); see the introductory note to no. **81**.

[2] There is a 'probatio pennae' after this line consisting of the alphabet and the abbreviation sign for *et*.

74

⟨The *Confiteor*⟩

Confiteor[1] deo *et* omnib*us* san*c*tis ei*us* et t*ibi* frater quia peccaui in cogitatione, in locutione *et* op*er*e, propterea p*r*ecor te ora pro me.
⟨*minister*⟩:
Misereatur tui om*nipoten*s deus *et* dimittat t*ibi* om*n*ia peccata tua; liberet te ab om*n*i malo, conseruet *et* confirmet in omni op*er*e bono *et* p*er*ducat te ad uitam et*er*nam./

---

[1] There are many forms of the *Confiteor* found in the liturgy throughout the Middle Ages. No exact analogue for this version in *G* has yet been found, the closest being in *M* (II. 489–90). See the introductory note to no. **62** for bibliographical information concerning the development of this prayer in the Middle Ages.

154

75

⟨The *Benedicite*⟩

°0ʳ Ben⟨ed⟩icite^{a1} omnia oper⟨a⟩^a domini dominum, laudate
et superexaltate eum in secula;
benedicite angeli domini dominum . . .
benedicite celi ⟨domino⟩^a . . .
benedicite aque omnes que super celos sunt^b domino . . .
bene*dicite* omnes uirtutes domini dominum . . .
benedicite sol et luna domino . . .
benedicite stelle celi domino . . .
benedicite omnes ymber et ros domino . . .
be*nedicite* omn*es* spir*itu*s dei domino . . .
benedicite ignis estus domino . . .
b*enedicite* frigus et estus domino . . .

°0ᵛ b*enedicite* rores et pruina / ⟨domino . . .
benedicite gelu e⟩t^c frig⟨us domino⟩^c . . .
benedicite glacies et ⟨niues⟩^c domino . . .
bene*dicite* noctes et dies domin⟨o⟩^c . . .
bened⟨ic⟩it⟨e⟩^c lux et tenebre domino . . .
b*enedicite* fulgura et nubes domino . . .
benedicite terra dominum laudet et superex⟨a⟩ltet^d eum in secula;
benedicite montes et colles domino . . .
b*enedicite* uniuersa germinantia in terra domino . . .
bened*icite* fontes domino . . .
b*enedicite* maria et flumina domino . . .
benedicite cete et om⟨nia⟩^c que mouentur in aquis domino . . .
b*enedicite* omnes uolucres celi domino . . .
b*enedicite* omnes bestie et pecora domino;/

1ʳ ⟨benedicat⟩^e Isr*ahel* dominum, ⟨laud⟩et^e et superexaltet eum in seculo;

---

^a *MS. damaged*   ^b *MS.* celo sunt: *there is ligature between the 'n' and 't'*
^c *MS. damaged*   ^d *MS.* superexaltatet   ^e *MS. damaged*

---

¹ This is an almost complete version of the *Benedicite*, consisting of verses 57–81, 83–88
and 56 of Daniel 3. The capital *B* is four spaces high and decorated slightly; it
has been executed with red ink. There are indications that a line may have been lost at
the top of this page.

be⟨nedici⟩te^e sacerdotes d*omini* d*omino* . . .
benedicite s⟨erui⟩^e d*omini* d*omino* . . .
benedicite spiritu*s* et anime iustor⟨um⟩^e d*omin*⟨o⟩^e . . .
benedicite sanct⟨i⟩^e et humiles ⟨corde domino⟩^e . . .
benedicite Annanias, Azarias, Misahel d*ominum*,
laudate et sup*er*exaltate eu*m* in s*e*cula;
benedicamus patre*m* et filiu*m* cum s*ancto* sp*iritu*,
laudemus et superexaltemus eum in secula.
Benedictus es in firmamento celi et laudabilis
f. 121^v   et gloriosus² / ⟨in secula⟩.^e ★★★(1–3 wd)^e

---

² *f. 121^v*. The upper left-hand corner has become separated from the rest of the page and is not properly aligned at present. The recto is visible through the page at the top.

76

⟨The *Athanasian Creed*⟩[1]

Qui⟨cumque u⟩ult[a] saluus esse ante omnia opus *est* ut teneat
catholic*am* fidem quam nisi quis*que* integram inuiolatamque seruauerit
absq*ue* dubio in eternum peribit. Fides aute*m* catholica hec est, ut
unu*m* deu*m* in trinitate et trinitatem in unitate uenere*mur*, neque
confudentes p*er*sonas neque substantia*m* separantes; alia *est* enim
p*er*sona patris, alia / ⟨filii, alia spiritus sancti;⟩[a] s⟨ed⟩[a] p⟨atris⟩[a] filii et
sp*iritus* ⟨sancti⟩[a] una *est* diuinitas equalis gloria, coeterna maiestas;
qualis pater talis filius talis et sp*iritus* sa*nctus*; increatus pater,
increatus filius, increatus et sp*iritus* sa*nctus*; inmensus pater, inmensus
filius, inmensus et[A] sp*iritus* sa*nctus*; eternus pater, eternus filius,
eternus sp*iritus* sa*nctus*; et tamen non tres eterni, sed unus eternus
sicut non tres increati nec tres inmensi, sed unus in- / ⟨creatus et⟩[b]
unus inmen⟨sus⟩.[b] Similiter omnipotens pater, om*nipotens* filius,
omni*potens* sp*iritus* sa*nctus*, et tam⟨e⟩n[b] non tres omnipotentes, sed
unus omnipotens de*us*;[B] ita de*us* pater, de*us* filius, de*us* sp*iritus*
sa*nctus*, et tamen non tres dii[c] sed unus *est*[C] de*us*; ita d*ominus* pater,
d*ominus* filius, d*ominus* sp*iritus* sa*nctus*, et tamen non tres d*omi*ni sed
unus *est* d*ominus*; quia, sicut singillatim unamqua*mque* personam
deu*m* et d*ominum* confiteri chr*ist*iana ueritate compellimur, ita tres
deos / aut dominos dicere ca⟨tholica r⟩elig⟨ion⟩e[b] prohibemur. Pater
⟨a⟩[b] nullo ⟨est⟩[b] factus nec creatus nec genitus; filius a patre solo *est*,
non factus nec creat*us* sed genitus; sp*iritus* sa*nctus* a patre et filio, non
factus nec creatus nec genitus sed procedens. Vnus ergo pater non tres
patres, unus filius non tres filii, un*us* sp*iritus* sa*nctus* non tres sp*iritus*
sa*ncti*; et in hac trinitate nihil prius aut posterius, nihil maius aut
minus sed tote tres p*er*sone / ⟨coe⟩ter⟨ne⟩[b] sibi sunt et coequ⟨ales⟩.[b]
Ita ut p*er* omnia, ⟨sic⟩ut[b] iam sup⟨ra⟩[b] dictum ⟨es⟩t[b] et trinitas

22[r] (margin)
22[v] (margin)
23[r] (margin)
23[v] (margin)

---

[a] *MS. damaged*   [b] *MS. damaged*   [c] *MS.* die

[A] et: *om. Denz.*   [B] deus *om. Denz.*   [C] est: *om. Denz.*

---

[1] The text used to reconstruct the damaged parts of *G* is in *Enchiridion Symbolorum*
Definitionum Declarationum, edd. H. Denzinger and A. Schönmetzer, Freiburg, 1965,
pp. 40–42 (abbreviated *Denz.* hereafter).

⟨in unita⟩ te^b et unitas in trinitate u⟨e⟩neranda^b sit. Qui uult er⟨go⟩^b
saluus esse, ita de trinit⟨ate⟩^d se⟨n⟩tiat.^d Sed necessari⟨um est⟩
ad eternam salutem ut incarnationem quoque domini nostri Ihesu
Christi unus quisque^D fideliter credat. Est ergo fides recta ut credamus
et confiteamur quia dominus noster Ihesus Christus dei filius ⟨et deus⟩^d
f. 124^r   pariter et homo est; / d⟨eus⟩^d es⟨t ex substantia patri⟩s^d ⟨a⟩nt⟨e secula
ge⟩nitus,^dE et ho⟨mo est ex s⟩ubstantia^d matris in ⟨se⟩cula^d natus;
perfectus deus, ⟨pe⟩r⟨fe⟩ctus^d homo ex ani⟨m⟩a^d rationali et humana
carne subsistens; equalis patri secundum diuinitatem, minor patre
secundum humanitatem; qui licet deus sit et homo non duo tamen sed
unus est Christus; unus autem non conuersione diuinitatis in carne,
f. 124^v   sed ad⟨sump⟩tione^d humanitatis in deo; / ⟨un⟩us^d om⟨nino non
confusione⟩^d substantie, ⟨sed unitate persone⟩.^d Nam sicut anima
rationalis ⟨et⟩^d car⟨o u⟩nus^d est homo, ita d⟨eus et ho⟩mo^d ⟨un⟩us^d est
Christus qui passus es⟨t⟩^d pro salute nostra, descendit ad inferos, tertia
die resurrexit a mortuis, ascendit ad celos, sedit ad dexteram
dei^F patris omnipotentis;^G inde uenturus est iudicare uiuos et
mortuos; ad cuius aduentum omnes homines resurgere habent cum
f. 125^r   corporibus suis et reddituri sunt^e de facti⟨s⟩^f / propriis ⟨r⟩atione⟨m⟩;
et^H qu⟨i⟩^f bona egerun⟨t, ibunt in uitam⟩^f eternam et qui uero mala,
in ⟨ignem⟩^f eternum.
Hec est fides catholi⟨ca⟩:^f quam nisi quisque fideliter ⟨fi⟩rmiterque^f
crediderit, salu⟨us⟩^f esse n⟨on⟩^f poterit.

---

^d MS. damaged   ^e sunt: the 'n' and 't' in ligature   ^f MS. damaged

---

^D unus quisque: om. Denz.   ^E saeculo Denz.   ^F dei: om. Denz.
^G omnipotentis: om. Denz.   ^H et: om. Denz.

77

Sancti Aðeluuoldi episcopi[a]

Deus[1] qui[A] preclari sideris sancti pontificis Aþelwoldi inlustratione nouam populis Anglorum tribuisti lucem hodierna die[B] clarescere, tuam suppliciter imploramus clementiam ut cuius magisterio totius[C] religionis ⟨do⟩cumenta[b] cognouimus illius ⟨et⟩[b] exemplis informemur et ⟨patr⟩ociniis[b] ⟨ad⟩iuuemur,[b] per . . . /

---

[a] episcopi: '-i' add. interl.   [b] MS. damaged

[A] qui: *J adds* in   aþelwoldi: *J adds* episcopi   [B] die: luce P   [C] totium G

---

[1] A prayer to be said at Vespers on the vigil of the feast of St. Æþelwold (August 1). The analogues for this text are *J* (p. 193), *H* (p. 132) and *P* (I. 136).

159

78

⟨Unidentified Fragments (folios 125ᵛ–129ʳ)⟩[1]

f. 125ᵛ Sanct ★★★(3–4 wd)ᵃ Sancte Machute ★★★(1 wd)ᵃ episcopus egregi
★★★(1–2 wd)ᵃ Christi presul dele me ★★★(1 wd)ᵃ intimis te precor
★★★(1 wd)ᵃ scelera mea posce ★★★(1–2 wd)ᵃ cordis mei uulneribus
★★★(1 wd)ᵃ mihi inclitam magnam ★★★(1 wd)ᵃ nec me uelis con-
tempnere pro peccatorum pondere. Exaudi me miserulam tuam,
Machute, famulam; confer mihi angelicum tuum clemens auxilium
tuam super me dexteram protende serenissimam a cunctis me contagiisᵇ
tuis munda suffragiis. Dele me de cyrographo[2] peccatorum ne quis

f. 126ʳ ★★★(1 wd)ᵇ simque ★★/★(5–7 wd)ᵇ intercedere ★★★(4 ll.)ᵇ ⟨ce⟩lestibus
★★★(1 wd)ᵇ asta ut sim et ★★★(1 wd)ᵇ humiles egregia ★★★(2–3 wd)ᵇ
et stabilis etᶜ actus patrocinatus.ᵈ Hostes omnes uisibiles procul et
inuisibiles a me clementer abice gratamque deo profice. Tu recita
altissimo precamina haec domino et pete ut humillima haec summa

f. 126ᵛ desideria. Angeli me custodiant ★★★(3–4 wd)ᵇ Sit ★★/★(5 ll.) Christo
★★★(3–4 wd).ᵇ

Domine deus omnipotens ineffabilis tuorum sanctorum gloria qui per
archangelum Gabrihelem precursoris tui natiuitatem manifestari
uoluisti, concede quesumus ut ★★★(1 wd)ᵇ eius hodie conceptionem
illiu⟨s⟩ᵇ nobis salutaria intercessione donentur. Exaudi, domine, preces
nostras gemen ★★★(3–4 lt)ᵇ ⟨i⟩nᵇ conspectu tuo fundentes et
intercessione sancti Cipriani et Rustini ⟨ui⟩rginis multiplic ★★★(1–2
wd)ᵇ dele ★★★(1 wd)[3] /

f. 127ʳ Veni[4] ★★★(1–2 wd)ᵉ pro cogitationibus meis et uerbis et factis ex⟨audi
me⟩,ᵉ exaudi me, exaudi me miserat ★★★(1–2 wd)ᵉ misericors me
★★★(1 wd)ᵉ dei et ★★★(2 wd)ᵉ quia tu es Christus filius qui in hunc
mundum uenisti saluare ★★★(1–2 wd)ᵉ Parce peccatis meis quia

ᵃ *MS. damaged*   ᵇ *MS.* cotagiis   ᵇ *MS. damaged*   ᶜ et: *corr. interl. from*
earlier uel   ᵈ *MS.* patrocinus   ᵉ *MS. damaged*

---

[1] For a discussion of the method of transcription used in this damaged part of the text
see the Introduction, p. xxv–xxvi.
[2] Cp. Col. 2: 14.
[3] There are three totally illegible lines squeezed into the lower margin of this folio.
[4] This prayer, which probably begins on f. 126ᵛ at 'Domine deus', should be compared
with nos. **19**, **24** and **25** above.

innumerabilia[5] sunt delicta mea et per baptismum tuum et sacrum
ieiunium quadraginta dierum et noctium te deprecor, da mihi ueram
humilita⟨tem⟩,[e] indulgentionem delictorum meorum ★★★(3–4 wd)[e]
lorum tuorum

27[v] ★★★(2–4 wd)[e] lorum ⟨tu⟩orum / ★★★(1 wd)[e] mortifica ★★★(4 ll.)[e]
uiuificationes in ★★★(3–5 wd)[e] meorum et inclinationem corporis
mundissima sana. Et per orationes tuas sacratissimas obsecro, Christe,
corpus et anim⟨am⟩[e] meam ab hostis antiqui temptationibus et ab
omni pollutione purifica peccato ★★★(1–2 wd).[e] Et per passionem et

28[r] resurrectione⟨m⟩[e] ★★★(1–2 wd)[e] tuam ★★/★(3–5 wd)[e] a morte anime
resurgam ★★★(2–3 wd)[e] ab huius seculi periculis et ⟨di⟩aboli[e]
⟨tempta⟩tionibus.[e] Et per sanctum Michahelem et Gabrielem et
Raphielem respice in me et miserere magne potens, et da mihi
ueritatem et ★★★(1 wd)[f] ter et medicinam mentis et corporis. Et per
merita gloriosa sanctorum angelorum et archangelorum, uirtutum et
po⟨testatum⟩[f] aufer a corde meo cogitationes otiosas inimicorum
meorum. Extingue nequitias et prosterne principatus et potestates
tenebrarum, et propitius esto mihi. Et per clarissimas intercessiones

28[v] ★★★(1 wd)[f] et seraphim, da mihi sapientiam ★★/★(5–7 wd)[f] ardore. Te
★★★(2–3 wd)[f] patriarcharum et prophetarum ★★★(1 wd)[f] me fauto
deus. Et per Mariam matrem ★★★(2–3 wd) me ab omni iniquitate et
inquinamento ★★★(2–3 wd).[f] Et per beatos apostolos tuos prote⟨ge⟩
★★★(1 wd)[f] pastor, et pretium ★★★(2–3 wd)[f] in temporibus meis. Et
⟨per⟩[f] merita beatorum martyrum tuorum ★★★(1 wd)[f] me de manibus
inimicorum meorum et benedic animam meam cum sanctificatione
★★★(1 wd)[f] tuorum in celis et in terris. Et per omnium sanctorum

29[r] supplicationes da me ★★/★[f] omni malo ★★★ (4–6 wd)[f] honor et gloria
omnipotens deus in secula seculorum. Amen.

---

[f] *MS. damaged*

---

[5] Cf. Ib. 14: 16.

79

⟨A Prayer before Communion⟩[1]

Ante communionem

Domine sancte pater omnipotens æterne deus, da mihi[A] corpus et sanguinem Christi[B] filii tui domini nostri[C] ita[D] sumere ut merear per hoc remissionem[E] peccatorum[F] accipere et tuo sancto spiritu repleri[G] quia tu es benedictus deus, in te est deus et preter te non est alius, cuius regnum gloriosum permanet et per infinita secula seculorum. Amen.

[A] mihi: *M adds* hoc   [B] christi: *om. M*   [C] nostri: *M adds* ihesu christi
[D] ita: tam digne *M*   [E] remissionem: *M adds* omnium
[F] peccatorum: *M adds* meorum
[G] *repleri: M continues*, atque ab eterna dampnacione liberari et in die iudicii cum sanctis et electis tuis in perpetua requie collocari quia tu es deus solus et preter te non est alius cuius regnum et imperium sine fine permanet in secula seculorum. Amen.

---

[1] The analogue for this prayer is *M* (II. 517–18), where it is found in the 'ordo misse' with the rubric 'Oracio sacerdotis consequenter dicenda'.

80

⟨Unidentified Fragments (folios 129ʳ–130ʳ)⟩

Post communionem

★★★(1 wd)ᵃ obsecro d*omine* I*hesu* Chri*st*e hoc sacra ★★★(1–2 wd)ᵃ
.29ᵛ aduisos ★★★(1 wd)ᵃ misericord ★★/★(2 ll.)ᵃ pecca⟨torum⟩ᵃ meor*um* ut
non adiudic ★★★(2 wd)ᵃ ad remedium p*er*cip*er*e merear.
Suscipe ★★★(3–4 wd)ᵃ oblationes n*os*tras ★★★(4–5 wd)ᵃ macris d*omi*ni
★★★(2–3 wd)ᵃ et archangelor*um* et ★★★(2 wd)ᵃ et omni*um* martyr*um* et
★★★(1–2 wd)ᵃ tuor*um* et omni*um* uirgin*um* t⟨u⟩a⟨rum⟩ ★★★(1 wd)ᵃ
eor*um* p*ro* pace et sanitate ★★★(1 wd)ᵃ tuor*um* et fructib*us* t*er*re
30ʳ ★★★(2–3 wd)ᵃ et ordine ★★★(2–3 wd)ᵃ n*os*tra et ★★/★(2 ll.)ᵃ tuis qui
p*ro*pe ★★★(2 wd)ᵃ in tuo nomine ★★★(4–5 wd)ᵃ d*omi*ne s*anct*e pater
★★★(1 wd)ᵃ d*eus* ante ★★★(1–2 wd)ᵃ maiestati tue.

ᵃ *MS. damaged*

81

⟨Blessings for the Monastery⟩[1]

E⟨xau⟩di[a] nos, d*omine* s*ancte* pater om*nipotens* aeterne[A] d*eus*, et
mittere dignare[b] angelum tuum s*anctum* de celis qui custodiat, foueat,
pr*otegat*, uisitet[c] et defendat om*nes* habitantes in hoc habitaculo.

In coquina

D*ominus* pascit me . . .[2]

Coll*ecta*. D*eus*[B] æt*erne* ante cuius conspectum adsistunt angeli et cuius
nutu ⟨r⟩eguntur[d] uniuersa qui etiam ne⟨cessar⟩iis[d] humane fragilitatis
tua ⟨pietate⟩[d] con⟨sul⟩ere[d] non desinis, te humiliter imploramus ut
f. 130ᵛ   ⟨ha- / bitaculum istius⟩[d] officine ⟨illa⟩[d] benedictione p*er*fundas qua
⟨per man⟩us[d] Helisei pr*ophete* ⟨i⟩n[d] oll⟨a⟩[d] heremitica gustus
amariss⟨imos⟩[d] dulcorasti et semp*er* hic tu⟨e bene⟩dictionis[d] copia
redund⟨ante⟩[d] laudes ⟨t⟩ibi[d] refe⟨r⟩ant[d] ser⟨ui⟩[d] tui qui das escam
omni ca⟨rni⟩[d] et reples omne animal benedictione saluator[C] ⋆⋆⋆(1 wd)[d]
eor*um*, d*eus* qui uiuis et regn*as*.

In cellario

Om*nipotens* et misericors d*eus* qui ub̄ique pr*esens* es, maies⟨tatem⟩[d]
tua⟨m supp⟩licit*er*[d] dep⟨recamur⟩[d] ut hu⟨ic promptuario[D] gratia⟩[d] tua
f. 131ʳ   ⟨adesse dignetur que / cuncta ad⟩uer⟨sa ab eo repellat et h⟩abundantiam[d]
benedictionis ⟨tue larg⟩iter infundat, p*er* . . .⟩[d]

---

[a] *MS. damaged*   [b] *MS.* dignere   [c] *MS.* uistat   [d] *MS. damaged*

[A] sempiterne JÞ   [B] dominus *P*   [C] saluator: *JPP cont.* mundi qui uiuis (*P*
adds et regnas)   [D] promptuariae *P*

---

[1] The analogues for these texts are *J* (pp. 277–78), *P* (I. 164–65) and *P* (pp. 220,
223–26). Two texts appearing above in *G* as nos. **71** and **73** are from the same group of
prayers as these, and oftentimes they appear together with them in other manuscripts,
as they do in *P* and *J*. They may have been together originally in *G* as well. The two
earlier prayers were to be said 'at the entrance to the monastery' and 'before the
Church'; there are eight prayers together here, to be said, 'after the aspersion of water',
'in the kitchen', 'in the cell', 'in the furnace room', 'in the refectory', 'in the dormitory',
'in the larder' and 'in the home of the sick'. (Analogues for these in order in *De* are
nos. 1456, 1484, 1477, 1486, 1475, 1476, 1485 and 1480.) Christopher Hohler has
suggested that the order in which these prayers appear might help determine which
monastery the manuscript was compiled for.
[2] Ps. 23: 1.

In caminata

Domine^E sempiterne de*us* cuius sapie⟨n⟩tia^e hominem docuit ut
domus hec careret aliquando frigore ⟨a⟩^e uicinitate ignis, te q*uesumu*s,
ut om*n*es habitantes uel conuenientes in ⟨ea⟩^e careant in corde
infidelitatis frigore a feruore ignis^F sp*iritu*s s*an*c*ti*, p*er* . . .

In refectorio

Timete^f d*omi*num . . .³
Collecta. O⟨m⟩*nipotens*^e ⟨et⟩^e misericors de*us*, qui famulos ⟨tuos in
hac⟩^e dom⟨o⟩^e alis^g refec⟨tione carnali^G cibum uel potum, te
benedicente cum gratiarum actione / percipiant^H et celesti mense
conuiuio⟩^eI ★★★(4–5 wd)^e salui esse mereantur ★★★(1–2 wd).^e

31^v

In dormitorio

Ecce non d⟨ormitabit⟩^e . . .⁴
⟨B⟩enedic,^e d*omi*ne, hoc famulorum tuorum dormitorum qui non
dormis neque dormitas qui custodis Isr*ahe*l famulos^h tuos^iJ in hac domo
quiescent⟨e⟩s^j post laborem custodi ab inlusionibus fantasmaticis
satane;^K uigilantes^k in precept⟨is⟩^j tuis meditentur, dorm⟨i⟩entes^jL p*er*
soporem senti⟨ant⟩^j et hic et ubique defen⟨sionis tue⟩^j auxilio
mereantur.^M

32^r

Collecta/ Sanctus^N misericors de*us*, qui neces⟨sitatem⟩^j hu⟨m⟩ani^j
generis clementer ⟨preuidens^O a⟩dminicula^j tempor⟨alia contulisti⟩,^jP
humiliter implora⟨mus ut⟩^j benedice⟨re⟩^j digneris hoc ⟨lardar⟩ium^j
⟨famu⟩lorum^j tuor⟨um^l ut quod h⟩ic^jQ tua misericordia pi⟨e contulit
nost⟩ro^j merito non depereat.

---

^e *MS. damaged*   ^f timete dominum collecta: *added by another hand*
^g *MS.* aliis   ^h famulos: *gl.* -as   ^i tuos: *the '-os' is a gl. on earlier '-as'*
^j *MS. damaged*   ^k *MS.* uigilates   ^l tuorum: *gl.* tuarum

---

^E domine: omnipotens *JP*   ^F ignis: *om. J*   ^G carnali: *P adds* concede ut
^H percipiant: *PP cont.* et hic et in aeternum per te semper (*P om.*) salui esse mereantur, per.
^I conuiuio: *J cont.* in aeterna claritatis gaudia laetantes participare mereantur, per
^J tuos famulos *P*   ^K satane phantasmaticis *J*   ^L dormientes: *JP add* te
^M muniantur *JPP*   ^N sanctus: omnipotens et *JPP*   ^O presidens *P*
^P contulisti: *P adds* te   ^Q hic: *om. P*

---

³ Ps. 33: 10
⁴ Ps. 120: 4

⟨Omnipoten⟩s^m et misericors d*eus*, q*uesumu*s inmen⟨sam^R p⟩ietate*m*
tua*m* ut ad intr⟨o⟩itu*m* humi⟨litatis nostre⟩ nos famulos tuos in hoc^S
⟨tabernaculo^T fessos⟩ iacentes salutife⟨re⟩^n uisitare ⟨digneris,^U sicut
uisitasti⟩,^n d*omi*ne, Tobiam^5 et Sarr⟨am, socrum Petri puerumque⟩^n
centurionis^V et ⟨isti pristini^W sanitate anime⟩^n corporisq*ue* recep⟨ta
gratiarum tibi in ecclesia tua⟩^n refera⟨t⟩^X accione*m*. /

f. 132^v   ★★★(1 1.)^6 astor adest ★★★(2–3 wd)^n spes ara ★★★(2–3 wd)^n fiunt
★★★(3–4 wd)^n hic ★★★(2–3 wd)^n quo iure sacerdos ★★★(2 wd)^n uiuens
meos ★★★(2–3 wd)^n unde cohors Wentana^7 ★★★(1–2 wd)^n plaude
patrono qui miranda facit quo sunt ★★★(1 wd)^n busta sacello.
Loripedos rectos statuens lumina cecis exaudi ★★★(1 1.)^n qui duce
★★★(3–4 wd)^n /

---

^m *a line was left blank for a rubric before this collect*   ^n *MS. damaged*

---

^R inmensam quesumus *J*: quos *P*   ^S hoc in *JPP*   ^T habitaculo *PP*
^U digneris: *PP add* et   ^V centurionis: *PP add* ita
^W pristina *PP*   ^X referant *PP*

---

^5 Tb. 12: 6–15; Mt. 8: 14–15; Mt. 8: 5–13.
^6 This badly damaged page contains a hymn text with interlinear musical notation.
^7 *Wentana*. 'Winchester'; see Introduction, p. xiv.

82

⟨Verses from Psalm 68⟩

133ᵛ ⟨Obsc⟩urent*ur*ᵃ¹ o⟨c⟩uliᵃ ei ne uid⟨eat et⟩ᵃ dorsu⟨m⟩ᵃ eius se*mper* incuru⟨um⟩.ᵃ²

⟨E⟩goᵃ su*m* paup*er* et dolens, salus ⟨t⟩uaᵃ d*eus*, suscepi⟨t⟩ me.³ ★★★(1 wd)ᵃ

⟨De⟩leaturᵃ de ⟨libr⟩oᵃ uiuentium e⟨t⟩ᵃ cu*m* iustis non scribatur.ᵇ⁴

⟨Eff⟩undeᵃ sup*er* eu⟨m⟩ᶜ ira*m* tua*m* et ind⟨igna⟩tioᵃ tua ⟨compreh⟩endat eumᵈ⁵ ★★★(1 wd)ᵃ uerte ★★★(1 wd)ᵃ dolor eiusᵉ ★★★(2–3 wd)ᵃ inimici et iniquiᶠ ★★★(5–7 wd)ᵃ /

ᵃ *MS. damaged*   ᵇ *MS.* scribentur   ᶜ eum: *gl.* -os   ᵈ eum: *gl.* -os
ᵉ eius: *gl.* -orum   ᶠ *the word lost after* iniqui *was gl.* -orum

---

¹ *f. 133ᵛ.* The recto of this folio has been left blank.
² Ps. 68: 24. These verses from the psalm have been converted to the singular; they were later glossed with plural endings although some are almost invisible now.
³ Ps. 68: 30.
⁴ Ps. 68: 29.
⁵ Cf. Ps. 68: 25; the psalm reads, '. . . tuam et furor irae tuae comprehendat eos'.

Folios 134ʳ–139ᵛ have been omitted from this edition of *G* because of the degree to which they were damaged by both fire and water. A few notes follow here concerning their contents; a diplomatic transcription of them can be found in Appendix A below.

134ʳ: contains a hymn with interlinear musical notation.

134ᵛ: but for three words, totally illegible.

135ʳ: only a few scattered letters legible.

135ᵛ: contains another almost totally illegible hymn with interlinear musical notation.

137ʳ: only has four or five legible words, one of which may be 'Abel'.

137ᵛ: several words legible, but scattered; this may be a text from the Easter Vigil since it mentions 'pharaoh' and the 'Red Sea'.

138ʳ: only three words legible; another hymn with interlinear musical notation.

138ᵛ: several words legible; another hymn, perhaps the conclusion of the preceding one.

139ʳ/136ʳ: folio 136 is bound out of place as the MS. now stands, and properly belongs here after f. 139. The text is in Old English and was catalogued by Wanley as Article XII with the description, 'Virtutes quae insunt dentibus superioris maxillae, dextro pedi, lumbis (broc.) et felli Mellis sive Taxi, cum Exorcismis praeparandis. Saxonice', and the incipit, 'Ðas cræftas syndon be ðam deore þe we urum geðeode Broc hata ð' (*op. cit.* p. 231). If the order of the items in Wanley's *Catalogue* is faithful to the original, as it indeed seems to be, then this item originally followed that found below on what is known as f. 151ᵛ, which is Wanley's Art. XI.

136ᵛ: is totally illegible. /

83

⟨Unidentified Fragment⟩

140^r Da ★★★(2–3 wd)^a confessores uirgines et omnes *sancti* dei. Da me ★★★(1 wd)^a celi et terra mare et omnia que in eis sunt. ★★★(1–2 wd)^a sol et luna et ★★★(1 wd)^a te^b accusantes ante ★★★(2 wd)^a die ★★★(2–3 wd)^a intermissione ★★★(1 wd)^a ibi semp*er* dolor et tristitia ★★★(1 wd)^a tibi mors sine cessatione fiat, fiat, fiat. Amen. /¹

---

^a *MS. damaged* ^b te: *gl.* eos

---

¹ Note that f. 140^v is omitted; it is totally illegible.

169

84

⟨Biblical Verses⟩

f. 141ʳ sicut[1] cera liquefacta ★★★(2 ll.)[a] super eum[b] et descend ★★★(1 l.)[a]
maledicant[c] ei[d] ⟨qui⟩[e] maledicunt die⟨i⟩[e] qui parati s⟨unt suscita⟩re[e]
leuiathon.[2]
Eripe me de inimicis meis[f] ★★★(1 wd).[e3]
Eripe me de ope ★★★(1 wd)[e] tibi. Exsurge domine ad iuuan ★★★(1 l.)[e]
Ostende nobis, domine, misericordi⟨am⟩[e] . . ./[4]

---

[a] *MS. damaged*   [b] eum: *gl.* -os   [c] *MS. maledicunt*   [d] ei: *gl.* -os
[e] *MS. damaged*   [f] meis: *gl.* nostris

---

[1] The two legible parts of these lines may refer to Idt. 16: 18 and Ps. 54: 16.
[2] Ib. 3: 8.
[3] Cf. Ps. 58: 2 or 142: 9.
[4] Note that f. 141ᵛ is omitted; it is totally illegible. Ps. 84: 8.

85

⟨Unidentified Fragments⟩

142ʳ qui[1] passione ★★★(1–2 wd)[a] propter ★★★(1 wd)[a] domine miserere
nobis ★★★(1 wd)[a] ⟨pro⟩phetice[a] promisisti mors tua a mor ★★★(1 wd)[a]
domine ★★★(1 wd) ligno moritur infernus ★★★(1–2 wd)[a] despoliantur
⟨d⟩omino qui ★★★(1 wd)[a] in cru⟨ce⟩[a] manibus ★★★(1 wd)[a] omnia
★★★(1–2 wd)[a] secula domine ★★★(2 wd)[a] ut ★★★(1 wd)[a] nos a dedica
★★★(1–2 wd)[a] quandoque transferre digneris de sancta Maria /

---

[a] *MS. damaged*

---

[1] *f. 142ʳ*. This text is a hymn with interlinear musical notation; it continues on the
verso. See Appendix A for f. 142ᵛ.

86

⟨Collect for the Vigil of St. Andrew the apostle⟩

f. 144ʳ ⟨Quesumus⟩[1] om*nipoten*s d*eus* ut beatus Andreus ap*osto*lus tuus pro ⟨nobis⟩[a] imploret ⟨auxilium⟩[a] ut a n*ost*ris reatibus absoluti ⟨a cunctis et⟩iam[a] p⟨er⟩icu⟨lis eruamur, per . . .⟩[a2]

---

[a] *MS. damaged*

---

[1] Note that ff. 142ᵛ–143ᵛ are omitted as only a few scattered words are visible; see Appendix A. F. 143ᵛ may have been a prayer to St. Brigid. The analogue for this text is *M* (II. 1012); see also *De* (no. 766). On both the recto and the verso of this folio lines 1–7 are in a large script, lines 8–13 in a small, finer one.

[2] Note that the rest of this folio is illegible; see Appendix A.

87

⟨Unidentified Fragments⟩

44ᵛ gestans munera ★★★(1 wd)ᵃ lita rite crucis sit nobis arma salutis ★★★ (1 wd)ᵃ crucis auxilia nobis tutamena facis in patris et ★★★(1 wd)ᵃ flatus et nom ★★★(1 wd)ᵃ

Omnipotens pater ★★★(1 wd)ᵃ naculum ★★★(1 wd)ᵃ a me omnium ★★★(1 wd)ᵃ fiat ⟨mi⟩hiᵃ lex et ★★★(1 wd)ᵇ lux per te ⟨om⟩nipotentemᵇ qui es benedictus ★★★(1 wd).ᵇ Amen./

46ᵛ beatissimi¹ ponificis Ceadd⟨e⟩ᵇ in sorte iustorum tu⟨orum⟩ᵇ pietate censemur, per . . . concep² ★★★(1 wd)ᵇ

Omnipotens sempiterne deus qui unigenit ★★★(1 wd)ᵇ filii tui sancti⟨ficat⟩ionemᵇ hodierna die nasc ★★★(3–4 wd)ᵇ declarasti conced⟨e⟩ᵇ familie tue pie effectum deuoto ★★★(1 wd)ᵇ quem eius anima recolit te ★★★(2 wd)ᵇ assequatur pacis ★★★(3–5 wd)ᵇ gaudia ★★★(3–4 wd)ᵇ /

ᵃ *MS. damaged*   ᵇ *MS. damaged*

---

¹ *f. 146ᵛ*. This folio is bound back to front and out of place in *G* as it now stands. It is clear from the first words on this page that this folio originally did not follow what is now f. 144.

² This word, which is in the line above it in *G*, was probably part of a rubric for the text following it since it is some form of the word *conceptio*, and the next text mentions 'the only-begotten son'.

88

⟨The Feast of St. Michael⟩[1]

f. 146ʳ Benedicite[2] d*omi*n*um* om*nes* ⟨angeli⟩ᵃ eius potentes uirtutesᴬ qui
facitis uerbum eius ad audiend⟨am⟩ uocem sermonemᴮ eius, p*er* . . .

⟨B⟩enedicᵃ anima mea d*omi*n*um*.[3]

Benedicite d*omi*n*um*ᶜ omnes ⟨a⟩ngeliᵃ eius potentes uirtutesᴬ qui[b]
facitis uerbu*m* eius.

f. 145ᵛ *Versus* : Benedic an⟨i⟩m⟨a⟩ᵃ mea d*omi*n*um*ᴰ et o⟨mnia in- /⁴ te⟩rioraᵃ
m⟨ea⟩ᵃ nomen s*anctum* eius. All⟨elu⟩ia.ᵃ

⟨In⟩ᵃ conspectu angelorum ⟨p⟩sallamᵃ tibi, d*omi*ne deus meus.

Offe*rtorium*

Stetit angelus iuxta aram templ⟨i⟩ᶜ habens turribulum aureum in
manu sua et data sunt ei incen⟨sa⟩ᶜ multa et ascendit ⟨fumus⟩ᶜ
f. 145ʳ aromatum in con- / spectu d*ei*. Alleluia.

In conspectu angelorum psallam tibi, d*omi*ne, et adorabo ad templum
s*anctum* tuum, et confitebor tibi, d*omi*ne.

Et ascendit . . .

ᵃ *MS. damaged*   ᵇ qui: *corr. from* quid   ᶜ *MS. damaged*

ᴬ uirtute *MHY*   ᴮ sermonum *H*   ᶜ domino *M*   ᴰ domino *MHY*

---

[1] This is a mass-set consisting of five prayers for the feast of St. Michael the archangel
(III kl. Oct. = 29 Sept.). In order, they are: the opening prayers, the gradual, the
offertory, the communion and the collect. This series of prayers for a particular feast
or season is one of three in *G*, the others being a set for Eastertide (no. **29**) and a set
for Trinity Sunday (no. **69**). The analogues for these texts are *M* (II. 960–63), *H*
(pp. 168–69) and *Y* (pp. 199–200, 203).

[2] Ps. 102: 20.

[3] Ps. 102: 1, 102: 2 or 103: 1.

[4] *f. 145ᵛ*. This folio is bound back to front in *G* as it now stands.

Communio

⟨Be⟩nedicite^c omnes angeli domini domino,[5] hymnum dicite et super-exaltate eum in secula.

9^v   P*salmus* : Benedicite omnia opera domini[6] ★★★(1–2 wd)^c/[7]
Deus[8] qui miro ordine ⟨a⟩ngelorum^c ministeria hominumque dis-pensas, concede propitius ut quibus tibi ministranibus in celo semper assistitur ab his^E in terra nostra uita^F muniatur, per . . .

---

^E his: *J adds* etiam   ^F uita nostra *M*

---

[5] Cf. Dn. 3: 58.
[6] Cf. Ps. 102: 22 and Dn. 3: 57.
[7] Two additional analogues for this prayer are *J* (p. 215) and *P* (I. 110); see also *De* (no. 726).
[8] *f. 149^v.* This folio is mounted back to front and out of place as *G* now stands.

89

⟨Collect for the Feast of SS. Dionysius, Rusticius and Eleutherius⟩

f. 149ʳ

D*eus*[1] qui hodierna die beatum Dionisium uirtute constant⟨ie⟩ᵃᴬ roborasti quiq*ue* illi ad / predicandum ⟨g⟩entib⟨us⟩ᵃ gl*ori*am tuam Rusticum et Elutherium sociare di⟨gna⟩tusᵃ es, tribueᵇ nobis q*uesumu*s, ex eorum imitatione pro amore tuo prospera mundi despicere et nulla eius aduersa formidare, ⟨per⟩ᵃ . . .

ᵃ *MS. damaged*   ᵇ tribue: *corr. from* tribues

ᴬ constantie: *MHPY add* in passione

---

[1] The analogues for this text are *M* (II. 969), *H* (p. 172), *P* (I. 145) and *Y* (p. 203); see also *De* (no. 671).

90

⟨A Collect for the Feast of the Birth of an Apostle⟩

Exaudi[1] domine, populum tu⟨um⟩ ★★★(1 wd)[a] sancti Cristofori[A]

8[v]   ★★★(1 wd)[a] /[2] turis tui patrocinio sup⟨p⟩licantem[a] ut tuo semper auxilio[b] secura tibi possit deuotione seruire, per . . .

---

[a] MS. damaged   [b] MS. auxilia

[A] tuum . . . cristofori: tuum cum sancti apostoli tui H

---

[1] The analogue for this text is H (p. 194). A line was left blank before its beginning.
[2] f. 148[v]. This folio is mounted back to front.

91

⟨Collect from the Mass in Honour of a Bishop and Confessor⟩

Om*nipoten*s[1] sempiterne d*eu*s maiestatem tuam suppliciter exoramus ut intercessione beato Machuti[A] confessoris tui atque pontificis[a] cuius hodie

f. 148[r] annuam / festiuitatem recolimus cum temporalibus ⟨i⟩n⟨cre⟩mentis[b] æterne prosp⟨e⟩ritatis[b] capiamus augmentum, p*er* . . .

---

[a] *MS.* pontifex tuus   [b] *MS. damaged*

[A] taurini *M*

---

[1] The analogue for this text is *M* (II. 903). A line was left blank before its beginning.

92

⟨A Prayer for the Feast of St. Stephen⟩[1]

Sacratissimum[A] *sancti*[B] Stephani protomartyris[C] diem inuentionis[D]
anniu*ersariam* deuotione celebrantes misericordiam tuam deprecamur
ut sicut ille totis uot[2] ★★★(1 wd)[a] /[3]

---

[a] *MS. damaged*

[A] sacratissimum: *P adds* domine   [B] sancti: *P adds* martyris tui
[C] protomartyris: *om. P*   [D] inuentione *P*

---

[1] The analogue for this text is *P* (I. 138). A line was left blank before this text.
[2] *P* concludes: 'totum uotum martyrii te adiuuante gaudens uoluntatem aeterna
misericordia consequi mereamur'.
[3] *f. 147ᵛ*. This folio is back to front and out of place.

93

⟨A Fragment concerning St. Andrew⟩

f. 147ᵛ martyrium Andreas suscepit ⟨it⟩aᵃ nos temporalia aux ★★★(1 wd)ᵃ
uoluptate despicient ★★★(1 wd)ᵃ æterna letitiam consequi mereamur,
p*er* . . .

ᵃ *MS. damaged*

94

⟨Collect for the Feast of the Invention of St. Stephen⟩

D*eus*[1] qui ad celebrandum ⟨n⟩obis[a] honorabile presentis diei festu*m* in b⟨eati m⟩artyris[aA] tui[B] Stephani ⟨in⟩uentione tribuisti, ⟨te⟩ supplicit*er* exoramus ⟨ut⟩ ipso inte⟨rc⟩edente /[2] ⟨mereamur in celestibus inueniri⟩, p*er* . . .

47[r]

[a] *MS. damaged*

[A] martyris: *H adds* et leuite   [B] tui: *om. H*

[1] The analogue for this text is *H* (p. 134).
[2] *f. 147[r].* Lines 1–3 are in a large script, 4–14 in a smaller one; likewise on the verso 1–4 are small, 5–11 large.

95

⟨A Prayer for the Feast of King Edmund⟩

XII Kł De*cembris*:[1] Natalis s*anc*ti Eadm⟨undi⟩[a]
D*eu*s ineffabilis misericord⟨ie qui⟩[a] beati⟨ssimu⟩m[a] regem Ead-
mu⟨n⟩d⟨um tri⟩buisti[a] pro tuo nomine ini⟨micum⟩[a] moriendo
uincere, concede *p*ropit⟨ius[A] fami⟩lie[a] tue ut eo interuenie⟨nte⟩[aB] in se
antiqui hostis incitamenta sup*er*a⟨ndo⟩ extinguere, p*er*. All*elu*ia.[bC]

---

[a] *MS. damaged*   [b] *added by another hand*

[A] propitius: *M adds* huic   [B] interueniente: *HM add* mereatur: *P adds* mereamur
[C] *om. HM*

---

[1] The analogues for this text are *H* (p. 182), *M* (II. 1004) and *P* (I. 149); note that they do not include no. **96**. The saint in question is Edmund, king of East Anglia, who was martyred by the Danes on 20 November 869.

96

⟨Fragment of a Prayer concerning St. Edmund⟩

Da nobis om*nipoten*s et misericors d*eu*s, ut s*ancti* tui Eadmundi regis celebrantes cuius celebr ★★★(1 wd)[a] triumph ★★★(1 wd)[a] fidem ueri-

50ᵛ   ★★/[1]★(4–5 wd).[a]

---

[a] *MS. damaged*

---

[1] *f. 150ᵛ*. This folio is mounted back to front.

97

⟨A Fragment⟩

D*eu*s qui (7–8 wd)ᵃ ⟨i⟩nsidiis hostilibus ★★★ᵃ (2 wd) trono regnis insignite ★★★(1 wd)ᵃ ethereis collocasti conced⟨e nobis⟩ᵃ q*uesumu*s ut que*m* signis ma ★★★(1 wd)ᵃ clare ★★★(1 wd)ᵃ sentimus eunde*m* ★★★(1 wd)ᵃ int*er*cessor ★★★(2–4 lt)ᵃ sentiamus continuu*m*, p*er*. Amen.

ᵃ *MS. damaged*

98

〈Fragment concerning Edward, King and Martyr〉

50ʳ Deus qui nobillissimum rege〈m〉 Eadwardum ★★★(1 wd)ᵃ interitu ★★/★(4 ll.)ᵃ celesti ★★★ (1–2 wd)ᵃ quesumus ut eiusdem sancti mar〈tyr〉isᵃ meritisᵇ suffragan ★★★(1 wd)ᵃ a cunctis mereamur aduer〈sariis〉,ᵃ per dominum nostrum Ihesum Christum.

ᵃ *MS. damaged*   ᵇ meritis: *1st 'i' interl.*

185

99

⟨A Prayer for Matins on the Feast of the
Commemoration of St. Dunstan⟩[1]

Be s*anct*e Dunstane[2]

D*eu*s qui hodierna[A] di⟨e⟩[a] s*anctu*m pontificem[B] Dunstanum ad
et⟨er⟩na[a] sul⟨leuasti gaudia⟩[a] eius, q*uesumu*s meritis illuc tua no⟨s
per⟩d⟨u⟩cat[a] misericordi⟨a, per Christum dominum⟩.[a] /

f. 151^r   ★★★(5 ll.)[a] quandoq*ue* letemur, p*er*. Amen.

---

[a] *MS. damaged*

[A] hodierna die: *om. M*   [B] *M reads* dunstanum pontificem *and adds* ac confessorem
tuum

---

[1] The analogue for this text is *M* (III. 1360).
[2] *Be sancte dunstane.* This rubric is repeated on the following line in *G*. Note the Old
English *be* with Latin forms; see also no. **34** above.

186

100

⟨A Fragment of a Prayer for the Feast of St. Milburg⟩

VII Kł Mar*tias*: ⟨In⟩[a] natale s*anc*te Milburge[b]

Fac nos, q*uesumu*s d*om*ine d*eu*s, beate ⟨uirg⟩inis tue Mil⟨burge⟩[a] annue sollempni ★★★(2 wd)[a] et ★★★(2 ll.).[a]

---

[a] *MS. damaged*   [b] martias . . . milburge: *traced over later*

101

⟨Postcommunion for the feast day of St. Milburg⟩

Percepta[1] d*omine* ⟨m⟩ens⟨e tue ut⟩[a] s*ancte* ⟨Mil⟩burg⟨e suffragia⟩[a] nob⟨is⟩[2] ★★★(2–4 wd)[a] p⟨a⟩r⟨iant⟩ ★★★(2–3 wd).[a] /

---

[a] *MS. damaged*

---

[1] The analogue for this text is *M* (II. 774); it is not a very close one in this instance.

[2] *nobis . . . (end).* *G* seems to omit some of the text found in *M*: '(tue) munera ut sancte Milburge suffragia et eterna nobis pariant remedia, per'.

102

⟨A Prayer to St. Ælfgyfe⟩[1]

51ᵛ   ⟨Gebed be sancte Æ⟩lfgyfe[a]

Deus[2] ⟨qui⟩[a] in omnibus operibus uel creaturis sed maxime in sanctis tuis constans, gloriosus et mirabilis, da omnibus fidelibus Christianis in commemoratione . . ./[3]

---

[a] *MS. damaged*

---

[1] Note that f. 151ᵛ, ll. 1–8 are almost totally illegible; see Appendix A.
[2] There is no analogue for this prayer which is designated Art. XI by Wanley. The rubric is reconstructed from Wanley; he notes that the prayer is 'Latine tantum' (*op. cit.* p. 231). The ending of the text has been lost.
[3] Note that f. 152ʳ is omitted since it is almost totally illegible; see Appendix A.

103

⟨A Fragment concerning St. Hemma (?)⟩

f. 152ᵛ   ★★★(1 wd)ᵃ rumq*ue* eius Hemman ★★★(1 wd)ᵃ modi succurre in
⟨cons⟩eruaᵃ me a cunctis a⟨d⟩uersariis mei⟨s⟩ ★★★(1 wd).ᵃ

ᵃ *MS. damaged*

104

〈Collect for the Feast of St. Patrick〉[1]

D*eus* 〈qui〉[a] *sanctu*m Patrici〈um〉[aA] episcopum[B] 〈tua〉[a] prouiden〈tia〉[a] elegisti ut Hiberniense〈s g〉entes in tenebris et in errore gentilitatis 〈erra〉ntes[a] eum[2] ★★★(2–3 wd) /

---

[a] *MS. damaged*

[A] patricium: *K adds* scotorum   [B] episcopum: *K* apostolum

---

[1] A line has been left blank before this text; the analogue for it is *K* (p. 55).
[2] The rest of the prayer is lost; *K* seems to continue differently: *errantes ad lumen uerum dei scientie* . . .

191

Note that folios 153^r–155^v have been omitted from this edition of *G* because of the extreme degree to which they were damaged by both fire and water. A few notes follow here concerning their contents; a transcription of them can be found below in Appendix A.

153^r: apparently a prayer for the intercession of the Blessed Virgin; several words visible, but nothing coherent.

153^v: scattered words visible; a post-fire marginal note indicates that this was a prayer to or concerning King Edgar.

154^r: a prayer or hymn to the Cross; many words visible.

154^v: another prayer to the Cross apparently; the three completely visible words on this page are *crux*.

155^r: omitted; totally illegible.

155^v: only a few words visible; apparently a series of petitions. The exact number of lines on this page cannot be determined.

INDEX OF INCIPITS

(1) of texts in Latin
(2) of texts in Old English

Note: the sigla for the analogues for each item are in brackets after the page references.

The following abbreviations are used:

(1) for Latin texts—
    C Christe   D domine   Ds deus   I Ihesu
    O. omnipotens   S sempiterne

(2) for Old English texts—
    C crist   D drihten   H hælend

The following incipits are damaged, but it may prove useful to others to have them listed:

The following are major items which do not appear in the above index:

INDEX OF BIBLICAL REFERENCES

The edition of the Vulgate Bible used is *Biblia Sacra uulgatae editionis Sixti V pontificis maximi iussu recognita et Clementis VIII auctoritate edita* (Rome, 1957). The following abbreviations from this edition are used:

Ac	Actus Apostolorum	Io	Euangelium sec. Ioannem
Ap	Apocalypsis	Ir	Ieremias
Cn	Canticum Canticorum	Is	Isaias
Col	ad Colossenses epistola	Iu	Iudae epistola
1 Cor	1 ad Corinthios epistola	Lc	Euangelium sec. Lucam
Dn	Daniel	Mr	Euangelium sec. Marcum
Dt	Deuteronomium	Mt	Euangelium sec. Matthaeum
Ecli	Ecclesiasticus	Ph	ad Philippenses epistola
Eph	ad Ephesios epistola	Ps	Psalmorum liber
Est	Esther	1 Pt	1 Petri epistola
Ex	Exodus	Rm	ad Romanos epistola
Ez	Ezechiel	1 Rg	1 Regum liber (1 Sam.)
Gn	Genesis	4 Rg	4 Regum liber (2 Reg.)
Heb	ad Hebraeos epistola	Sap	Sapientia
Ib	Iob	Tb	Tobias
Idt	Iudith	1 Tm	1 ad Timotheum epistola

INDEX OF LITURGICAL FORMS

The following abbreviations are used:

C Christe   D domine   Ds deus   I Ihesu
O. omnipotens   S sempiterne

205

Communion

Gospel Antiphon

Gradual

Introit

Benedicite Dominum omnes angeli eius potentes.................... 174

Offertory

Stetit angelus iuxta aram templi 174

Postcommunions

★★★ obsecro D I C hoc sacra ★★★..................................... 163
Percepta D mense tue ut sancte Milburge........................... 188

Super Populum

Da nobis D quesumus perseuerantem in tua........................... 81
Subueniad nobis quesumus D misericordia........................... 81

Verses of Graduals

Ego dixi: D miserere mei; sana anima 74, 147
In conspectu angelorum psallam tibi D Ds 174

Miscellaneous

'Adoro te' petitions 143
Athanasian Creed.. 157

Benedicite 155
Benedictiones in monasterio 164

Celtic Capitella... 113
Confessio inter presbiteros 130
Confiteor.. 154

Da nobis O. et misericors Ds ut sancti 183
Ds ineffabilis misericordie qui beatissimum 182
Ds qui hodierna die sanctum pontificem 186
Ds qui in omnibus operibus uel creaturis 189
Ds qui nobillissimum regem Eadwardum 185
Ds qui preclari sideris sancti pontificis.............................. 159
D Ds O. ineffabilis tuorum sanctorum gloria 160
D I C filii dei uiui miserere mei 119

Exaudi D preces nostras gemen★★★ 160

207

Hymns

Prayers

APPENDIX A

PAGES TOO SERIOUSLY DAMAGED TO BE INCLUDED IN THE EDITION

34ʳ   In ★★★★ *perfectus* alib ★
     ★★★★★★ quale*m* d*eu*m
     ★★★★★★★ beata uir
     ★★★★★★★ lle ★★
     chr*ist*ian ★★★★★★★
     ★★★★★★★★★★
     ★★★★★★★★★★
     ★★★★★★★★★★
     ★★★★★★★★★★
     et rege ★★★ re manens ★ /
34ᵛ   te chr*ist*e ★★★★★★★
     ★★ lu ★★★★★★★★
     tione ★★★★★★★★★
     illa ★★★★★★★★★★
     (The rest of this page is totally illegible.)/
35ʳ   ★★★★★★★★★★
     ★★★★★★★★★ mo
     ★★★★★★★★★★
     ★★★★★★★★★★
     ★★★★★★★★★★
     ★★★★★★★★★★
     ★★★★★★★★★ dec
     ★★★★★★★★★★
     ★★★★★★★★★ et
     ★★★★★★ as ★★ sione /
35ᵛ   ★★ et ★ patre ★★★★★
     preces ★★★★★★★★
     ★★★★★★★★★★
     ibat ★★ libri ★★★★★
     ★★★ os ★★★★★ nos

★★★★★★★★★★
★★★★★★★★★★
★★★★★★★★★★
bat intus arde ★★★★★
★★ pta facere ★★★★★ /

f. 137ʳ   ★★★★★★★★★★
★★ abel ★★★★★ male
★★★★★★★★★★
★★★★★★★★★★
★★★★★★ nos ab o ★★
★★★★★★★★★★
★★★★★★★★★★
★★★★★★★★★★
★★★★★★ ione ho ★
★★★★ maledicti Nomen mita
★★ ira ★★★★★★★★ /

f. 137ᵛ   ★★ pharaon misisti iram ★★
★ ari rubro ★★ Male ★★★
★★ tus sit domine ★★★★
★★ ternu ★★ oprimi te angeli
★ t archangeli N ★★★★★
prophete N ★★★★★★★
in et ★★★★★★★★★
pe ★ tus et ★★★★★★★
et ★★★★★★★★★★
pag ★★★★★★★★★★
apostoli et martyres ★★★★ /

f. 138ʳ   ★★★★★★★★★ ng ★
★★★★★★★★★★
★★★★★★★★★★
★★★★★★★★★★
★★★★★★★★★★
★★★★★★★★★★
★★★★★★★★★★
★★★★★★ nobilis ★
★★★★★★★★★★
★★★★★★ hec est ★
★★★★★★★★★★ e /

f. 138ᵛ   qui pretio ★★★★★★★
inclito ★★★★★★★★

conclamemus ★★★★★★★
Conserua nos tua clement ★★★
rex isr*ahel* ★★★★★★★
★★★★★★★★★★★★★
★★★★★★★★★★★★★
res et ★★★★★★★★★★
(The rest of this page is totally illegible.)

39ʳ ★★★★★★★★★★★★★
‹Ðas cræftas syndon be ðam d›eore þe we
‹on urum geðeode Broc hatað› ★★ ret
★★★★★★★★★★★★★
★★★★★★★★★★★★★
★★★★★★★★★★★★★
★★★★★★★★★★★★★
★★★★★★★★★★★★★
★★★★★★★★★ anweald
★★★★★★★★★★★★★
(The rest of the page is totally illegible.)

39ᵛ nesse *and* mid hned ★ is ★★ *and* do
★★★ swiðr ★★★★★★★★
★★★ þe gede ★ ian ★★★★
ne dæges ne nihtes ★★‹swi-›
þran fot ★★★★★★★★★
★★★★★★★★★★★★★★
þe on ★★★★★★★★★★★
★★★★★★★ ealle ★ g ★ sp ★ eð
★★★★★★★★ da þ ★★★★
★★★★★★★★★★ swiðe ★★
forþon h ★★★★★★★★ þ ★
for ★ or ★★★★★★★★★★
þo þ ★★★★★★★★★★★★ /

36ʳ ★★ nesse mæg *and* ★ nun his geallan
★ þæt ilce *and* mæng wið clæne win ★
★★★★★★★★★ eag ★★ te wearde
‹mid› feðre ‹drep i›n þæt bisne eagan
‹ðu meaht cuðlice oncn›awan þone
‹læcecræft› ★★★★★★★★★★★★
(several lines illegible after these)
★★★★★★★★★★★★★★★ et omnia
★★★★★★★★★★★ oppositate tuorum /

211

f. 136ᵛ ★★★★★★★★★★★★★★★★★★
disti ★★★★★★★★★★★★★★★
(The rest of this page is illegible.)/

f. 142ᵛ ⟨i⟩nuiolata singular ★★★★★★★★
ut omnibus a ★★★★★★★★★★★★
gratiam ★★★★★★★★★★★★★★
uale ★★★★★★★★★★★★★★★★
★ et ★★★★★★★★★★★★★★★★
★ la ★★★★★★★★★★★★★★★★
★★★★★★★★★★★★★★★★★★
ges ★★★★★★★★★
★★★★★★★★★★
★★★★★★★★★★
★★★★★★★★★★
★★★★★★★★★★
per ★★★★★★★★★ /

f. 143ʳ ★★★★★★★★★★
I ★★★★★★★★★★
C ★★★★★★★★★★
C ★★★★★★★★★★
★★★★★★★★★★
T ★★★★★★★★★★
D ★★★★★★★★★★
★★★★★★ culparum ★★
★★★★★★★★★★
★★★★★★★★★★
★★★★★★ los g ★ s ★★
★★★★★★★★★★ /

f. 143ᵛ ★★★★★★ Sancte ⟨Br⟩igide
omnipotens sempi ★★★★★
★★★★★★★★★★★
(The rest of the page is totally illegible.) /

f. 144ʳ ★★★ omnipotens deus ut beatus
andreus apostolus tuus
pro ★★★★ imploret
★★★★★ ut a nostris
reatibus absoluti
★★★ iam pe ★ icu ★
★★★★★★★★★★
★★★★★★★★★★

212

★★★★★★★★★★
fa ★★★★★★★★★
nam ★★★★★★★
★★ s const ★★★★★★
meis digne ★★★★★★ /
151ᵛ D ★★★★★★★★★
tuam ostendis ★★★★★
★★★★ tuum ★★★ ntis
★★★★★★★★★ is
★★★★★★★★★ ne
★★★★★★★★★★
★★★★★★★★★★
★★★★ suffrag ★ s ★★
★★★★★★ lfgyfe
Deus ★★ in omnibus operibus
uel creaturis sed maxime
in sanctis tuis constans gloriosus
et mirabilis. da omnibus fidelibus
christianis in commemoratione /
152ʳ ★★★★★★★★★★
uentus ★★★★★★★
tis ★★★★★★★★
★★★★★★★★★★
dignus ★★★★★★★★
★ nibus est ★★★★★★
★ co ★★★★★★★★
tuis ★★★★★★★★
Deus ★★★★ et sanguin ★
(The rest of the page is totally illegible.)/
153ʳ ★★★★★★★★★★
★ gare ★★★★★★★★
gestauer ★★★★★★★
Ne der ★★★★★★★★
famulo ★★★★★★★★
one mea ad ★★★★★★★
cem ★ lu ★★★ propter glori ★
nominis tui et per interces
sionem sancta maria atq ★
interc ★★★ beati ★★★
di confessoris ★★★★★ /

213

f. 153ᵛ   ★★★★★★ mittes ★
          ★★★★★★ iracula ★
          ★★★★★★★ ilem ★
          ★★★★ ge recte inten ★★
          ★★★ ntes roboras. ★★★
          ★★★ s ★ stit. exemplo ★★
          ★★★ ne ★ x ★★★★★
          ★★★ ne cuius stu ★★★
          ★★★ uderag ★ m regis ★★
          ★★★★★★★★★ gere
          ★★★★★★★★ a que
          ★★★★★★ s*anctifi*cas
          ★★★★★★★★ al ★★ /

f. 154ʳ   ab hoste sacri ★ signa ★★
          ★ rore salubri.
          ostendeat ut nobis uir
          tutum gloria chr*isti* ★
          ★★ melliflua crux
          ★ are ★★ tilis aue ★
          Salue p ★★ ifera crux
          sal ★★★★ bona sal ★
          aue ★★ di chr*isti* cr ★
          opti ★★★ salue ★★
          Crux d*omi*ni salue ★★★ /

f. 154ᵛ   Crux ★★★★ glor ★★ tendo
          ★★★★★★★★★★
          ★★★★★★★★★★
          ★★★★★★ crux s ★★
          ★★★★★★★ crux ★★
          ★★★★★★ ngn ★★★
          (The rest of the page is totally illegible.)/

f. 155ᵛ   ★★★★★★★★★★
          Quod miser ★★★★★★
          Sit m*ihi* recta holo ★★★
          Sit m*ihi* p ★ pti ★★ esterio
          Sit ★★★★★★★★
          S ★★★★★★★★
          (The rest of the page is totally illegible.)

The following is as much as can be transcribed of the marginal note on f. 7^{r-v}:

for ★★ englas hio awurpon of heofenas ★ eald þa xii ymbren dagas þe on twelf monð ★★★ *and* be ★ wiþ abl ★★ attor cra ★ tas scead ★★ gelere ★★ r s ★ a ★★ *and* giferu ★ ic pres ★★ *and* ★★★ ne ★★★★ do*mine* ★★ and b ★★★★★★ alde ★★ þwære ★★★ ines ★ glo ★★ þine teoþunge do to godes y ★ eat *and* searum *and* lufa cirican georne ★★ od mild ★★ *and* þu most mid ★★★★ ic bisne þe Ic ★★★/ ★★★ st gesorh ★★ ge ★★ þde ★★★ annis ★★ um þon ★★ efe on do ★ *and* dæge ★ ran go ★★ befo ★★ am ★★ waru*m* ★★ waru*m* e ★★ ell ★★ u ★★★★ tio ★★ p*re*ces ★★ oon ★★ subtil ★★ geþe ★ e permeatis u ★★ s conscientie reatus accus ★★ gentie ★★ erationis absoluat. p*er* do*min*um.

It is described in Wanley's Catalogue as Art. III:

Interrogationes Sacerdotis (ut uidetur) ad readmissionem Poenitentis in ecclesiam, cum absolutione, et concilio de ieiuniis obseruandis, etc. imperf. Sax.

Ker notes that this fragment is probably the end of the piece described by Wanley, and gives bibliographical data for an analogue for it, which however is not close enough to warrant being cited here (*op. cit.* p. 199).

APPENDIX B

The following table records the various foliations in N and G, and is
followed by a brief commentary. Entries followed by an asterisk are
referred to in this discussion.

Nero A.ii	19/17/–	49/47/93
3/1⋆	20/18/–	50/48/94
4/2	21/19/–	51/49/95
5/3	22/20/66	52/50/96
6/4	23/21/67	53/51/–
7/5	24/22/–	54/52/98
8/6	25/23/69	55/53/–
9/7	26/24/70	56/54/100
10/8	27/25/–	57/55/–
11/9	28/26/72	59/57/–⋆
12/10	29/27/73	58/56/–⋆
13/11	30/28/74	60/58/104
Galba A.xiv	31/29/75	61/59/105
2/–/–⋆	32/30/–	62/60/106
3/1/–	33/31/–	63/61/–
4/2/–	34/32/–	64/62/40⋆
5/3/–	35/33/–	65/62/108⋆
6/4/50⋆	36/34/80	75/64/10⋆
7/5/51	37/35/81	66/68/–⋆
8/6/–	38/36/82	67/63/109⋆
9/7/53	39/37/83	68/71/–⋆
10/8/54	40/38/84	69/80/–⋆
11/9/55	41/39/85	70/128/–⋆
12/10/–	42/40/86	71/–/–
13/11/–	43/41/87	72/–/–
14/12/58	44/42/88	73/–/–
15/13/59	45/43/89	74/72/–
16/14/–	46/44/90	76/65/111⋆
17/15/–	47/45/91	77/75/–
18/16/–	48/46/92	78/68/–⋆

79/76/–★	105/98/17	131/125/45
86/73/–★	106/99/–	132/126/46
80/77/–	107/100/19	133/127/–
81/78/–	108/–/–	134/129/–
87/74/–★	109/–/21	135/130/–
82/79/–★	110/103/22	137/132/–★
83/67/–★	11/–/23	138/133/–
84/69/–★	112/–/–	139/134/–
85/70/–	113/–/26★	136/131/–★
89/82/–★	114/–/27	140/135/–★
90/83/–	115/108/28	141/136/–
91/84/–	115/109/29	142/137/–
92/85/4★	117/110/30	143/–/–
93/86/5	118/111/31	144/–/–
94/87/6	119/112/–	146/–/–
95/88/7	120/113/33	145/–/–
96/89/8	121/114/34	149/–/–
97/90/9	122/115/35	148/–/–
98/91/10	123/116/–	147/–/–
88/81/–★	124/117/37	150/–/–
99/92/11	125/118/38	151/–/–
100/93/12	126/119/39	152/–/–
101/94/13	127/121/41★	153/–/–
102/95/14	128/122/42	154/–/–
103/96/15	129/123/43	155/–/–
104/97/–	130/124/44	

There are three foliations of *G*; the two most complete and orderly are recorded in the upper right-hand corner of the modern paper frames in which the folios are now mounted (see above, p. xi, n. 11). The series running from 2 to 155 has been adopted for reference in this edition since it is the most consistent of the three, best reflects the order of items in the pre-fire catalogues, and has been used in the past by Ker and others. This series, as modified in the table above, reflects the reorganization of *G* according to the information contained in the table on p. xii of the Introduction. If and when the manuscript is again rebound, a new foliation will have to be made to reflect this reordering of the folios (which, unhappily, will complicate reference to earlier editions and to Ker's *Catalogue*, but this will be less troublesome with a less well-known manuscript such as *G* than it has proven to be with e.g. the *Beowulf* manuscript). The third series

recorded in the table, running from 50 to 46 and usually recorded at
the bottom of the folio (see plate 7 where a faint *23* is visible under the
-rum of the last line of text), was probably the first made immediately
after the fire when the binding had been destroyed and there was not
yet time to reorganize the folios in consultation with the pre-fire
catalogues. If this assumption is true, however, it is not immediately
apparent why this series should be incomplete. From this earliest
foliation we can see that the last part of the manuscript (from 92/85/4)
was at that time placed at the beginning, which contradicted the
details in the catalogues.

The series *1–137*, which runs parallel to *2–155* for the most part, but
is less complete, reflects the first attempt to reconstruct the manuscript with reference to the catalogues. It follows *2–155* by 2 down to
65/62/108 where 62 is recorded for a second time through oversight.
From here, *1–137* becomes erratic for about fifteen entries until
89/82/– where it once again becomes systematic, but now trails by 7
until 127/121/41 where it hiccups and reduces this margin to 6. At this
point, series *50–46* also jumps a notch, omitting 40, which was out of
its proper position when this foliation was made, and is now positioned
as 64/62/40. Interestingly, this is the point at which *1–137* duplicates
the number 62. At 134/129/– *1–137* again reduces the margin of
difference by 1 to 5. It stops at 137, perhaps reflecting the despair of the
person charged with re-establishing the proper sequence of the manuscript when he came to these hopelessly disfigured folios.

Of the early catalogues, that which has been of most use in reordering the final folios of *G* is MS. Gough London 54—Wanley's
copy of Smith's *Catalogus* of 1696 containing his own marginal
annotations; it contains more detailed information than his own
Catalogue of 1705. These annotations were made for an official report
which was delivered on 22 June 1703, and are reproduced here; the
two asterisked items are no longer identifiable. The reference number
to this edition is given in parentheses after each item.

Epistola I. Christi ad Abgarum Regem (**18**); Confessionis Oratio
(**25/26**); Collectae Paschales (**29**); Orationes Cotidianis diebus
(**29**); Formula Confessionis (**62**); Oratio in die S. Athelwoldi
Episcopi (**77**); Oratio ad S. Machutum Episcopum (**78**); Hymnus
de S. Swithuno Episcopo★; de S. Dionysio (**89**); S. Chrystophoro
(**90**); de S. Machuto (**91**); de S. Stephano (**92/94**); de S.
Eadmundo Rege (**95**); de S. Eadward R. et Mart (**98**); de S.

Dunstano (**99**); in Nat. S. Milburge (**100/101**); Oratio Eugenis Toletani Episcopi⋆; Metrica in Nat. S. Brigide (**35**, but perhaps there was a second prayer, now illegible, on f. 143v).

And finally, the following modern annotations appear on the frames of the folios indicated: de S. Maria (142ʳ); Holy Cross (144ᵛ); S. Malo (148ᵛ); S. Christopher (149ᵛ); Margt. (153ʳ); K. Edgar (153ᵛ).

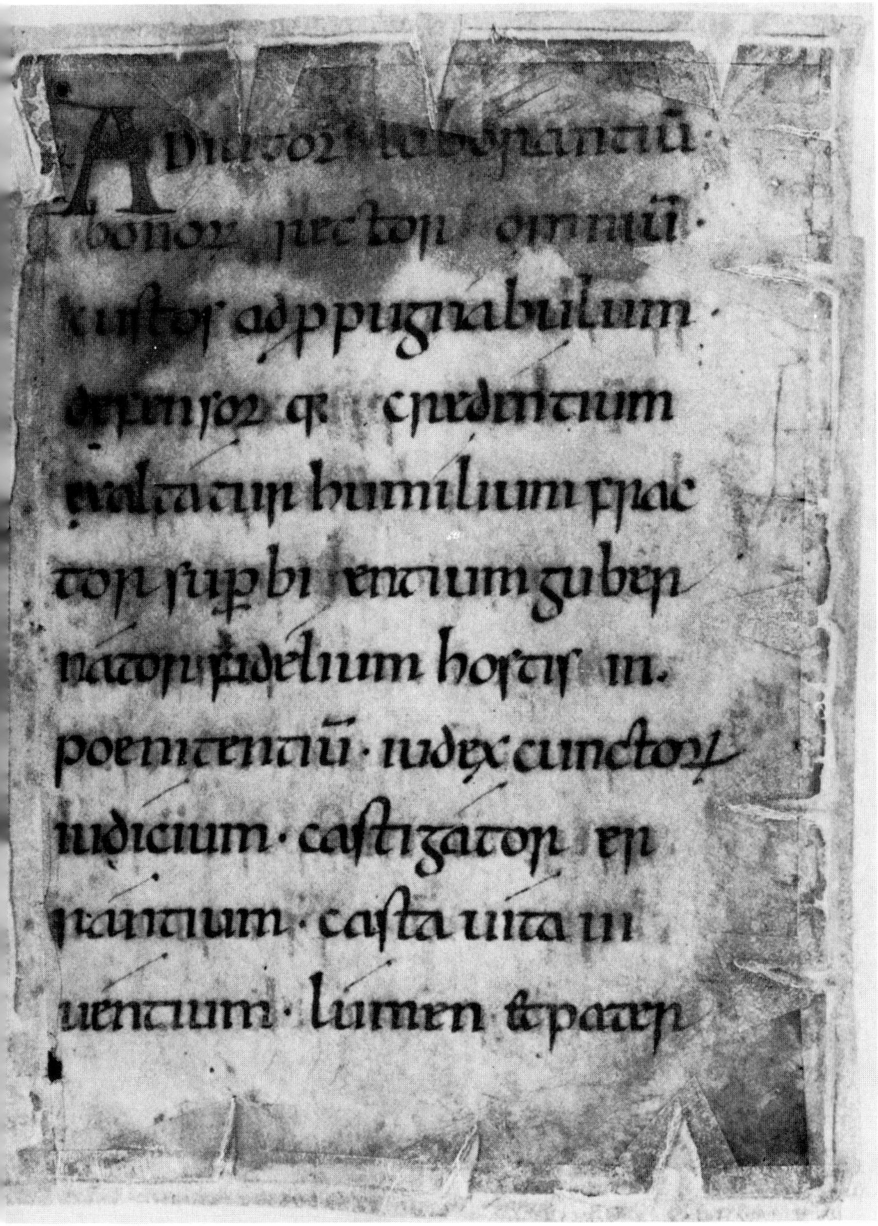

Adiutor laborantium
bonorum rector omnium
custos adppugnabilium
expectentium que expectentium
exultatium humilium spes
tor superbientium guber
nator fidelium hortus in
poenitentium · iudex cunctorum
iudicium · castigator er
rantium · casta vita in
ventium · lumen et pater

PLATE 1
20ʳ

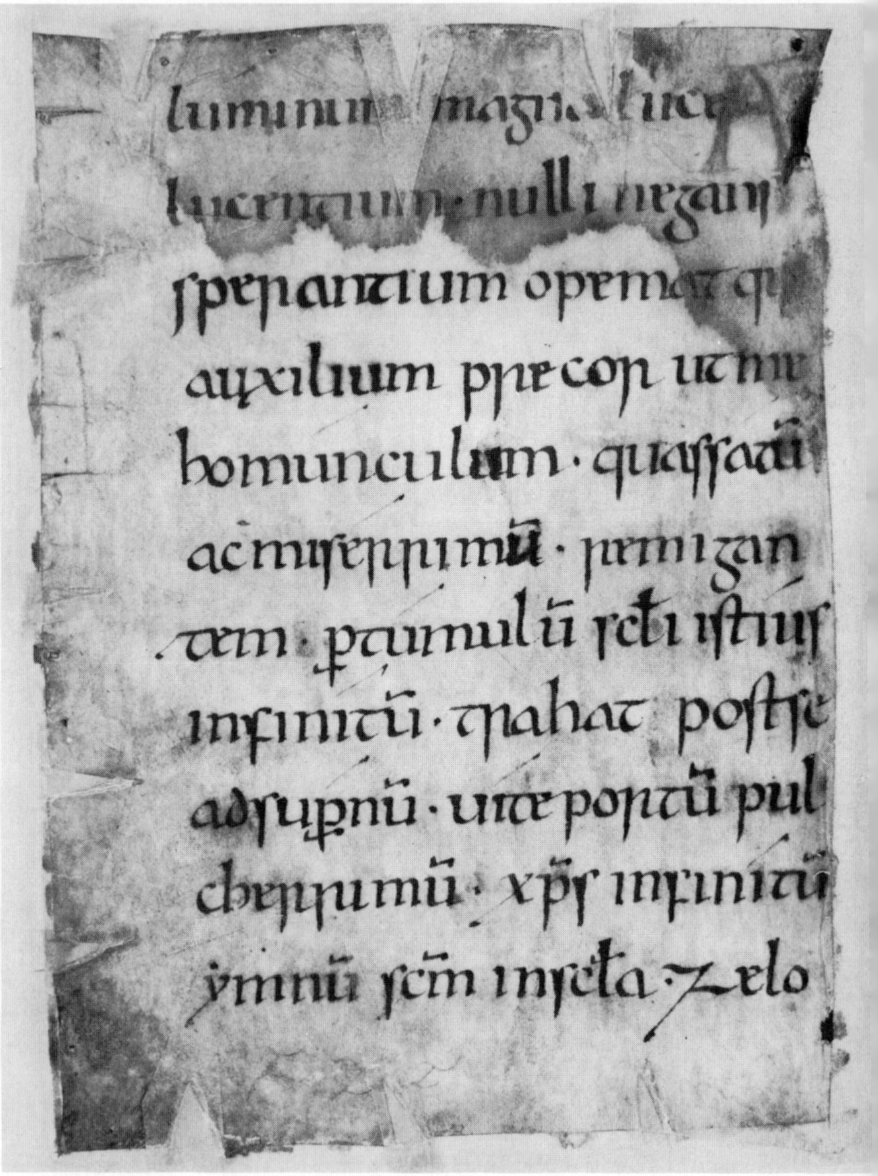

luminum magna luce
luernarum nulli negam
sperantium opem ... q
auxilium precop utmr
homunculum · quassatu̅
ac miserrimu̅ · prmizan
æm · paruulu̅ reti istiuf
infinitu̅ · trahat posse
adsupnu̅ · uitæ portu̅ pul
cherrimu̅ · xpr infinitu̅
ymnu̅ scm inycta · zelo

PLATE 2
20ᵛ

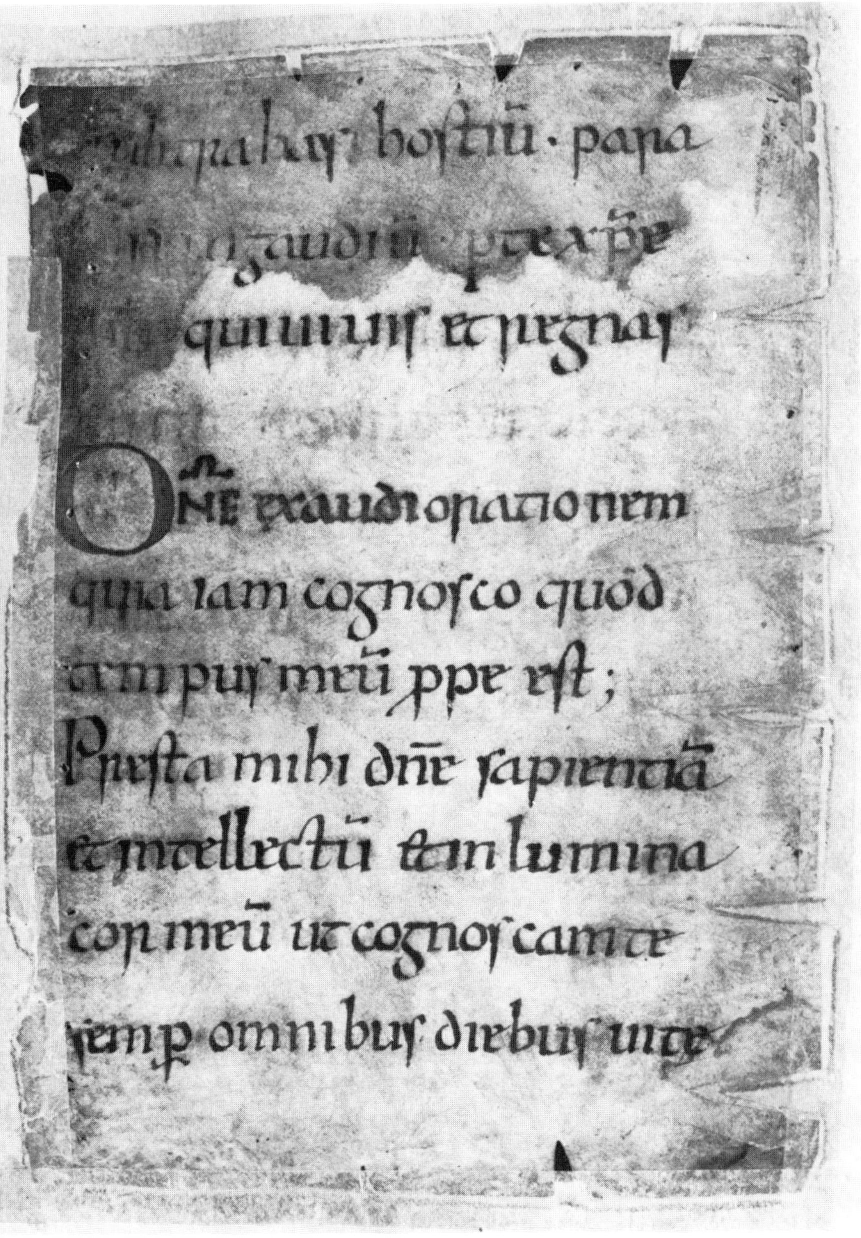

... hostiũ · papa

... gaudiũ ... xp̄e

qui uiuis et regnas

ONE exaudi oratio nem
qua iam cognosco quod
a ... pur̄ meũ ppe est ;
Presta mihi dn̄e sapientiā
et intellectũ et in lumina
cor̄ meũ ut cognoscam te
semp omnibus diebus uite

PLATE 3
21ʳ

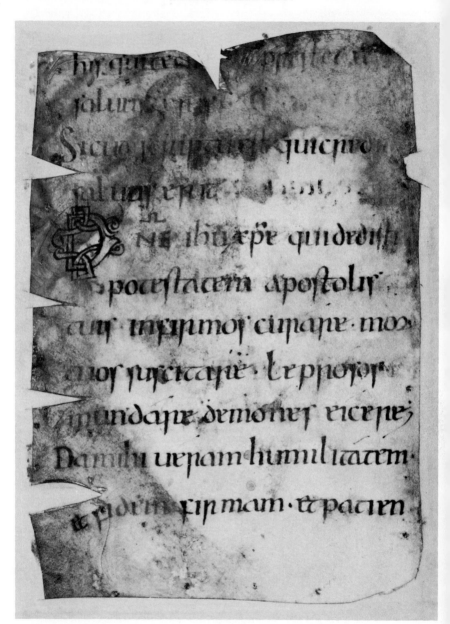

PLATE 4
28^v

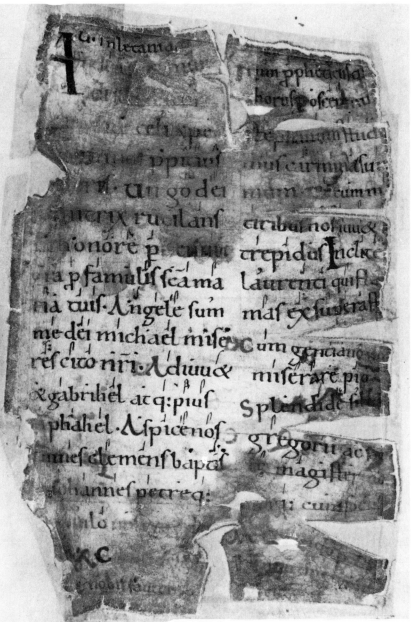

PLATE 5
103^r

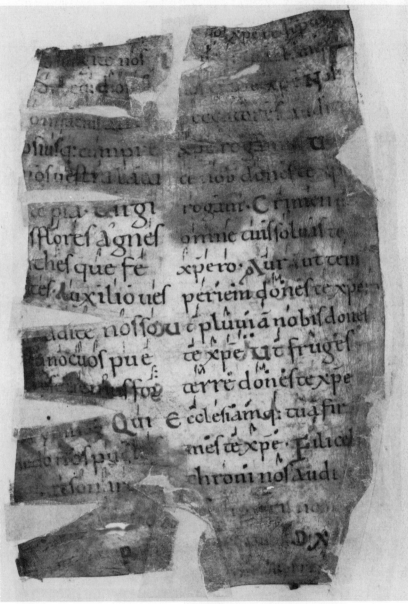

PLATE 6
103ᵛ

PLATE 7
111ʳ

COTTON GALBA A.xiv

PLATE 8
111ᵛ